Pvt. Ltd.

Mobile Telephony & Socio-Economic Transformation

by

Balwant Singh Mehta

2019

Studium Press (India) Pvt. Ltd.

Mobile Telephony
&
Socio-Economic Transformation

ISBN: 978-93-85046-37-7

Published by:

Studium Press (India) Pvt. Ltd.
4735/22, 2nd Floor, Prakash Deep Building
(Near Delhi Medical Association),
Ansari Road, Darya Ganj, New Delhi-110 002
Tel.: + 91-11-43240200-15 (15 lines); Fax: 91-11-43240215
E-mail: pubdir@studiumpress.in

Printed at India

About the Author

Dr Balwant Singh Mehta has over one and half decade experience in information and communication technology for development (ICT4D) sector. He is currently working as 'Fellow' at Institute for Human Development, New Delhi. His interest areas areranging from ICT4D, employment, unemployment, children wellbeing, poverty, inequality and gender. He has published several books, reports and articles in reputed national and international journal on these issues. He has visited and presented his work in several countries around the world and also worked as a consultant in various international organisations such as ADB, SDC and others. He has received international recognition for his work in ICT4D as 'Amy Mahan International Fellow' from UPF, Spain; Research Fellowship in ICT4D from SIRCA, Singapore; and Emerging Researcher from IDRC, Canada. He also writes inmagazines, blogs and newspaperson the national relevant issues.

Acknowledgement

I have been writing articles on topics relating to information and technology in various journals, newspapers and magazines for the last one decade and more on telecom. However, efforts of putting it all together in a book form would not have been possible without inspiration from Prof Shakti Kak, my PhD supervisor, and support from my colleagues Prof. Sandip Sarkar and Prof Alakh N Sharma, Director, IHD, Delhi. Their valuable guidance, generous help, comments, constant inspiration, and overall moral support made it possible for me to complete this work. I am thankful to Professor Atul Sarma, visiting Professor ISID, New Delhi for his concern, valuable suggestions, and moral support to me since the beginning of my research work. The theoretical basis of my research was set during my PhD work after several round of discussion with my PhD supervisor, who still regularly debates with me on various topics including the telecom market.

My sincere thanks to the anonymous reviewers of various journals, whose comments have helped me to improve my articles, which are part of this book. I am thankful to Dr J.N. Govil, Publishing Director & Managing Editor, Studium Press LLC, Houston, TX - 77072, USA, who have approved my proposal in very short time. I am also indebted to my family members, my wife Ms Nidhi and my son Puluk, whom I deprived from the attention and care they deserve from me, yet I always receive smile, attention, care and support from them. I shall always be grateful to them.

Last but not the least I am thankful to all those people who have helped me directly or indirectly during the process of writing this book but whose names could not be mentioned here.

Balwant Singh Mehta

Preface

India's emergence as one of the fastest growing economies of the world during the last three decades has been led by the service sector. It was argued that for developing countries at India's level of per capita income, economic growth should have been led by industry rather than the services sector. Some regard it as a temporary phase and unsustainable in the long run. Several others, however, claimed that because of technological progress, service can serve as a lead sector in economic growth. A few recent studies seek to reconcile these contrasting views by explaining 'two waves of service-sector growth', the first wave consists of 'traditional services'-'wholesale and retail trade', 'hotels and restaurants' and 'transport and storage' which emerged at an early stage of development. The second wave comprises of 'modern services'–communications (which include mobile phone services), financial services and business services (which include information technology or software services) at a relatively advanced stage of development.

India's services sector growth led by modern services appears to confirm the second wave. In particular, information and telecommunications-mobile phone services have emerged as a growth engine of the service sector. India's mobile phone sector is the fastest growing sector in the world and stands globally at second today after China, both in terms of mobile phone subscribers and internet users. Its contribution to the economy, foreign investment is growing over the years and also creating employment for a large number of youth in the country with a high spillover effect to other sectors. It is argued that proactive policies and regulations by the Indian government are mainly responsible for the high diffusion of mobile phone services. These policies and regulations ensure competitive behaviour and ensure public interests in terms of affordable and wider service coverage. In turn, the sector has huge socio-economic impact on people particularly mobile phone consumers.

This books presents a comprehensive picture of India's mobile phone sector (interchangeably also used as telecom sector in the book). It has highlighted every aspect, policy and regulatory bodies; growth of subscribers; digital divide, current financial status of mobile phone operators; economic contribution, socio-economic impact on mobile phone consumers, future growth drivers of the sector and assessment of current policies and regulation, summarises the analysis beautifully and provides useful suggestions by explaining the challenges. In addition, it also critically examines the government policy decisions in the past and latest development of RJio entry in the telecom market. So, the book is not only useful for the post graduate students, research scholars and other researchers but also a treasure for the policy makers and operators. In the book, advance statistical techniques such as granger causality tests, herfindahl-Hirschman index (HHI), data envelopment analysis, efficiency analysis, ratio analysis and other statistical have been used appropriately to analyze various aspects of the sector. This will greatly benefit, firms or operators to understand their efficiency or productivity and policy makers to understand the sector performance. Additionally, students, research scholars and other researchers can use it as a guide to understand the past performance of the sector and learn new techniques and methods, which they can apply in their future research work. The mobile phone sector is a dynamic sector, and things change very fast. So, it is very difficult to assimilate all the recent changes, and I have tried my best to capture as many as possible to make this an interesting, informative and insightful experience for the readers.

Table of Contents

List of Tables

List of Figures

Abbreviations

ADC	:	Access Deficit Charges
ARPU	:	Average Revenue Per User
BSO	:	Basic Service Operators
BTS	:	Basic Telecom Services
BSNL	:	Bharat Sanchar Nigam Limited
RoW	:	Broadband Rights of Way
BWA	:	Broadband Wireless Action
BICP	:	Bureau of Industrial Cost and Prices
CPP	:	Calling Party Pays
CMTS	:	Cellular Mobile Telephone Service
CSO	:	Central Statistical Organisation
CDMA	:	Code Division Multiple Access
CAGR	:	Compound Annual Growth Rate
CR	:	Current Ratio
DEA	:	Data Envelopment Analysis
DER	:	Debt Equity Ratio
DMUs	:	Decision-Making Units
DoT	:	Department of Telecom
EPS	:	Earnings per Share
EBITDA	:	Earnings before Tax, Depreciation and Amortization
EGoM	:	Empowered Group of Ministers
5G	:	Fifth Generation Technology
1G	:	First Generation Technology
FCFS	:	First-Cum-First-Serve
FDI	:	Foreign Direct Investment
FIPB	:	Foreign Investment Promotion Board
4G	:	Fourth Generation Technology
GSM	:	Global System for Mobile
GDP	:	Gross Domestic Product
GDPPC	:	Gross Domestic Product Per Capita
GoT	:	Group on Telecom
HHII	:	Herfindahl-Hirschman Index

ICT : Information and Communications Technology
IHD : Institute for Human Development
ILD : International Long Distance
IOT : Internet of Things
ITU : International Telecom Union
IUCs : Interconnection Usage Charges
ISPs : Internet Service Providers
MTNL : Mahanagar Telephone Nigam Limited
NLD : National Long Distance
NNP : National Numbering Plan
NSSO : National Sample Survey Organisation
NTP99 : National Telecom Policy, 1999
NTP94 : National Telecom Policy 1994
NTP12 : National Telecom Policy, 2012
OECD : Organization for Economic Co-operation and Development's
OTE : Overall Technical Efficiency
PFP : Partial Factor Productivity
PTT : Posts, Telephone and Telegraph
PSU : Public Sector Units
PTE : Pure Technical Efficiency
QoS : Quality of Service
RPP : Receiving Party Pays
RoCE : Returns on Capital Employed
RPA : Revenue per Asset
RPE : Revenue per Expenditure
SE : Scale Efficiency
2G : Second Generation
SDCA : Short Distance Charging Area
SMS : Short Message Services
SIMs : Subscriber Identity Module
SACFA : Standing Advisory Committee on Radio Frequency Allocation
SC : Supreme Court
TC : Telecom Commission
TDSAT : Telecom Disputes Settlement and Appellate Tribunal
TRAI : Telecom Regulatory Authority Of India
TRE : Telecom Regulatory Environment
TTO : Telecom Tariff Order
3G : Third Generation
4G : Fourth Generation
5G : Fifth Generation
UASL : Unified Access Service Licensing

UAL	: Universal Access Levy
USO	: Universal Service Obligation
VAS	: Value Added Services
VAT	: Value Added Tax
VSNL	: Videsh Sanchar Nigam Limited
WLL	: Wireless in Local Loop
WPC	: Wireless Planning and Coordination Wing
WTO	: World Trade Organisation

1

Introduction

1.1. BACKGROUND

The process of economic development has been historically linked with the general pattern of structural changes of capitalist economies. This was associated with falling share of agriculture, which was at first offset by a rising industrial sector in the early stages of development, and services took over the lead role only after a fairy high level of development had been achieved (Eichengreen and Gupta, 2010; Nayyar, 2012; Ghose, 2013). The structural change pattern was first derived by Lewis (1954) and Kuznet (1957), and afterwards confirmed by Chenery (1960), Arrow (1962), Kaldor (1966) and Rowthorn and Wells (1987). This process of economic development is referred as the 'stylized pattern of structural change'.

Asian economies namely South Korea, Taiwan, Thailand, Malaysia, and China have experienced the same pattern of growth after the mid-eighties and early nineties, with a larger share of industry (Brandt and Rawski, 2008; Todaro and Smith, 2009; Nayyar, 2012). The Indian economy, which was dominated by agriculture sector (56 per cent) followed by services (30 per cent) and industry (14 per cent) at the time it became a republic in 1950 also witnessed the stylised pattern of structural change between 1950 and 1981, when the primary sector share in GDP decreased by 17 percentage points and share of both industry as well as services increased by 10 percentage points and 7 percentage points respectively.

However, after the mid-eighties, from 1982 to 2018, the share of the primary sector decreased again by 21 percentage points, but the share of industry increased by only 4 percentage points and services led the growth of the country with a 17 percentage point change (Economic Survey, 2018; Ghose, 2013). Today, primary sector stands at 18 per cent, industry at 24 per cent and services dominate at 54 per cent share of GDP. These two periods confirm the contradictory pattern and the fact that the recent period is deviating from the 'stylized pattern' of capitalist economies.

It was argued that India's services-led growth after the mid-eighties rather than industry or manufacturing led growth, unlike the other Asian economies, came at an early stage of development (Dasgupta and Singh, 2006;Todaro and Smith, 2009; Nayyar, 2012; Ghose, 2013). But several studies in the past had alternative views and found no relationship between the share of services and GDP growth (Kuznet, 1957; Chenery, 1960). In the case of India also, Joshi, (2004) and Dasgupta, (2005) explained that the service-led growth is a short term phenomenon and unsustainable in the long run. On the other hand, other scholars claimed a significant positive relationship between the share of services and GDP growth (Chenery and Syrquin, 1975; Kongsamut *et al.,* 2001).

Some recent studies seek to reconcile these contrasting views by explaining 'two waves of service-sector growth'. The first wave consists of 'traditional services'-'wholesale and retail trade', 'hotels and restaurants' and 'transport and storage' which emerged at an early stage of development. The second wave comprises of 'modern services'-communications (which include mobile telephone services), and business services (which include information technology services) that emerged at a relatively advanced stage of development (Eichengreen and Gupta, 2010; Ghose, 2013). India's pattern of economic structure seems to confirm that the second wave of services growth led by 'modern services' emerged on account of technological progress (Ghani, 2011; Nayyar, 2012).

Modern services - Information and Communications Technology (ICT) - in India grew at a very fast rate in recent years. It is not only contributing to the economy but also has high spillover or multiplier effects in other sectors (Sarkar and Mehta, 2010; Ghose, 2013). These modern services are called the 'growth engine' of the Indian economy (Dasgupta and Singh, 2005). Jha (2012) also stated that modern services are responsible for India's emergence as a global economic power. Importantly, the communications service with advent of mobile telephony has changed the definition of the service sector, which has characteristics of both manufacturing as well as service. In this context, it is important to understand how historically communications (mobile phone, telecommunications or telephony, telecom terms have been used interchangeably henceforth) services have emerged as an important indicator of economic growth.

1.2. ECONOMIC GROWTH AND MOBILE PHONE TECHNOLOGY

Economic growth has been at the heart of economic analysis and in essence, the topic of Adam Smith's treatise on the "Wealth of Nations" (Todaro and Smith, 2009). The relationship between economic growth and various factors has been the subject of debate since decades. It is beyond the scope of this work to provide a detailed history of the economic growth debates and emphasis has only been given on evolution of technological change based prospective of economic growth in this section.

In the early 1950s, the Harrod (1939) and Domar (1946) theory of growth stated that accelerated capital accumulation by mobilization of foreign investment and domestic saving was necessary for economic growth, especially in the case of developing countries. Neo-classical economist Solow (1957) opposed their model and explained the major determinant of long term growth also depends on an exogenous parameter, the rate of technical change, which was first discussed by Marx in the nineteenth century and later by Schumpeter in the twentieth. They considered technical change as an important factor to drive economies but their views were not taken seriously (Freeman, 2005).

Lewis's (1954) structural change theory focuses on transformation of underdeveloped economies from agrarian to industrial and services economies. This process of labour transfer and output growth from traditional agricultural sector to the modern urban industrial sector became the general development theory of most of the surplus–labour developing nations in 1960s and 1970s and many still support it and subsequently confirmed by Kuznets (1957) and Chenery (1962).

Arrow (1962) and Kaldor (1967) extended the structural changes theory and viewed industry as the main engine of economic growth in the classical division of agriculture, industry and services. They argued that it is a central issue to understand the growth process of modern economies.

Romer's (1986, 1990) new growth theory called the endogenous model originated from the limitation of the neo-classical theories. In the neo-classical theories, technological change is treated as exogenous in contrast to Romer's model, which treats technical change as endogenous. Endogenous growth simply means technical change generates within the system, *versus* technological change being treated as a 'black box'[1] in the case of exogenous growth models of neo-classical theory. The sources of technological change provide a good quality explanation for the level of growth since 1990s, which was much higher than in the earlier period.

Lucas (1988) laid emphasis on human capital and Sanchez-Robles (1998), Canning and Bannathan (2002), emphasized public infrastructure as important sources of technical change. Roller and Waverman (1996, 2001, 2005), Sridhar and Sridhar (2004), The Economist (2009), Lee *et al.* (2009) and Qiang (2009) focused on telecom infrastructure, in particular mobile phones, which has ability to generate a significant contribution to economic growth, also referred to as a Neo-Schumpeterian wave extending Schumpeter's views of technical innovation[2] or change.

The Neo-Schumpeterian view classified long innovation or wave as occurring due to the introduction of new technology, the diffusion of which imparts a deep material change in the reproduction process and is instrumental to growth, and placed information technology and mobile phones in the most recent wave (Daniel, 2009). It was argued that changes or development of new telecom technology and state policies played a major role in the

[1] 'Freeman, (1994) referred 'Black box' to the view that "technical change was thought to be tackled by an engineer and a scientist instead of an economist". This approach fitted quite well with the convenient (but erroneous) assumption that science and technology could be treated as exogenous and need not be examined in any depth for most purposes"

[2] They viewed technical innovation as destruction of the old technology and replacing it with new technology.

growth of mobile phone services. Therefore, it will be interesting to know, how telecom technology and role of the governments (state and government terms have been used interchangeably henceforth) have evolved historically with growth of mobile phones.

1.3. EVOLUTION OF MOBILE PHONE TECHNOLOGY

A mobile phone is a device that allows two-way communication by means of radio signals among groups of people. This includes voice, data services, audio services, video services, SMSs and internet services. The first mobile phone, also called first generation (1G) technology was launched commercially in the early 1980s. It was based on analog radio signals through which a voice call gets modulated to a higher frequency and transmitted between radio towers. This technology upgraded to digital technology[3] called second generation (2G) launched in Finland in 1992. It used a digital system for voice calls, short messages, and data transfer such as email or software, etc. Third generation (3G) mobile telecom system was launched in 2002 that allowed more advanced services including video calls, broadband wireless data, mobile television, GPS (global positioning system) and video conferencing. Now, fourth generation (4G) mobile phone system is available with high data speed and high quality audio/video streaming facility.

1.4. GLOBAL DIFFUSION OF MOBILE PHONE SERVICES

The mobile phone subscribers surpassed those of fixed line phone in 2002. There were an estimated 7.7 billion mobile subscribers with Tele-density crossed 100 per cent globally (103.5 per cent) by 2017 (ITU, 2018). About 79 per cent of the mobile subscribers reside in developing countries. But the tele-density of developing (98 per cent) countries is still far behind that of developed countries (127 per cent). The proportion of mobile phone subscribers out of total telecom (fixed and mobile phone) subscribers in developing

[3] "Digital system uses discrete values of numbers or non-numeric symbols such as letters or icons for transmission, storage, or display, rather than a continuous range of values as represented in an analog system" available athttp://www.digitalpeasants.com/

countries has increased from about 30 per cent in 2000 to 92 per cent in 2017, with China (18 per cent) and India (14 per cent) sharing together 32 per cent of the pie.

1.5. ROLE OF STATE IN MOBILE PHONE SERVICES

The provision of telecom services is determined by the state's role in policy formulation, regulations and administrative decisions. Telecom services across the globe are subject to government regulations, whether provided by a state-owned operator or a private operator. The state policy directions are reflected in each case, whether it is a decision taken with respect to technology, the allocation of resources or the type of distribution of services (Melody, 2001).

It is argued that proactive government policies are responsible for the phenomenal growth of telecom services in both developed and developing countries. The governments of these countries have formulated various affirmative telecom policies and regulations for providing competitive markets[4] and universal services at affordable prices. They also established an independent regulator, which could regulate the telecom sector by formulating rules and regulations (Cave, 2006). There are various economic and non-economic interrelated factors in telecom, where state intervention is necessary for its smooth functioning. The economic factors include interconnection, market entry and competition, spectrum management, and tariff management; and non-economic factors consist of ensuring universal service at affordable prices (Ure, 2010) as discussed in the following sections:

1.5.1. Interconnection

Interconnection allows subscribers of one telecom operator to access networks of the other operators. In the absence of interconnection regulations, the operator with largest network will have a superior market position and use its monopoly power to keep out competitors from the market (Melody, 2001). For example, in USA, its largest telecom operator (AT&T) refused to

---

[4] "Spulber, (2002), discussed that inefficiency of monopoly operator (universal and affordable services) has led to the opening of the sector around the world".

offer interconnection to local operators for long distance connectivity, so local operators filed anti-trust cases against the operator in 1913. This was also backed by the Justice Department. The operator granted the interconnection under pressure, with an agreement for joining an AT&T-led cartel. But new entrants had no right to interconnection. Over the next sixty years, AT&T ruled the USA telecom market, and only in the 1970s, one company - Microwave Communication Inc - won a court ruling against AT&T that allowed it interconnection for long distance services. This eventually led to the breakup of AT&T and the government formulated interconnection policy in 1982, further amended in 1996 (Noam, 2006). Therefore, pro-active policy and regulation for interconnection are necessary for competitive telecom markets.

1.5.2. Market Entry and Competition

Cave (2006) and Ure (2010) stated that a monopoly market restricts the opportunities for new entrants, and reduces the competitive pressure, efficiency and innovation. It weakens consumer choice and price protection. They argued that competition is the most effective means to achieve efficiency and innovation in the supply of goods and services. A well-functioning competitive market protects consumers by providing them various choices, affordable telecom prices, and characterized by easy entry and exit.

Most of the telecom markets in the world do not fully satisfy the conditions of a perfect market. Therefore, the state needs to limit the monopolist's behaviour and improve market performance. It attempts to maintain active competition in the market by formulating policy for easing entry and exit barriers and prohibiting abuses of monopoly power.

1.5.3. Spectrum Management

Since spectrum is a limited natural resource used by mobile operators for communication, it is awarded through a state-managed administrative process of lotteries or by auctions (Melody, 2001). However, it is now also considered as a revenue raising process by the governments. The spectrum set aside for mobile phone services by the government in a country limits its total capacity and determines competition in the market. The competition in the mobile phone market grows as the number of competitors grows; as four operators may be few and six are many.

The important issue in a market is the number of licences offered for a spectrum and the number of existing telecom operators. These operators would like to stay in the business and are willing to stop the potential new entrants. In such a scenario, the existing operators can collude among themselves and bidding will be dismal. On the other hand if too many licenses are offered, that could also bring down the auction revenue. Therefore, the licences have to be one or two more than the existing operators to attract new operators and increase revenue (Cramton, 2006). This needs state intervention in terms of proper spectrum management, which provides the right balance between competition and government revenue generation.

1.5.4. Tariff Management

It is observed that the dominant mobile operator (monopoly market) exercises its power to decide the price of services in absence of tariff regulations in a particular market (Ure, 2010). However, this power disappears once the market gets competitive, but still, access price control may be necessary. In the case of competitive markets, a forbearance (self-control) regulation is allowed where new operators start offering lower tariff to get additional subscribers, an action that would benefit consumers. But the same may also stifle the competitive market as it will have an adverse effect upon the business plan of both new entrants and incumbents. Some have argued that rebalancing of tariffs in long and international calls by a targeted subsidising scheme for low income, backward areas or those who are making relatively few calls, is the right approach (Sappington, 2006). Therefore, the right balance of tariff regulations is necessary for a competitive mobile telecom market.

1.5.5. Universal Service Obligation

Universal service obligation (USO) means geographical coverage of telecom services in the whole country, so that all the people or households can access the services at an affordable price. The rationale for universal service is to bridge the digital divide emerging between the information-rich and information-poor groups or areas (Cave, 2006).

States impose universal service obligations on operators to provide telecom services all over the country with a uniform tariff, despite significant cost differences. However, there is a view that after the introduction of competition in the market, mobile operators would only focus upon high-value customers defined either by their calling patterns or their place of residence, and abandon the objective of universal service obligation. Therefore, to avoid such a possible outcome, the cost of the USO has to be shared on some equitable basis between the operators providing services and the other competitors. The state has to formulate appropriate regulations or policy regarding the same to provide universal services (Ure, 2010).

The governments of developing countries have initiated several pro-active policies and regulations on these issues discussed above, that resulted in competition in the market, reduction in tariff, quality services and rolling out of the mobile phone services in remote and rural areas. However, many a time the state policies and regulations have produced poor results because of continuous development of new mobile phone technology. In addition, sometimes policies and regulations are also hampered by various constraints such as political interference and lobbying. In this context, it will be interesting to discuss how the Indian mobile phone sector has evolved over the years.

1.6. DEVELOPMENT OF MOBILE PHONE SERVICES IN INDIA

Telecom services were not perceived as one of the key infrastructures[5] during the formative years of the India's economy. The government initiated some policy initiatives in the middle of the 1980s by allowing the private sector in telecom equipment

[5] "The sixth five year plan document, of Planning Commission, Government of India, 1980 mentioned that the primary need of the people is food, water and shelter, telecom development can wait. In place of doing any good, development in the telecom infrastructure tended to intensify the migration of population from rural to urban areas. There is need to curb growth of telecom infrastructure, particularly in the urban area (Dossani, (2002) pp. 30).

manufacturing in 1984, and by setting up the Department of Telecom (DoT) in 1985 and creating two Public Sector Corporations (PSUs), Mahanagar Telephone Nigam Limited (MTNL) and Videsh Sanchar Nigam Limited (VSNL), to provide domestic and international telecom services in 1986. The government took a major policy step by allowing private participation in the telecom sector in 1992 and announcing the National Telecom Policy (NTP94) in 1994, which established a duopoly regime with two operators (one government and the other private) competing in four metros and eighteen regional divisions- called circles - of the country.

The introduction of private competition in the sector was extended to foreign ownership which ranged from 49 percent in basic, mobile and other voice telephone services-subject to licensing and security requirements. The NTP94 placed considerable emphasis on protecting consumer interests and ensuring fair competition, which led to the establishment of an independent agency - Telecom Regulatory Authority of India (TRAI) - in 1997 to regulate the sector.

The private operators bid a high fixed licenses fee in 1995 for telecom circles depending upon the perceived revenue potential of each circle. These licensees were to pay a fixed amount of licence fees annually based on the agreed amount during the bidding process. The licence fee per customer worked out to around Rs 500 per month in expectation of a high profit margin from the rollout of the services (Upadhyay, 2009; Desai, 2006). However, the telecom sector was posting losses worth $92 million every month. Industry expert argued that overestimation of market size and usage was the main problem, which had projected 300 minutes in a month. Beside, average revenue per user was only $23 compared to projections, which had ranged between $41 and $58 per month. As a result by July 1999, telecom operators owed almost $900 million in licence fees to the government (Achar, 1999).

The government faced a situation where the telecom operators would have to default on their payments and their licenses would have to be cancelled. Facing this problem, the government responded with a New Telecom Policy in 1999 (NTP99) that mandated moving to a revenue-sharing regime, where the operators were to pay their license fees (15 per cent of their adjusted gross revenue[6]) through a share of their annual revenue, over a 20 year period.

The government gradually opened the telecom sector, increased the number of operators and introduced policies that increased competition. In the year 2000, the National Long Distance (NLD) market was opened to private operators and Bharat Sanchar Nigam Limited (BSNL) as a corporate body, by separating the operational part from DoT, was established. Public sector operators (BSNL/MTNL) were allowed as the third operator in the mobile phone market. Further, the government created a new body, separate from TRAI, namely the Telecom Dispute Settlement Appellate Tribunal (TDSAT), to handle the disputes among licensees and licensors, between two mobile operators, and between operator and a group of consumers.

In 2001, the entry of a fourth operator was allowed in the mobile phone market, and the international long distance (ILD) market opened up to private operators; and Videsh Sanchar Nigam Limited (VSNL) was privatized in 2002. The government also set up Universal Service Obligation Fund (USOF) under the DoT, funded through a 5 per cent tax on annual revenues of operators to develop the mobile phone infrastructure in rural and remote areas, and TRAI implemented calling party pays[7] in 2003. The unified access licence regime was implemented allowing any operator to offer services using any technology, and the broadband policy was unveiled in 2004. Next, in 2005, the government step to hike the foreign direct investment limit from the earlier 49 per cent to 74 percent led to the desired momentum in the mobile phone sector. These steps taken by government had allowed competition and growth of mobile phone services in India. In 2006, India became the fifth country to cross the 100 million mark of subscribers, and it overtook China as the fastest growing mobile telecom market in the World.

[6] Upadhyay, (2009) in his paper mentioned as adjusted gross revenue is calculated after excluding all interconnection charges, roaming charges, access charges being paid to other operators for using their network and revenues like though handset sale.

[7] Only caller has to bear the cost of calls.

The government phased out access deficit charges[8] and removed the cap on the number of players in a circle in 2007. Subsequently, 122 new licenses for second generation spectrum on 'first come first served' basis were allocated to operators in 2008 at a price determined in 2001. Entry of more operators in the mobile phone market increased competition - on an average 10-12 operators in each circle - and call tariffs came down drastically resulting in expansion of mobile phone subscribers by almost two and half times, from around 300 million to 800 million in 2012. Further, successful third Generation (3G) and Broadband Wireless Auction (BWA) held in 2010 brought more than expected revenue to the government (Rs 6775 billion). Mobile Number Portability (MNP) was introduced in 2011, which enabled subscribers to get a wider choice and the facility to switch between service providers easily. The National Telecom Policy, 2012 was announced after a gap of more than one decade in 2012 to promote the next growth wave with unified licence regime-wherein an operator can provide all kind of services with a single licence and delinking spectrum from licence. The government announced draft policy branded as National Digital Communication Policy, 2018, with main focus on broadband for all.

The favourable policies and regulatory steps taken by government has transformed the Indian mobile phone sector and it emerged as one of the fastest growing sector with 20 per cent per annum compound growth rate during the period 1993 to 2018. India today is second largest country in terms of telephone phone subscribers in the World (around 1206 million subscribers after China) with around 92.8 per cent tele-density[9] by March, 2018. In particular, mobile phones have proved to be more useful in developing countries like India, where existing fixed-line infrastructure was weak and underdeveloped (Ducombe and Boating, 2009). The mobile phone dominates the present Indian telecom market with almost 98 per cent share of total phone subscribers. Hence, the telecom sector is termed as mobile phone sector in the present study interchangeably.

This diffusion of mobile phones is not only providing affordable telecom services to consumers but also contributing directly and

[8] Desai, (2006), mentioned in his paper that access deficit charges introduced to compensate BSNL for operating in rural areas on all type of calls.

[9] The number of phone subscribers for every 100 people of the country.

indirectly to India's GDP, Foreign Direct Investment and Employment. This led to the socio-economic empowerment and rise in income level of both individuals and telecom operators (World Bank, 2011) and has high spill over effect to other associate sectors like Information Technology and Information Technology Enabled Services such as business process outsourcing, financial services and community services such as education and health (Kotwal *et al.,* 2010; Islam, 2011).

Indian policy makers and their critics often cited the positive policies and regulations initiated by state as responsible for the success of the mobile telecom sector, which has been carried out in very fast and efficient ways (Bagchi, 2000;Uppal*et al.,* 2006). After a healthy growth, the Indian mobile telecom sector experienced downward movement between 2009 and 2013 and recovered later (Thomas, 2011; Guha and Roy, 2012; Gupta, 2015; Mehta, 2015). During the same period industry experts and scholars raised concern about falling or stable revenue[10], drop in foreign investment[11], intense competition[12], fall in tariff[13], rise in debt[14], reduction in net addition of subscribers and widening rural-urban divide[15]. They argued policy uncertainty was responsible for the fall in financial health of the sector after successful journey before it[16](PwC, 2011; Thomas, 2011; Amulaya

[10] TRAI, (2012) mentioned that average revenue per user of telecom operators in India,which was only Rs 100 in 2011, is one of the lowest and approximately one-third compared to other developing countries.

[11] FICCI, (2013) report discussed that the SC cancellation of 122 2G licenses awarded in 2008 has deteriorated the telecom environment and generated negative publicity and discouraged investors from additional investment in the sector.

[12] PwC, (2011) report highlighted that average 10 to 13 operators per circle in India.

[13] PwC, (2011) mentioned that India's mobile phone tariff was only Rs 0.30 per minute in 2011.

[14] PwC, (2011) report elaborated that mobile operators invested heavily for acquiring 3G licenses and taking loans for rolling out network which may resulted in huge debt in the sector.

[15] According to TRAI, (2013) reports tele-density in India was more than 140 per cent in urban areas and 35 per cent in rural areas.

[16] Guha and Roy, (2012) highlighted that the telecom policy was last announced in 1999, after that mobile technology and services have changed a lot and the allocation of 2G spectrum licences to favour a few in 2008 turned the market into an intense competitive zone with the lowest tariff in the world. The cancellation of 2G spectrum licences by the Supreme Court (SC) has shown signs of policy uncertainty in the sector.

and Annad, 2012; Mani, 2012; Guha and Roy, 2012; FICCI, 2013; Mehta, 2015; ICRA, 2016). Again, after the recovery, the entry of Reliance Jio in 2016 has changed the industry scenario by providing free services for initial two quarters and services at low prices afterwards. As a result, RJio has captured around one-sixth of the total telecom market within one-year time. But affected other operators' market badly particularly smaller ones, who have either merged with big players or have exited from the market due to continuous fall in their subscribers' and reduction in revenue in the last year.

In this process, the market is consolidating and consumers have benefited with low price voices, high speed data and other services. In particular, the people from low socio-economic strata and from rural or backward areas are able to get access to mobile voice and data services at low prices. But, the price war among the operators is also hurting the growth of the sector, which is an area of great concern for its future development. Many questions appear in this context. How did the mobile phone sector become one of the most successful sector in the last decade?; How did state policies contribute in the success of mobile phone sectors?; What are the factors responsible for the growth of sector, mobile phone operators and consumers?; How the sector is contributing to Indian economy and its job market?; How mobile phone sector is responsible for the socio-economic empowerment of people?; Are the present policies and regulatory environment favourable for the growth of the sector?; and, what is the future of mobile phone sector and its challenges?, and what steps are needed for its future growth?

1.7. RATIONALE FOR THE STUDY

The above discussion indicates that Indian economy has changed enormously during the last few decades. This is partly because of the country's huge advances in information and communication technology, and also due to new thinking with respect to the theory of economic development. Economic history indicates that for developing countries at India's level of per capita income, economic growth was normally led by the industry or manufacturing sectors. However, the leading sector in contemporary Indian economic growth has increasingly been services rather than industry. There is a view which suggests that because of technological development and other factors, services may in the future replace industry as the engine of growth, even in developing countries. In that sense, India may be regarded as pioneering a new development path which gives primacy to services rather than to industry as the leading sector (Nayyar, 2012; Ghose, 2013).

But in the literature of development economics, the debate on role of the service sector in economic development process is limited unlike agriculture and industrial sectors, which have been extensively debated. The increasing importance of services in India, in particular the growth engine of sector, *i.e.,* mobile phone services, deserves attention in the present context and needs detailed investigation on the issues raised above. Literature on mobile phone services has emerged only after the opening of the sector in mid-nineties focusing on three main issues. The first set of literature looked performance of mobile phone sector and its relationship with economic growth by using various macro-economic approaches (Vittal, 1997; Waverman *et al.,* 2005; Strother Neil, 2004; Sridhar and Sridhar, 2007; Ramachandran, 2005; Kathuria *et al.*, 2009). Second set of studies examined mobile phone operators productivity and efficiency analysis focusing mainly on developed and only selected Asian countries (Giokas and Pentzaropoulos, 2000; Rusdi, 2000; Lee, Park and Oh, 2000; Pentzaropoulos and Giokas, 2002; Lam and Lam, 2005; Liao Chun-Hsiung *et al.,* 2007; Sharma *et al.,*2010). Third set of literature examined telecom policies and regulatory environment impact on the growth of the sector and operator's business (Noll, Roger, 2000; Fink *et al.*, 2002; Samarajiva *et al.,* 2007; Samarajiva, 2009; Goswami and Malik, 2007; Malik, 2006). In addition, selected studies also examined the impacts of mobile phone services on people in India (Baijal, 2004; Chowdary, 2000; Guha and Kaushal, 2010; Gual and Trillas, 2006; Jensen, 2007; Abraham, 2006; Souter, *et al.,* 2005; Mittal, *et al.*, 2010; Sood, 2006).

However, the studies examining whole picture of mobile phone sector and its economic and social impact particularly with emerging new technology in recent years are not available in India. In addition, the studies on performance analysis of operators, assessment of continuous changing regulatory environment and emerging or future of the sector are limited. Hence, a book containing systematically analysis of economic and social impact of mobile phone sector with changing policy and regulatory environment is need of the hour. This book would help the policy makers and mobile phone operators in formulating future policies and strategies. In the light of above concerns, the following are main objectives of the book.

1.8. OBJECTIVES

The general objective is to understand the economic and social impact of mobile phone sector during the last one and half decade period. Further, the sub-objectives or specific objectives include, To review the state telecom policies and regulatory system; To study the performance of the mobile phone sector, operators performance and factors responsible for its growth; To study direct and indirect economic contribution of the sector; To study the social impact of mobile phone; To study the future of mobile phone sector; To study the stakeholders' view on current mobile phone sector policy and regulatory environment and To provide suggestions and future strategies.

1.9. STUDY FRAMEWORK AND METHODOLOGY

As discussed earlier the favourable policies and positive regulatory environment has made Indian mobile telecom sector as one of the successful sector. It is well known fact that apart from the government's positive steps, other stakeholders also played an important role in the formulation of favourable policy. Nørgaard and Møller (2002) has developed a framework to understand the government policies and regulatory environment and its impact on economy. This analysis framework after few modifications has been adopted for the analysis. Accordingly, the three stage analysis - macro, me so and micro level has been performed to examine the objective of the book. At *macro level-* journey of mobile phone sector and its impact on economy, at *meso level* –performance *of* mobile phone operators and its impact on the telecom sector', and at *micro level mobile phone* impact on socio-economic empowerment of consumers have been taken for the analysis. In addition, the future growth drivers and various stake holders' views are also taken on present regulatory environment.

The analysis in the present book is based on both secondary and primary sources of data and information. Secondary sources include Telecom Regulatory Authority of India, Central Statistical Organization, Annual financial statements of various operators and other published material and websites, while primary data was collected by conducting interview from 90 different stakeholders, (operators, consultants, academicians) in India and 394 mobile phone users in rural Bihar. The advance statistical analysis such as concentration index (herfindahl-hirschman index), data envelopment analysis, partial productivity, ratio analysis for data analysis and statistical tests like unit root test and granger causality test performed for the validation the data.

Detailed data sources and methodologies used for the analysis have been discussed in the respective chapters. Although there are few limitations of the study such as the only services part of the telecom sector is analysed in this book. The TRAI data has limitation as it is self-reporting information by telecom operators. In the study, sometimes it is very difficult to segregate the financial data for mobile and other services. In such a scenario, overall telecom sector's financial data has been analyzed instead of just mobile phone services sector. The financial data reported by mobile operators has its limitations as some time they indulge into creative accounting to artificially boost their profit figure to attract investors.

1.10. CHAPTERS OF THE BOOK

To meet the objectives of the book, its scope is defined by an analysis of the questions presented above in five substantive chapters (Chapter 3 to 7), each of which endeavours to make an original contribution to the literature on the subject. Although each chapter of the book is a self-contained piece of research and they are closely interrelated. The result of the first two chapters sets the stage for the analysis in the next four chapters, so a set of results from one chapter validate important assumption in subsequent chapters. This book is an attempt to understand the mobile phone sector comprehensively at macro (overall sector), meso (operators) and micro (consumers and other stakeholders) level analysis.

First chapter 'Introduction' introduces the topic with economic growth and technology relationship and economic characteristics of mobile phone services. The chapter highlights emergence of service sector and mobile phone service in India and discusses success, challenges, motivate for study, objectives, study framework and layout of the book. Sector chapter 'Evolution of State Telecom Policies and Regulatory Institutions' describe evolution of policy, regulations and institutions with their role in development of telecom sector in the country. Third chapter 'Journey of Mobile Phone Sector' analyse performance of the sector and mobile phone operators with changing scenario of the sector during last one decade.

Fourth chapter 'Economic Contribution of Mobile Phone Sector' presents a comparative analysis sector contribution in terms of revenue to national income, public funding or income through various regulatory charges or fees such as spectrum auctions, licence fee, spectrum usage charges and other taxes, and job creation by the sector. In addition, the chapter also discusses the indirect contribution of the sector in the economy through multiplier or spill over effects. Fifth chapter 'Impact on Mobile Phone Users' discusses the socio-economic impact on mobile phone consumers by a detail survey among selected consumers of mobile phone in rural or remote areas. Sixth chapter 'Growth Drivers of the Sector' highlighted the future growth drivers such as untapped rural area, broadband or data services, 5G and internet of things etc. and positive government initiatives. Seventh chapter 'Evaluation of State Telecom Policy and Regulatory Environment' is based on analysis of interviews of various stakeholders on the mobile telecom regulatory environment in the country. Last chapter 'Conclusion and Policy Implications' summarizes the findings with important conclusive remarks and future policy suggestions for the development of the mobile phone sector, keeping into account the welfare of both the operators as well as the consumers.

2

Telecom Policies and Regulatory Institutions

2.1. BACKGROUND

The history of the Indian Telecom sector goes way back to 1851, when the first operational landlines were laid by The British Government near Kolkata (Calcutta). Their primary interest was to use telecom services as a tool for maintaining law-and-order (Headrick, 1998). In 1876, Alexander Graham Bell issued a patent for inventing the telephone and created the Bell Telephone Company. Five year later, in 1881, British firms brought telephone to India and British government granted licence to operate till 1944 (Subramanian, 2008). Indian Telegraph Act was enacted in 1885, which gave exclusive privilege of establishing, maintaining and working of "telecom services" to the Government. It also empowered the Government to grant licence to any person to establish, maintain or operate telecom services within any part of India. Total 321 telephone exchanges and 338 long-distance public call offices were set up with 82 thousand subscribers till India's Independence, in 1947 (Mody, 1995).

After independence, all the foreign telephone firms were nationalised to form Department of Posts, Telephone and Telegraph (PTT) and became a vehicle for employment and welfare (Subramanian, 2008). Under the PTT monopoly, telephones were not considered as an essential service but a luxury. In a period of next 40 years after independence, new telephone lines were added only to cities and metro areas with only 1per cent tele-density.

Only after mid-1980s, Indian government paid greater attention to telecom sector and announced new electronic policy in 1984 and set up the Centre for Development of Telemetric (C-DoT). C-DoT produced switches and soon went into mass production and started the concept of the PCO or Public Call Office, which is a small shop located in markets, grocery shops, and other public places. The PCO phone worked well and successfully reached across the cities and towns of India (Subramanian, 2008).

The Department of Telecom (DoT) was set up after splitting PTT in 1985. The DoT became exclusive provider of both local and long distance telecom services and the profits that accrued from telecom remained with it (Mody, 1995). But the combination welfare-type employment[17]and poor technology made telecom services far from satisfactory (Subramanian, 2008; Jeffery and Doron, 2013). Within one year, government, businessmen and private users started complaining about the poor service from DoT. This led to the creation of the two Public Sector Units (PSU) in 1986, Mahanagar Telephone Nigam Limited (MTNL) to run the telecom services in Delhi and Mumbai metropolitan and Videsh Sanchar Nigam Limited (VSNL) to run international telecom services. This corporatization of the government's department was a move to professionalise telecom sector. However, DoT still controlled these corporations directly or indirectly (Mukherji, 2009).

A high powered Telecom Commission was established to direct policy formulation, licensing, wireless spectrum management, administrative monitoring of PSUs, research and development and standardisation/validation of equipment with DoT in 1989. Despite the above mentioned attempts, the growth of telecom sector was abysmally slow due to limited resources or funds. In a year period, the government formed a high level committee on the reorganisation of telecom department, which recommended that the DoT needs to be restructured, Value Added Services (VAS)[18] must be open for competition and policy and regulation should be separated from operations (Mukherji, 2009).

[17] Provided employment to thousands of Indians and thus became a vehicle for employment and welfare.

These recommendations of the committee were not taken up seriously by the government. In 1992, ministers and bureaucrats also rejected the recommendations of Rangarajan Committee for disinvestment of PSUs up to 49 per cent. The committee was formed to recommend the disinvestment of shares in Public Sector Units. This rigidness of the government, apart from limited resource and absence of proper policy or plan were primarily responsible for slow progress of the telecom sector till early nineties (Kathuria, 2000; Bagchi, 2000).

2.2. TELECOM POLICIES

The telecom sector was opened up for private participation to attract capital and followed by announcement of the National Telecom Policy in May, 1994.

2.2.1. National Telecom Policy 1994 (NTP94)

The main objectives of NTP94 were to provide affordable telecom services to all people, cover all villages, availability of telephone on demand, to make the country a major manufacturing base of telecom equipment and to ensure defence and security needs. Private participation opened in basic services, mobile services as well as VAS except National Long Distance (NLD) and International Long Distance (ILD) telecom services. The first mobile phone service was launched in Calcutta in July, 1995. NTP94 also envisaged setting up of an autonomous regulator, Telecom Regulatory Authority of India (TRAI) in 1997 as an independent authority to regulate the sector.

However, the NTP94 policy did not fully yield the desired results of private participation or deregulation in telecom sector. It failed to define clearly how universal access and service goals were to be achieved, while there had been a rapid rollout of cellular mobile network in Metros[19] and States (circle)[20] with over one million subscribers, but most of the operators were in

---

[18] "DoT, (1994) defined Value added services, which includes electronic mail, voice mail; data services; audio text services; video text services; video conferencing; radio paging and cellular mobile telephone" accessed on 12 March, 2013 from http://www.dot.gov.in/telecom-polices/national-telecom-policy-1994

loss (Jain, 2001). The companies who had taken licences failed to fulfill their licence conditions. Their actual revenues realised from the projects were far lesser than the projections and they were also unable to arrange finances for their projects. The high licence fee further eroded their business viability. The licence fee worked out to be around 500 INR per month. As the detail given in the first chapter, the revenue of the operators was less than expected, it became difficult for the operator to pay the instalment of licence fee and the sector was virtually on the brink of the collapse (Upadhyay, 2009). As a result, some of the targets envisaged in NTP94 remained unfulfilled and concerns were raised regarding the further development of the sector (Chaudhary, 2004).

The government asked two agencies, ICICI and Bureau of Industrial Cost and Prices (BICP) to review the progress of the sector in quick succession. First was to examine the sector's performance and report on the need for a licence extension for cellular services and second to review the viability of private cellular operations. The government also constituted a high level Group on Telecom (GoT) to review the NTP94. Both the agencies and GoT accepted that the sector was in trouble, private operators and investors suggested for government intervention. The Government viewed this with great concern as it was adversely affecting the future development of the sector and recognized the need to take a fresh look at the policy framework. As a result, NTP99 was formulated and declared in July 1999 (JPC Report, 2013[21]).

[19] Four Metros cities of Delhi, Mumbai, Kolkata and Chennai

[20] "Jain, (2001) mentioned in his paper that circles have been classified as category A, B and C based on their revenue potential, subscriber potential and DoT's already present infrastructure, *i.e.,* largely state. Type A circles were considered most attractive commercially and type C the least. For administrative convenience, the larger states were divided into two circles, while some smaller states were amalgamated together. For cellular services, DoT decided to have two operators per service area, while for basic services there would be one more operator besides DoT in each service area"

[21] Joint Parliamentary Committee (JPC) report to examine matters relating to allocation and pricing of Telecom Licences And Spectrum', LokSabha Secretariat, New Delhi, accessed on 21 March, 2012 from http://www.prsindia.org/uploads/media/JPC%20Report%20on%202G/JPC%20Report%20on%202G.pdf

2.2.2. New Telecom Policy 1999 (NTP99)

The NTP99 laid down a clear roadmap for future reforms and contemplated opening up of all segments of telecom sector for private sector participation. The main features of NTP99 were strengthening of regulator, opening of NLD and ILD services[22] to private sectors, licence to private telecom operators on a revenue sharing basis[23], plus a one-time entry fee, resolution of problems of existing operators' envisaged and direct interconnectivity and sharing of network with other telecom operators within the service area. Government further amended NTP99 in 2002 by providing licence for Unified Access Services permitting licensee to provide basic and cellular services using any technology in a defined service area. The NTP99 policy also facilitated corporatisation of DoT by the formation of Bharat Sanchar Nigam Limited (BSNL), which was carved out from DoT to promote a fairer competitive field and also terminated its monopoly by opening NLD and ILD telecom services for private sector (Jain, 2002)

2.2.3. Universal Service Obligation (USOF)

The Government is committed to provide basic telecom services to all at affordable and reasonable prices. The government set up a Universal Service Obligation Fund (USOF) in 2002, to increase access to telecom services within rural areas and help to achieve universal service obligations as laid down in the NTP99. The fund is used to subsidise the developments of telephone services in rural/remote areas. Mobile services are also included under USOF in 2006 for creation of infrastructure for provision of mobile and broadband connectivity services in rural and remote areas in a

[22] "TRAI, (2012) report discussed that the NLD Service refers to the carriage of switched bearer telecommunication service over a long distance network *i.e.,* a network connecting different Short Distance Charging Areas (SDCAs). The ILD Service is basically a network carriage service (also called Bearer) providing International connectivity to the Network operated by foreign carriers".

[23] DoT, (2013) discussed that Initially, the percentage of licence was fixed in three slabs (10%, 12% and 15%) of adjusted gross revenue depending upon the category of the circle. The licence fee was reduced in 2004 with 10% of AGR for Metro, 8% for B circles and 6% for C circle (DoT, 2013) accessed on 15 April, 2012 from http://www.dot.gov.in/access-services/introduction-unified-access-servicescellular-mobile-services

phased manner. The resources for meeting the USOF are raised through a 'universal access levy' of 5 per cent from Adjusted Gross Revenue of the operators under various licenses.

The implementation of the USOF for rural and remote areas is undertaken by all service providers, who are reimbursed from the funds collected from the universal access levy. Earlier, DoT was solely responsible for the use of USOF for infrastructure development in rural and remote areas. It is revised later and now opens to every stakeholder, who wants to develop its infrastructure in rural and remote areas. Although USO levy increases the cost burden for the telecom operators but helps in building telecom infrastructure and increase telecom penetration in rural areas. However, over the year, low disbursement and around one third of the unutilised amount of USOF raised the question on its management and planning (JPC Report, 2013; Mehta, 2013).

2.2.4. Broadband Policy

The government announced a national broadband policy in October 2004. This emphasised on creation of infrastructure using technologies such as optical fibre and wireless technologies. The government also proposed to inter-connect all knowledge institutions in the country through an electronic digital broadband network under the broadband policy. Broadband has the potential to contribute in economic growth and quality of life improvement through access of high speed information on education, medicine, governance, entertainment (TRAI, 2012). However, the penetration of the broadband in the country is quite slow with coverage of just 2.2 per cent population till 2012-13.

2.2.5. Foreign Direct Investment (FDI) Policy

The telecom sector is the third major sector attracting FDI inflows after services and computer software sector. In 2005, the government enhanced the FDI limits from 49 per cent to 74 per cent, which resulted in greater amount of foreign investment. In Basic and Cellular Mobile services FDI is limited to 49 per cent and up to 74 per cent permitted in the Internet Service (with gateways). The government decided that proposal for foreign investment greater than 49 per cent shall be submitted to Foreign

Investment Promotion Board (FIPB) for approval on a case-to-case basis. However, the government has permitted 100 per cent FDI in telecom manufacturing under the automatic route. Further, the government has hiked FDI limit to 100 per cent from earlier 74 per cent in July, 2013 to encourage investment in the sector.

2.2.6. Telecom Policy, 2012 (NTP12)

This telecom policy was formulated after a gap of more than a decade. There was a wide gap between rural and urban tele-density, and broadband penetration. NTP99 most targets not only achieved that significantly contributed to overall development of the sector. NTP99 was not relevant and exposed by the controversies of licensing and auctions process. The sector dynamics changed drastically in terms of market, technology and consumer. Hence, the government recognised the need and formulated a new telecom policy in June 2012.

The NTP12 aim was to change the licensing framework to adopt a single (unified) licence across services and telecom circles and de-link licence from service delivery by making it technology neutral and flexible to operate any services. The network sharing in the policy reduced entry barriers and new entrants have now less investment for their network construction. On the other hand, incumbent operators enhanced its network utilization rate and increased revenues by sharing their network. Spectrum Act of allowed spectrum pooling, sharing, and trading for optimal and efficient utilisation of spectrum. Further, re-farming[24] and availability of additional spectrum ensure its efficient use. The policy also initiated for new licensing framework, migration of licensees to the new framework, mergers and acquisitions policy and exit policy, etc.

In addition, rural tele-density targeted from 39 to 70 per cent in next 5 years. The NTP12 mentioned about cloud computing, next generation networks, IPV6 and Voice over Internet Protocol (VoIP) as thrust areas. Government has allowed One Nation - Full Mobile Number Portability (MNP) recently. This has enabled the

[24] TRAI, (2012) document mentioned that re-farming is re-planning or reassigning the spectrum more efficiently and permit introduction of new services that were simply not available with earlier technologies.

subscribers to change their licence service area and still retain their mobile number. MNP also allows subscribers to retain their existing mobile number when they switch from one telecom service provider to another irrespective of technology or service area limitation. This would help in developing mobile numbers as an identity of individuals for providing various government services and harness the power of JAM (Jan Dhan-Aadhar-Mobile) Trinity. But, the policy was unclear cut time line for implementation of re-farming, exit policy, spectrum trading and sharing and merger and acquisition and national roaming policy, out of these targets some are still pending and not achieved till date such as tele-density of rural areas (57 per cent) and VoIP.

2.2.7. Draft Telecom Policy, 2018 (NTP18)

The draft of National Telecom Policy (NTP) 2018 referred as National Digital Communications Policy 2018 has been released recently for public consultations. Some of the highlights are recognising spectrum as a key natural resource for public benefit to achieve India's socio-economic goals, optimise availability and utilisation by making adequate spectrum available to be equipped for the new broadband era; the pricing of spectrum should be optimal to ensure sustainable and affordable access to digital communications and simplifying the process of obtaining permissions from various agencies such as Wireless Planning and Coordination (WPC) and Standing Advisory Committee on Radio Frequency Allocation (SACFA) in order to promote efficiency.

It proposes identifying and making available new spectrum bands for access and backhaul segments for timely deployment and growth of 5G networks and making available harmonised and contiguous spectrum required for deployment of next generation access technologies. Further liberalizing of the spectrum sharing, leasing and trading regime, coordinating with government departments for freeing under utilised/substitutable spectrum, and its auctioning and/ or assignment along with unutilised spectrum for efficient and productive use. There would be transparent and fair mode of spectrum allocation by developing a fair, flexible, simple and transparent method for spectrum assignments and allocations. The policy accomplish some of the strategic objectives by 2022 including — Provisioning of Broadband for all, creating four million additional jobs in the digital communications sector, enhancing the contribution of the digital communications sector to eight per cent of India's GDP from around six per cent in 2017, enhancing India's contribution to global value chains — and ensuring digital sovereignty.

2.2.8. Other Important Initiatives

To enable India's transition into a digital economy and knowledge society large investment in infrastructure, both optical fibre cable and towers, for wireless transmission is required. The Government is committed to extending the reach of the mobile network to the remaining 50,000 remote and rural villages with support from the Universal Services Obligation Fund. In addition, investments are being made to lay optical fibre cable for high speed broadband connectivity in rural areas. The following initiatives have been taken in the last year:

BharatNet

For the deeper digital penetration in rural areas, the Government has taken up BharatNet initiative to link each of the 2.5 lakh Gram Panchayats of India through Broadband optical fibre network. On its completion, BharatNet would facilitate Broadband connectivity for over 600 million rural citizens of the country. This is the largest rural connectivity project of its kind in the world, and is rightfully identified as the first pillar of Digital India Programme. It will facilitate the delivery of various e-Services and applications including e-health, e-education, e-governance and e-commerce. Implementation of the programme has been ramped up since last year. Phase-1 of the project that targeted connecting 100 thousand Gram Panchyat (GP), through Optical Fibre Cable, is nearing completion. As of 5th Nov, 2017, 103.3 thousand GP have been connected by laying 238 thousands kms. Optical Fibre Cable. Of these, 75 thousands GP locations are ready for broadband services.

Network for left wing extremism areas

Department of Telecom executed a project for providing Mobile Services in 2199 locations in Andhra Pradesh, Bihar, Chhattisgarh, Jharkhand, Maharashtra, Madhya Pradesh, Odisha, Telangana, Uttar Pradesh and West Bengal, which are affected by Left Wing

Extremism (LWE). This large project was completed in a short period of 18 months and has brought connectivity to about 3000 villages and helped in the operation of security forces.

Connecting the unconnected

The Government has approved a Comprehensive Telecom Development Plan for North East Region to be funded from Universal Service Obligation Fund (USOF). The total cost of plan is INR 53.36 billion. This project will connect 8621 villages through installation of 321 mobile tower sites. The Department is also implementing a project for laying 2164.23 km of Submarine Optical Fibre Cable between Mainland (Chennai) and Port Blair and five other islands namely Car Nicobar, Little Andaman, Havelock, Kamorta and Great Nicobar Islands of Andaman & Nicobar Islands.

Wi-Fi hotspots

The Department decided, in April 2016, that Outdoor Public Wi-Fi Access Points (OPAP), for last mile connectivity are to be provisioned in the BharatNet network to provide discernible value addition in the BharatNet for citizens. Accordingly, the Department has now approved a proposal to setup 25 thousand Public Wi-Fi Hotspots using the block-level infrastructure of BSNL's Telephone Exchanges in rural areas, at an estimated cost of INR 7.89 billion to be funded from USOF. Community Service Centre (CSC) - SPV has setup of 5,000 Wi-Fi Chaupals at Gram Panchayat levels in 14 States, at an estimated cost of INR 1 billion, funded through USOF. In addition to the above, BharatNet Phase-2 aims provision of community Wi-Fi services at all 250 thousand Gram Panchayats.

Right of way rules

The Central Government has notified the Indian Telegraph Right of Way Rules, 2016 to regulate underground infrastructure (optical fibre) and over ground infrastructure (mobile towers). This rule is applicable to all telecom service providers holding a licence issued under sub-section (1) of section 4 of the Indian Telegraph Act, 1885.These rules have simplified the grant of right of way permissions for creation of telecom infrastructure by making it transparent and time-bound. Under the new Rules, applications for laying fibre underground cable as well as for setting up telecom towers have to be accepted or rejected within a period of 60 days failing which application will be deemed to have been approved. All Government agencies and municipal bodies will also have to establish an electronic interface to receive and process Right of Way permission within one year from coming into force of these Rules in November, 2016. Further, telecom infrastructure cannot be shut down without following due process. This measure is expected to facilitate an increase in the pace of creation of infrastructure both in both rural and urban areas.

Aadhaar based e-KYC for new subscribers

The Government has prescribed an 'Aadhaar based E-KYC services' for issuing mobile connections from September, 2016. Under this, a subscriber can authenticate himself using his biometrics at the point of sale and obtain a new activated sim-card in 30 minutes. When manually done, this process takes almost a day and involves a lot of paper work. In addition to simplifying the process this also ensures security assurance and is an environment friendly measure saving more than 50,000 trees annually.

Introduction of virtual network operators (VNO)

The Government has issued guidelines for UL(VNO) on 31st May, 2016. VNO system allows Telecom Service Providers to utilise their networks and spectrum efficiently by sharing active and passive infrastructure. Further, VNOs can provide services in small towns and rural areas using the network of existing TSPs having unutilised capacity or by last mile connectivity. This apart, the VNOs can be effective in providing services in airports or buildings or in smart cities. DoT has issued VNO licenses to 106 entities as on 31st Oct, 2017

Active infrastructure sharing

The Government issued a notification on 11 Feb, 2016 permitting sharing of active infrastructure amongst service providers based on mutual agreements. The active sharing would cover antenna, feeder cable, Node B, Radio Access network (RAN) and transmission systems. This measure would help in provision of better and speedy services to the consumers while alleviating the cost burden incurred by the operators for laying telecom infrastructure.

Abolition of wireless operating license for telecom service providers

To facilitate ease of doing business, Department of Telecom has abolished Wireless Operating License (WOL) for Access Service Providers from 2nd November, 2016. Earlier WOL was required for any trans-receiver deployed in the telecom network by telecom service providers. This would obviate the need for endorsement by Department of Telecom and result in consequential convenience to Telecom companies. Furthermore, this would prevent the delay in utilization of scarce infrastructure as radio transmission can be started immediately on installation of base stations without waiting for obtaining clearance from Department of Telecom.

2.3. LICENSING FRAMEWORK

2.3.1. Cellular Mobile Telephone Service Licences

After the NTP94, private participation in Basic Telecom Services (BTS) and Cellular Mobile Telephone Service (CMTS) market end the monopoly of the government. The telecom market was duopoly with government incumbent and one private player in BTS, and between two private players in the CMTS market. A maximum of two licences in each service area, 8 CMTS licences in the four metros were awarded to private companies on the basis of a beauty contest[25] in November 1994. This followed by 34 CMTS licences in 18 circles to 14 private operators through a competitive bidding process in November 1995 of Global System for Mobile Communication (GSM) technology. These licensees were to pay

[25] According to TRAI, (2012) report, 'beauty parade' is the bidding processes, which evaluated the bids on certain pre-qualification criteria including bidders' financial net worth, and prior experience in telecom service provisioning. Licence fee was pre-determined and bids were called on selected parameters (such as rural coverage or the fulfilment of roll out obligations).

fixed amount of licence fees annually based on the agreed amount during the bidding process (JPC Report, 2013).

As mentioned earlier fixed licence fee regime of NTP94 was transferred to revenue share based licence fee in NTP99. Public sector undertakings (MTNL/BSNL) were issued licenses for provision of CMTS as third operator in 1999. In January 2001, Basic Service Operators(BSO) were permitted to provide mobility, using Wireless in Local Loop (WLL) technology, to their subscribers with wireless access systems limited within the local area *i.e.,* Short Distance Charging Area (SDCA) in which the subscribers were registered. The government issued fourth cellular licenses in four metros and 13 non-metro circles in October, 2001 through multi-stage bidding[26].

2.3.2. National and International Long Distance Licences

The NTP99 envisaged the opening up of NLD service beyond the service area to private operators and without any restriction to carry inter-circle traffic with effect from August 13, 2000. The licence for NLD was issued on non-exclusive basis, for a period of 20 years and extendable by 10 years at one time. The government further opened the ILD service also from April 1, 2002 to private operators without any restriction on the number of operators. The ILD services are providing network carriage service and international connectivity to networks operated by foreign operators for 20 years period from the date of licence agreement (TRAI, 2012).

2.3.3. Licensing of Internet Services

Videsh Sanchar Nigam Limited (VSNL) launched internet services in India in 1995. The internet services were opened for private participation by government in November 1998. NTP1999 encourage the Internet services by putting the policy in place and further decided to permit to carry voice signal over internet service

[22] TRAI, (2012) document mentioned that 'multistage auction' was specifically a 3 stage ascending auction procedure. By this time the CMTS market had matured and operators could bid at more realistic levels in comparison to earlier auctions. The three stage auction allowed bidders to revise their bids at each stage, thus reducing the probability of the winners curse.

protocol in April, 2002. In 2007, the government decided to issue a single licence to internet service protocols that permitted restricted Internet telephony. These policies have helped the internet services provision to both private and public operators in the country, which still largely limits to urban areas in the country.

2.3.4. Unified Access Service Licences

As mentioned earlier BSO permitted technological neutrality to offer limited mobility services over WLL using Code Division Multiple Access (CDMA) technology in their coverage areas in a condition that the last mile linkage should be only with copper wire, but this condition was relaxed, allowing more advanced technologies in 2001. Moreover, they were also able to offer all-India mobility using the CDMA WLL technology. However, the prices of these services were generally lower than that for GSM cellular mobile services. This created a potential disadvantage for the GSM cellular operators as they had paid substantial amount to obtain their licences and WLL services were increasingly seen as substitute for GSM services (TRAI, 2012).

The TRAI proposed wireless services within the local loop (WLL) for fixed service operators using the CDMA technology. This facility allowed the fixed service operator to provide cell phone type services within a defined short distance charging areas. The GSM Operators felt the pain because the fixed operators paid a lower licence fee, enjoyed a favourable interconnection regime, and, did not pay for utilising the spectrum. These benefits were accorded to the fixed operators in return for fulfilling costly rural commitments (Mukherji, 2009; Jeffery and Doron, 2013).

The cellular operators using the GSM technology were negatively affected by this regulatory development. They approached TDSAT, but it gave two opinions that GSM operators had already benefited from migration to the revenue sharing regime they should bear some extra competition in local area and faster roll-out of fixed wireless lines would help to boost tele-density in rural area. GSM operators approached Supreme Court in 2003. As a result, the government introduced Unified Access Service Licensing (UASL) regime in November, 2003 and eliminated the need for separate licences for different services. It permitted a service provider to offer both fixed and mobile services under the same licence, using any technology. Basic and cellular services licensees were permitted to migrate to UASL regime and the service providers migrating to UASL continue to provide wireless services in already allocated/contracted spectrum. The GSM operators subsequently withdrew the cases, when Unified Access Service Licensing (UASL) was allowed for both GSM and CDMA technology. From 2003 onwards, only UAS licenses were issued and Government decided to permit dual technology for an existing licensee by payment of additional specified charges (TRAI, 2012).

Further, government also announced criteria for additional spectrum and removed cap on number of players in a circle in 2007. In the following year, 122 new UAS licences were auctioned and granted on first come first serve basis to the operators in 2008. After the grant of these new licences, the number of operators in all the service areas increased from earlier on an average 6 per circle to 14 per circle, which argued high-competitiveness in the market (PwC, 2011).

2.4. SPECTRUM MANAGEMENT

The electromagnetic spectrum[27] is the most essential input for the growth of wireless services. In India, spectrum is considered as a scarce natural resource and shared among Defence, Railways and other government departments and the two streams of CMTS providers, that is, GSM and CDMA. In India, the DoT conducts auctions of licenses for spectrum. As mentioned earlier the government first issued licenses of GSM standards to two operators per service area for offering cellular services after competitive bidding for a 10-year period, extendable by five years. Further, third operator (DoT/MTNL) in 1999 and fourth operator provided licences through multistage auction in 2001.

[27] TRAI, (2012) document mentioned that 'multistage auction' was specifically a 3 stage ascending auction procedure. By this time the CMTS market had matured and operators could bid at more realistic levels in comparison to earlier auctions. The three stage auction allowed bidders to revise their bids at each stage, thus reducing the probability of the winners curse.

In order to prioritise spectrum allocation among competing bidders, DoT introduced a subscriber linked spectrum allocation process in 2002, which provided for a maximum allotment of 12.5 MHz of spectrum per operator in each circle. The initial allotment of spectrum along with the licence was 4.4 MHz for GSM and 2.5 MHz for CDMA. This was further increased up to 6.2 MHz for GSM and 5 MHz for CDMA operators depending on availability and the operator's ability to justify the need for it. However, this criteria was not used anywhere in the World and the fixed amount of spectrum given to the operators in the country was also far below compared to the International average of 17.18 MHz (TRAI, 2012).

2.4.1. UASL Licence Auction

DoT modified the criteria for additional spectrum in 2007 and announced that additional player could get UASL licenses and start-up spectrum based on availability. It subsequently issued 2G spectrum 122 new licences on the basis of First Come First Serve auction process to the operators in 2008. However, the method of licence allotment process and prices of spectrum-at a price determined in 2001-raised questions of favoritism to certain companies in the auction and loss of government revenue by Comptroller and Auditor General (CAG) in 2010. In response, the Supreme Court of India later cancelled all these licenses in February 2012 and directed for re-auctioning of the same to the DoT (TRAI, 2012).

2.4.2. 3G and BWA Spectrum Auctions

The department of telecom issued guidelines for auction of 3G spectrum in the 2.1 GHz band and BWA spectrum in the 2.3 GHz band through e-auction in August 2008 at market determined price through a transparent process. The action was held in May, 2010 and a total 9 private operators participated in the 3G and 11 private operators for BWA auction. Out of which 7 operators won 3G, and 6 operators BWA auction in various telecom circles. The auction brought in revenues for the government far beyond expectations (Rs 165 billion), which was almost five times for 3G and seven times for BWA reserve prices.

The public sector operators, BSNL and MTNL were granted 3G licenses by the DoT before the auction without participation in the process. These two operators allotted the required 3G spectrum on the condition that each would pay an amount which would be equal to higher bid in the auction, which they paid later after the auction. But the process of awarding 3G spectrum without participation and before the auction to public sector operators showed government biasness towards private operators (PwC, 2012).

2.4.3. Recent Spectrum Auctions

The Supreme Court of India had given direction to DoT to auction 2G spectrum licences in November, 2012 and again in March 2013. Consequently, DoT had invited bid for both GSM and CDMA band in October, 2012. But the response of the auction was poor and no bidder turned for CDMA spectrum auctioned, which was subsequently cancelled. Although, Tata and Videocon had applied to participate in the auction of CDMA but withdrew their application later saying the high reserve price of the spectrum. On the other hand, similar response was also seen for GSM, only five operators participated in the auction and no bidder turned for Delhi, Mumbai, Karnataka and Rajasthan circles and more than half of the auctioned spectrum remains unsold (TRAI, 2012).

Immediately after the first round of auction, the government reduced the reserve price of spectrum by 30 per cent and again invited application for second round of auction in March, 2013. However, no bidder expressed interest in 1800 MHZ and 900 MHZ bands, and only few operator bids for 800 MHZ. Out of total spectrum put for auction only 40 per cent was sold. The poor response of the auction attributed by operators was the high reserve price of spectrum and their high debt condition and weak cash flow (PwC, 2012; Mehta, 2013). Some suggest it may be cartelization of some big private players, who did not turn up for the auction.

Further, three spectrum auctions held between 2014 and 2016 as given in Table 2.1.The 2014 and 2015 spectrum auctions was essentially focused on safeguarding business interests, where the telecom companies bid aggressively to maintain business continuity in key circles, resulting in around 82 per cent and 89 per cent of the spectrum offered was sold across the bands. In contrast, the 2016 auction underpinned the telecom companies' interest to plug the gaps to enhance their spectrum portfolio. They filled up gaps in their spectrum holdings to provide better data services considering the intense competition in the industry, especially since Reliance Jio launched its 4G services in October, 2016.

Therefore, selective bidding was witnessed across bands. In 2016 spectrum auction only 41 per cent of the spectrum offered got sold with no activity seen in 700MHz and 900MHz band. This approach of service providers' underlined their strategic focus areas. Since telecom ecosystem has evolved significantly to cater to the growing needs of data. So, 4G bands, including 2,300MHz and 1,800MHz, with well-developed ecosystem received maximum attention with 100 per cent of 2,300MHz band and 90 per cent of 1,800MHz band put out for auction got sold. The auction also fetched a total amount of Rs 66,000 crore, and highest ever upfront payment of Rs 33,000 crore since 2012. The auction of October, 2016 was the most complex and sophisticated auction of natural resources and was conducted smoothly and transparently, without any glitch. The auction addressed the issue of spectrum scarcity in the country and call drops.

Table 2.1: Spectrum Auction held between 2010 and 2016

Year	*Band (MHz)*	*Spectrum on offer*	*Spectrum sold*	*%Sold*	*Major participants*
2014	900, 1800	431.0	353.2	81.9	Bharti, Vodafone, Idea, Rjio, Telenor
2015	800, 900, 1800, 2100	470.5	418.1	88.9	Bharti, Vodafone, Idea, Rjio, Tata tel, Aircel
2016	700, 800, 900, 1800, 2100, 2300, 2500	2354.5	965	41.0	Bharti, Vodafone, Idea, Rjio, Aircel, Tata, Reliance

Source: ICRA, 2017

The government is now proposing auctions for unsold portion of the previous auctions along with the inclusion of two new bands *i.e.*, 3300-3400 MHz and 3400-3600 MHz. These bands are academically suited for 5G services, wherein deployment across the world is limited. In India, the requirement of this spectrum is some time away, especially when seen in the light of the fact that spectrum in the 2300 MHz band, auctioned in 2010 has not been fully deployed. As of now, the operators in India hold 4345 MHz of spectrum across six bands. The industry appears adequately stocked with spectrum and would look to commit its resources towards deploying the spectrum already acquired instead of buying more.

2.4.4. Re-farming of Spectrum

The technological progress often necessitates re-planning, possibly reassigning the government regulated spectrum. Use of spectrum in more efficient way (from 900 MHz spectrum to 1800 MHz) and permit introduction of new services that were simply not available with earlier technologies. Accordingly, it was felt that for faster and better services such as wireless broadband and data- spectrum must be freed either for a similar use in a particular band or other uses. This process is called re-farming, and in recent times, many countries have undertaken this exercise (Guha *et al.*, 2012). However, spectrum re-farming is a challenge for both operators and regulators. When frequencies have been used for one purpose for long period of time, it is difficult to reallocate these frequencies for a different use. The regulator, therefore, taking the expiration of existing 2G licences as an opportunity to update licence terms in 2014-15 to benefit from the developments in the mobile industry (TRAI, 2012). That requires updating of mobile telecom infrastructure to adapt with refarming spectrum.

This spectrum harmonization of spectrum in 800 MHz and 1800 MHz bands was carried out from April to September, 2016 resulting in rationalisation of spectrum holdings of telecom service providers, and transferring defence holdings to the defence bands. Consequentially, about 197 MHz of additional spectrum was recovered from its erstwhile use as guard and separation bands and was sold for more than Rs. 15000 crores in the October, 2016 auction. Harmonization of spectrum has helped improve quality of service by making fragmented frequency spots contiguous for efficient utilisation by service providers and making more spectrum available for the auction conducted in October, 2016 (BSNL, 2018).

2.4.5. Mergers and Acquisitions Norms

In September 2014, government approved mergers and acquisitions norms. Upon the implementation of M&A the total spectrum held by the resultant entity should not exceed 25% of the total spectrum assigned for access services and 50% of the spectrum assigned in a given band in the concerned service area. Excess spectrum held by the relevant entity as a result of merger should be surrendered within 1 (one) year of the permission being granted. Any demand pertaining to the licenses of the merging entities shall have to be cleared by either of the two licensees before permission for merger / transfer of license/authorisation. The spectrum usage charges as prescribed by the government from time to time, on the total spectrum of the resultant entity shall also be payable. After the entry of RJio in 2016, the waves of mergers or acquisitions are on during the past one year. This shows that only three-four main players, Bharti Airtel, Vodafone and RJio would remain in the market in future.

Table 2.2: Merger/Acquisition in telecom market, 2016-18

Year	*Merger/Acquisition*
2016	Bharti Airtel buys Telenor
2017	Rcom-Aircel merger in a nutshell
	Idea-Vodafone merger
	Videocon's Quadrant exit
	Tata Tele merged with Tata Tele
	RCom discontinued its voice operations
2018	Aircel'saquisition by Airtel

2.4.6. Spectrum Sharing and Trading

The spectrum sharing and trading have been approved and guidelines were issued on September 24, 2015 and October 12, 2015 respectively. Accordingly, the Indian Telecom Industry has witnessed a spur in spectrum trading and sharing activity, largely driven to address the spectrum requirements to meet the data growth in the country. The large telecom operators have been preparing to ride on the data growth wave. The result of sharing and trading policy resulted in deals between Reliance Communications Limited (RCom) and Reliance Jio (RJio); Bharti Airtel Limited (Bharti) and Videocon Telecommunications Limited (Videocon); Bharti and Aircel Limited (Aircel) in the late 2016 and Vodafone and Idea in early 2017 as given below in Table 2.3. Further as discussed above the consolidation of the sector with presence of four-five operators only both by way of mergers between operators and by trading or sharing of spectrum holding is now reality.

Table 2.3: Mergers and spectrum trading & Sharing deals between operators, 2017-18

Participants	***Nature***	***Spectrum band***	***Rationale***
Bharti–Aircel	Spectrum trading	2300 MHz	Bharti improving its spectrum holding in 2300 MHz band for 4G services Makes Bharti a pan India 4G operator Aids in debt reduction for Aircel
Bharti–Videocon	Spectrum trading	1800 MHz	Bharti sharing up its 1800 MHz spectrum holding for 4G services was a contiguous spectrum and thus better suited for 4G services Paves way for gradual exit of Videocon from the sector
RCom–Sistema	Merger	800 MHz	RCom strengthening its 800 MHz spectrum holding for 4G services Exit of Sistema as a telco
RCom–Aircel	Merger	Across spectrum bands	Achieving synergies across services, subscriber base and spectrum holding RCom–RJio Spectrum sharing/trading 800 MHz Both players would be able to plug the gaps in 800 MHz spectrum holding
RCom-RJio	Spectrum trading	800 MHz	Jio would plug the gap in 800 MHz spectrum holding
Vodafone–Idea	Merger	Across spectrum bands	Achieving synergies across services, subscriber base and spectrum holding

Source: ICRA, 2017

This started when government allowed spectrum sharing for the first time in India on 21st April, 2016 when operators were allowed to pool their respective spectrum holdings for using the whole spectrum block (which was the sum of their respective holdings). As on today, spectrum is being shared by two service providers in 21 out of 22 service areas. Since spectrum efficiency increases exponentially with the size of the spectrum block, spectrum sharing has helped multiply spectrum efficiency many times without the need of additional spectrum, besides generating additional revenue for the Government. In another measure aimed at facilitating optimization of resources, the government has permitted trading of Spectrum by allowing an Access Service

Provider (Seller) to transfer spectrum usage rights and obligations to another Access Service Provider (Buyer).

This is meant to facilitate optimisation of resources. The first such trade took place on 17thMay, 2016 and this facility has thereafter been utilised by a number of telecom service providers. Spectrum trading enables telecom players to sell their spectrum and exit leading to consolidation in the sector. This has helped reduce the number of service providers from 10 to 8, thereby reducing fragmentation of spectrum. Trading also facilitates ease of doing business through greater competition, incentives for innovation, better/new services being available to consumers at cheaper tariffs

2.5. TARIFF AND REGULATORY CHARGES

The regulatory body TRAI is empowered to fix tariffs for telecom services under TRAI Act of 1997. First tariff regulation in the country was initiated with the notification of Telecom Tariff Order, 1999 (TTO, 1999). It specified in form of a package of monthly rental and call charges, for basic and cellular services that is termed the "standard tariff package." This package must be provided to the customer.

The review of mobile phone tariff was first done in the year 2002 in view of emerging market scenario, the TRAI came to the conclusion that a stage has reached when market forces could effectively regulate cellular tariff due to competition. Accordingly, the regulatory agency forbear the tariffs for cellular mobile services vide 23rd amendment to TTO dated September 6, 2002, under which service providers are left free to provide any "alternative tariff package". Since the standard tariff package is always available to the customer, any alternative tariff package has to be better in order to attract any customer (TRAI, 2012).

The alternative tariff packages being attractive only if the expenditure involved in them is lower than that for the standard tariff package. This method of flexibility was adopted because of the growing tendency in telecom markets to provide different tariff combinations for various baskets of services. Thus, the standard tariff package can be viewed as a ceiling tariff, with operators free to provide alternative tariffs that were below this level (TRAI,

2012). The possibility of giving alternative tariffs provided a means of addressing several concerns. Further, tariffs for basic service were forborne except for: (i) rural fixed line services; (ii) national roaming services; and (iii) leased circuits in November 5, 2003. Over time, with greater competition in the market, tariffs for basic services is stable with Rs 1 per minute and for cellular mobile have seen dramatic declines from Rs 7.3 per minute in 2000 to Rs 0.5 per minute in 2012 within such a framework.

2.5.1. Interconnection Usage Charges

Interconnection as discussed in the introductory chapter is the lifeline of telecom services and allows subscribers and service provider to access the network of other subscribers and service provider. Interconnection is very important for the service providers and users. No new entrant into the market will be able to compete effectively unless it is able to interconnect its network with the facilities of the incumbent operator either directly or indirectly *via* the network of another competitive entrant. The provision for interconnection and cost based interconnection pricing is essential for encouraging new entry.

Interconnection Usage Charges (IUCs) are charges payable by one telecom operator to the other for use of the later network either for originating, terminating, or transiting/carrying a call. The regulatory framework for interconnection was first established through the regulation issued by TRAI in May 1999 determined interconnection charges and revenue sharing arrangements. Subsequently, TRAI considered it important to specify an IUC regime that would give greater certainty to the Inter-operator settlements and facilitate interconnection agreements (TRAI, 2012).

IUC contained charges for origination, transit and termination of calls in a Multi-Operator environment. This IUC regulation introduced the regime of Calling Party Pays(CPP), which is perhaps the biggest factor in growth of telecom services in India. In the early period India followed the Receiving Party Pays (RPP) system where the subscriber used to pay for incoming calls from both mobile as well as fixed line networks. In CPP regime, the caller bears the three separate elements of cost of putting his call through to the called party: the costs, respectively, of origination, carriage & termination and all incoming calls could be received free of charge. This regulation was superseded by a regulation on October 29, 2003. In this regulation TRAI prescribed identical termination charges for all types of calls and, therefore, simplified the implementation of the regime.

The IUC regulations amended in 2009, by reducing termination charge in domestic to 20 paise per minute and increased international termination to 40 paise per minute. Termination charge for 3G voice calls would be same as 2G voice calls. Further, NTP12 announcement of free national roaming can alter or revised and adversely affect the IUC charge, which is still not clear (TRAI, 2012).

2.5.2. Access Deficit Charges (ADC)

Access Deficit Charges (ADC) was paid by telecom operators to basic telecom operators like BSNL and MTNL for the services on which they do not recover the cost of operation. Before the opening of the telecom sector, access deficit was being taken care of through a cross-subsidy from NLD and ILD tariffs. But with the decline in long distance rates owing to competition and the implementation of cost-based termination and carriage charges, the operators had less scope to take advantage of cross-subsidy through long-distance tariff. As a result ADC was first introduced in January 2003 to share a percent of the revenue earned with the service provider at the receiver's end and revised in the February 2005 and finally abolished in 2008 due to an increase in mobile subscribers in large numbers and falling per line capital cost resulting through new technologies (TRAI, 2012).

2.5.3. Spectrum Usage Charges (SUC)

The spectrum usage charge is payable by the licensees providing mobile access services, as a percentage of their Adjusted Gross Revenue (AGR). Spectrum usage charges is payable as per the spectrum slabs/ rates notified by the Government from time to time. The expensive auctions during past years resulting from high reserve prices with more spectrum usage charges have long been an issue of contention for the operators. The Government's has taken a positive move to reduce spectrum usage charges (SUC) from 5 per cent to 3 per cent of AGR in 2016 has come as a huge relief to financially stressed operators.

2.6. REGULATORY STRUCTURE AND INSTITUTIONS

The government telecom regulatory framework broadly classified into three sub-groups as given in Fig. 2.1: (I) policy making institutions, (II) regulatory institutions and (III) dispute settlement institution and given specific roles. Apart from government regulatory institutions, two private non-profit bodies represent telecom operators and interact on their behalf with regulators on policy and regulatory issues.

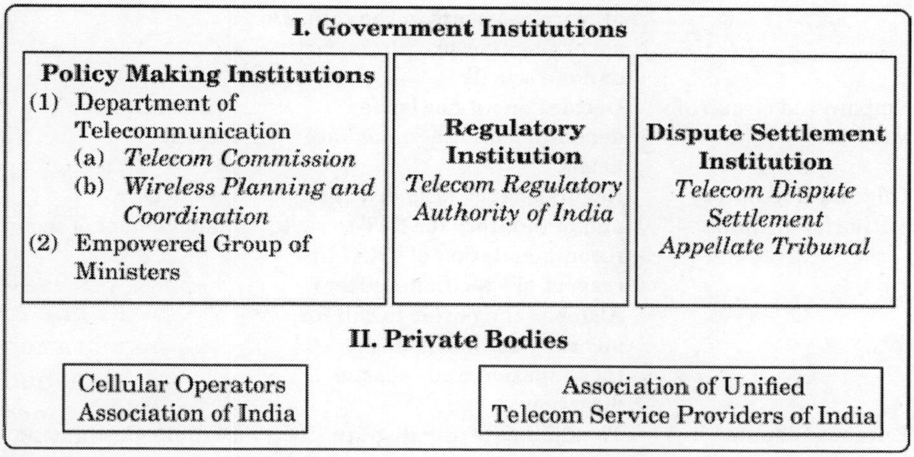

Fig. 2.1: Regulatory structure and institutions in India's telecommunications

The policies and regulation for the development of telecom services comes under the jurisdiction of Union government and formulated at the national level for the country as a whole. It is governed by the Indian Telegraph Act, 1885 (ITA, 1885) and the Indian Wireless Act, 1933. As per Act, the central government has the exclusive right of establishing, maintaining and operation of telecom services. However, the government can delegate this right to any service provider by granting a license. As the government is referred to as the *licensor*; and the service providers are referred to as *licencees*. The detail roles and responsibilities are given in Table 2.4.

2.6.1. Government Institutions

There are three government institutions classified as *Policy making institutions*, *Regulatory institution* and *Dispute settlement*

Table 2.4: Roles and functions of regulatory institutions

Name of Institutions	*Function or Role*	*Type of Institutions*
Department of Telecom	Licensing, licence fee, frequency management of telecom sector	Policy making and enforcing body
Telecom Commission	Executive and policy making function of ministry	Part of DoT
Wireless Planning Commission	The national radio regulatory authority responsible for spectrum management and licensing. Caters for the need of all wireless users in the country, government or private, security or non-security	Country's spectrum management
Empowered Group of Minister	Decides on ad-hoc issues depending on the immediate needs	Prime Minister's council
Telecom Regulatory Authority of India	Regulating, issuing directions and mandatory for DoT to seek recommendation of TRAI in respect of specified matters. Also has the power to call for any information, conduct investigation and to issue direction	Day to Day management of sector
Telecom Dispute Settlement Appellate Tribunal	To adjudicate any dispute between a licensor and a licensee; between two or more service providers; between a service provider and a group of consumers	Dispute Settlement Body

institution responsible for policy and regulatory formation and implementation in India. The policy maker is the Ministry of Communications and Information Technology, which operates through the Department of Telecommunications (DoT) and its two wings, Telecom Commission (TC), and Wireless Planning and Coordination (WPC). The Telecom Regulatory Authority of India (TRAI) is an independent regulator that reports to Parliament through the Empowered Group of Ministers (EGoM) and Disputes Settlement Institution, Telecom Dispute Settlement Appellate Tribunal (TDSAT) is responsible for effective settlement of disputes arising in the telecom industry. The evolution of these institutions is discussed in the following section:

2.6.1.1. *Policy making institutions*

Department of telecommunications

Department of Telecommunications (DoT) is a branch of the ministry of communications and information technology. It lies at the top most level in the hierarchy of the telecom service sector. Its responsibilities includes policy formulation, performance review, monitoring, international cooperation, research & development and grant of licences to operators for providing fixed, wireless and value added services in various cities and telecom circles in the country. DoT also allocates frequency or spectrum and manages radio communications in close coordination with the International bodies. It is also responsible for enforcing regulatory measures and monitoring the telecom transmission in the country. Since inception, DoT has been instrumental in drafting developmental policies for the accelerated growth of the telecom services. At present, the DoT is essentially performing the role of a policy maker and licensor. The national telecom policy, 1994, 1999 and the more recent 2012, are few of the major contribution made by DoT for the purpose of transformation of the Indian telecom services.

Telecom commission (TC)

The Telecom Commission was set up by the Government of India on April 11, 1989. This has administrative and financial powers of the Government of India to deal with various aspects of Telecommunications and an exclusive policy-making body, works under the DoT. The Telecom Commission is responsible for policy formulation, review of performance, licensing, wireless spectrum management, administrative monitoring of PSUs, research and development and standardization and validation of equipment and International relations among other matters.

Wireless planning and coordination wing (WPC)

The WPC wing of the ministry of communications was created in 1952. This is responsible for management of spectrum and its needs to both public and private operators. It is divided into three units, licensing and regulation, new technology group and standing advisory committee on radio frequency allocation. These units make the recommendations on spectrum allocation issues, formulate the spectrum allocation plans, and make recommendations on the various issues related to International Telecom Union (ITU), to sort out problems referred to the committee by various wireless users and clearance of all wireless installations in the country.

Empowered Group of Ministers (EGoM)

This is a group of Ministers of Union Government of India, who discuss and present the final recommendations in the cabinet for approval. Over the years, EGoM has emerged as the final authority for all the decisions, in spite of telecom commission and DoT. This group has become the final authority to approve any recommendation of TRAI and DoT. In recent 2G auction in 2012 and 2013, the reserve price for the spectrum was recommended by TRAI in consultation with DoT but EGoM, had reduced the final auction prices after the first auction in 2012 and blamed the organisation for their suggestions. This showed existence of multi-regulatory and policy institutions but most of them only play advisory role and final decision are only made by the EGoM and DoT. This raised the questions on autonomy of the regulatory institutions and increasing political interference in the system.

2.6.1.2. *Regulatory institution*

Telecom Regulatory Authority of India (TRAI)

In the context of privatisation of telecom services following NTP94, a multi-operator scenario emerged both in the basic as well as wireless services in which private operators were competing with government entities. In February 1997, India signed telecom services agreement at World Trade Organisation (WTO) for a regulatory mechanism. For an orderly and healthy growth of the telecom sector as also for protection of consumer interests, it was felt necessary to separate the regulatory functions of the government from the service providing functions. Accordingly, the government decided to set up an independent telecom regulatory authority. An ordinance was issued on January 25, 1997, establishing the Telecom Regulatory Authority of India (TRAI) as an independent regulatory agency for the telecom sector. TRAI in the initial stage regulate licences issued by the central government and also responsible to adjudicate and settle disputes.

In 2000, the TRAI Act, 1997 was amended and established the Telecom Dispute Settlement & Appellate Tribunal (TDSAT), as a separate authority to handle disputes in the telecom sector. It has also been made mandatory for the central government to seek the recommendations of the authority in respect of matters need and timing for introduction of new service providers, and terms and conditions of licence to a service provider. TRAI recommendations continued to be non-binding on the government part but required to provide any information requested by TRAI. The government would take the final decisions only after modification of TRAI recommendations if could not be accepted at first time.

Since its inception, TRAI initiated a number of important mandatory steps such as tariff rebalancing for basic service, issuing a regulation on interconnections, fixation of interconnection user charges with the access deficit charges, developing a national numbering plan, fixation of the parameters for the quality of services, funding of USO, introduction of unified licensing scheme and mobile number portability, trading and sharing of spectrum, re-farming exercise, trading and sharing of spectrum, spectrum auctions, reduction in spectrum usage charges and announcement of NTP, 2018. Apart from these TRAI also holds meetings, seminars and workshop with registered consumer organisations to address the problems of consumers and established a telecom consumer's education and protection fund to educate telecom consumers along with research studies on matters relating to consumer interests. To curve unwanted telemarketing calls and TRAI issued regulation. In order to identify fake or inactive subscribers, the TRAI issued the practice of counting only those subscribers who show up in the visiting location register.

However, its functioning was also marked by a number of bitter disputes, between the DoT and the service providers on providing WLL provision to the fixed line service providers in 2001, spectrum licence allocation in 2008 and 2012-13. TRAI authority and credibility were undermined by court rulings in 2003 in case of WLL controversy. The lack of power and government steps to construct TDSAT to settle disputes between the various stakeholders reflect one of the most important functions of telecom regulator also approved this fact. This decision effectively reduced the power of the regulator and it becomes only recommendatory body and the final decision is to be taken by the government. The power of TARI are now restricted to a number of technical issues such as fixing the terms and conditions of inter-connectivity between the operators, laying down the standards for quality of service and ensuring that these conditions are actually met by the operators and with the effective compliance of the universal service obligations.

In sum, TRAI recommendations on the above mentioned issues like tariff, interconnection, quality of services, spectrum management, MNP and NTP12 is considered satisfactory and helped in the growth of the sector. On the other side, TRAI remains to be only a policy recommendation body without any power of final decision.

2.6.1.3. *Dispute settlement institution*

Telecom disputes settlement and appellate tribunal

In April 2000, the GoI established the Telecom Dispute Settlement & Appellate Tribunal (TDSAT), a separate body to handle disputes in the telecom sector. The functions of TDSAT are to adjudicate any dispute between a licensor and licensee, between two or more service providers, and between a service provider and a group of consumers; and to hear and dispose of appeals against any decision or order of TRAI. TDSAT has the jurisdiction to hear and dispose off appeals against any direction, decision or order of TRAI. The decisions taken by TDSAT can be appealed only in the Supreme Court of India. The TDSAT is also expected to speed up the settlement of dispute between various agents involved in provisioning and pricing of telecom services in India. The appellate tribunal consists of a chairperson and two other members.

2.6.2. Private Bodies

Among other contribution to the growth of Indian telecom is the role played by private bodies that represent operators and interact with the government policy and regulators.

Cellular operators association of India (COAI)

The COAI was set up in 1995 as a registered non-government society. It is the official voice for the cellular industry and it interacts on its behalf with the government policy and regulatory agencies. The tower and telecom manufacturers are also member of the association. The COAI pointed out several issues in the past such as monopolistic proposition of DoT, WLL for fixed service provider and high reserve prices of spectrum in the last two auctions held in 2012 and 2013. It continuously also provides operator's opinion on any new policy recommendations of TRAI.

Association of unified telecom service providers (AUSP)

AUSP is representative bodies for unified access service licensees providing telecom services with CDMA, GSM technology and fixed line and value added services. It interact on policy and regulatory issues with government bodies such DoT, TRAI and others on behalf of its members. It formulates expert opinion on industry issues and submits recommendations to the concerned authorities. In some major issues both AUSP and COAI represent the case together on behalf of operators to government and regulators.

These private organisations lobby on some critical issues and represent on behalf of operators to several key members of the government and ministry. This type of lobbying, which won respect over time with the regulator and the DoT, is, central to the revolution in Indian telecom. However, BSNL and MTNL always complained about the lobbying of private operators and favouritism that they unable to do due to public sector operators.

2.7. CHAPTER SUMMARY

This chapter presents an overview of the evolution of telecom policy in India since independence with a special focus on new policy initiatives during nineties and post-2000 after the introduction of mobile phone. In addition, chapter also highlights the timing and sequencing of various policy changes during the last decade. It is evident from the analysis that the driver of the Indian mobile telecom success story is appropriate policies and transparent regulatory approach. The opening up of the sector in

1994 has led to the growth of the sector through mobile telephony over the last decade.

The new policy in 1999 changed the face of mobile telecom sector in India. Further, some decision like creation of USOF fund for financing rural telecom infrastructure, UASL licences for offering both fixed and wireless services, hike in FDI limit, implementation of CPP, removing ADC and additional UASL licence has given the desired momentum to the sector.

However, the success of the sector also marked by several controversial issues such as allowed licences for wireless services within the local loop to fixed service operators by using CDMA technology that created potential disadvantage to the GSM mobile operators in 2003, who paid licence fee for spectrum licence; allocation of spectrum licenses on first cum first basis due to lack of transparency in 2008, cancellation of the same by the SC in 2012 and allowing free services to RJio in 2016. The government favour to public sector operators (BSNL/MTNL) by granting 3G spectrum licenses were before the auction in 2009 and waiving the extra amount to be paid for keeping additional spectrum in 2013. Fixation of high reserve price for 2G spectrum auction in 2012 and 2013 just to enhance the government revenue and subsequent mute response also reflect the government poor regulatory decisions. This has created policy uncertainly and dented image of the telecom sector in the country.

The government introduced new telecom policy in 2012 and followed by merger and acquisition guidelines, 2014, reduction of spectrum usage charges and trading & sharing of spectrum norms in 2015 is a positive sign. In particular, re-farming exercise in 2016, trading & sharing spectrum policy in 2015 and spectrum auctions held in 2016 and 2017 has improved the operators' positions in the market in terms of spectrum holding and merger planning among operators particularly after the entry of RJio in 2017 helped in consolidation and efficiency of the sector. This would mainly help in growth of data services in the country. The existence of multiple regulatory and implementing agencies still delay the process of implementation of new policies or regulatory decisions. Like in the case of main regulatory body TRAI has only recommendatory power that creates confusion and problems in the decisions and policy implementation.

3

Indian Mobile Phone Sector Journey

3.1. BACKGROUND

The previous chapters provided the background information and telecom policies and regulatory institutions in India. This chapter further explores the impact of policies and regulatory environment on mobile phone sector's journey. The mobile phone sector is considered to be one of the most successful sectors in the country. This is possible due to high competitive market and huge foreign investment. However, this is a capital-intensive sector and mobile phone operator's needs continuous profit from their investment, to meet their operational cost as well as for their survival in the market. They are continuously under pressure to perform in the market. Investors regularly expect to get profit from their investment in the form of dividends or appreciations of share values. In such a scenario, operators have to look beyond attracting just customers to improve their profitability. Hence, in this chapter, apart from sector's performance in terms of subscribers, investment, competitiveness, efficiency and productivity analysis has also been done to understand their profitability and efficiency. Because it is argued that in the short-run, cost competitiveness can drive the sector growth, but in the long run, the efficiency improvement such as service quality, innovative marketing or other strategies and technological competitiveness can benefit the sector (Seth *et al.*, 2008; Mittal *et al.*, 2009).

In this context, the chapter examines the questions such as over the years, whether the telecom subscribes growth has stagnated and urban-rural gap is widening?; whether the result of intense competitive market lead to spectrum scarcity and poor quality of telecom services?; whether the competitive market led to lowering of cost prices of services that resulted in worsening of financial performance of the sector and operators?; whether the high prices of spectrum resulted in high debt and less capital for investment?; whether these factors leading to exit of some operators and increase the level of concentration in the next period?, and what are the new emerging trends?.

3.2. GROWTH OF TELECOM SERVICES

The Indian telephone subscribers (combined mobile and fixed services) increased from 0.1 million in 1947 to 5 million in 1991 and 36 million in 2001 to 1206.2 million by March 2018. It is the second biggest mobile market in the world in terms of subscribers, second only to China. The Indian market accounts for 28 per cent of Asia Pacific's total telecom subscribers and 15 per cent of the global subscriber base (ITU, 2018). Mobile phone has mainly contributed to the phenomenal growth of telecom services during the last decade, which crossed the fixed line subscribers in 2004 and presently dwarfs the fixed segment (23 million) by a ratio of 52:1. The mobile phone subscribers constitute almost 98 per cent and increased by more than 7.7 times between 2006 and 2018. Today India ranked second in the world in terms of mobile phone subscribers[28]is attributed to various factors such as low prices of services, rise in people's income, competition and introduction of micro prepaid connection and low hand set prices (Guha and Kaushal, 2010). Mobile phone subscriber growth rate had fluctuated from high at 13 per cent in 2010-11 to –7 per cent in 2012-13 and again –2 per cent in 2017-18.

This fluctuation was possibly due to shedding off inactive subscribers by the operators to improve their operational performance and compliance with subscriber verification norms. As TRAI introduced registration of active users *via* Visitor

[28] India is ranked second after china (TRAI, 2017).

Location Register (VLR)[29] and estimated number was around 50 per cent of the total subscribers in 2011. This is due to overestimation of subscribers, inactive connections and usage of multiple Subscriber Identity Module (SIM) cards. About 35 per cent of mobile connections were inactive and 15 per cent had multiple SIMs either in the same phone or in different phones. Applying filters of inactive users and multiple SIM holders, it translates to about only half of the total subscribers were active in 2011. Over the years, after shedding off inactive subscribers by the operators still 16 per cent of the total subscribers were inactive in March 2018. The recent decline in mobile operator is mainly due to entry of RJio, several small operators have either merged or exited from the market.

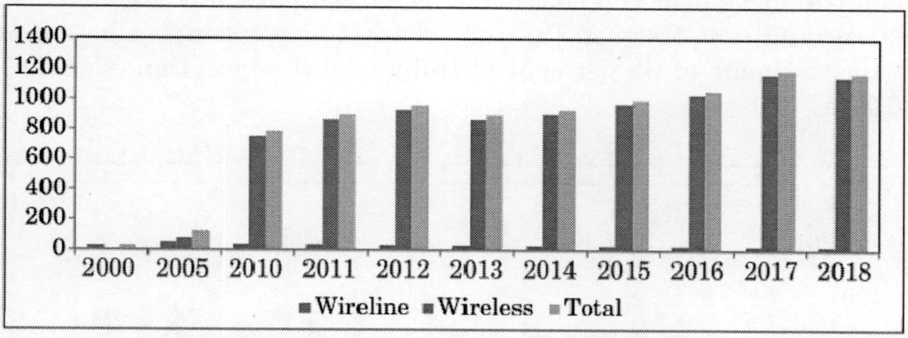

Fig. 3.1: Telecom subscribers (in millions)

Source: TRAI

The wireless technologies that are currently in use are of two types known as Global System for Mobile Communication (GSM) and Code Division Multiple Access (CDMA). GSM technology dominates the Indian market with 99.6 per cent of the share in March 2018. The CDMA technology wireless service is largely provided by Reliance and Tata, whereas GSM technology has been used by almost all the operators existing in the market. The

[29] The regulator is measuring the number of active subscribers *via* its Visitor Location Register (VLR), a temporary database of subscribers who have roamed in a particular area. Each base station in the network is served by exactly one VLR; hence a subscriber cannot be present at more than one VLR at a time. VLR data is calculated based on the date of Peak VLR of the particular month and gauged from the switches having a purge time of not more than 72 hours (TRAI, 2012).

government efforts to open telecom sector for private participation is evident from the continuous increase in share of the private telecom players, which are playing an important role in the expansion of telecom services. The share of private sector in total telephone subscription was 90 per cent by March, 2018 against a mere 10 per cent in 2001. The private operators (90 per cent) dominate in the mobile phone segment and public sector operators (75 per cent) dominate in the fixed line telephone segment.

Overall tele-density[30] has gone up to 93 per cent by March, 2018 from just 4 per cent in 2001 and 17 per cent in 2006. This clearly demonstrates the success story of Indian telecom sector, however, the diffusion of services are uneven in rural and urban India. There is a huge gap in rural-urban tele-density, which has been widening over the years. The rural (59 per cent) tele-density was around one-third to that of urban (166 per cent), albeit the former is home of 65 per cent of India's total population (Census, 2011).

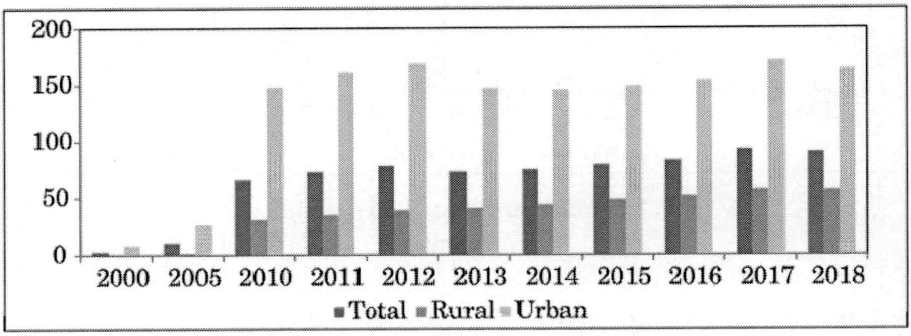

Fig. 3.2: Tele-density, Rural-urban and Total

Source: TRAI

In other words, one can say that about 65 per cent of the people are covered by only 59 per cent of phone connections. In order to understand the urban-rural difference an index has been prepared[31] (Mani, 2012). This value of index has been falling continuously over the years from 2006 (1636) to 2018 (295) demonstrate that telecom revolution largely concentrated in urban areas (Fig. 3.3). This rural-urban divide is more pronounced in

[30] Telecom subscribers per 100 population.

[31] This is a ratio of urban to rural tele-density multiplied by 100.

less developed states. The growing urban-rural divide is a reflection of the widening divide within the country as far as income and wealth is considered (Mani, 2012). This divide is wider in underdeveloped states compared to developed states (annexure).

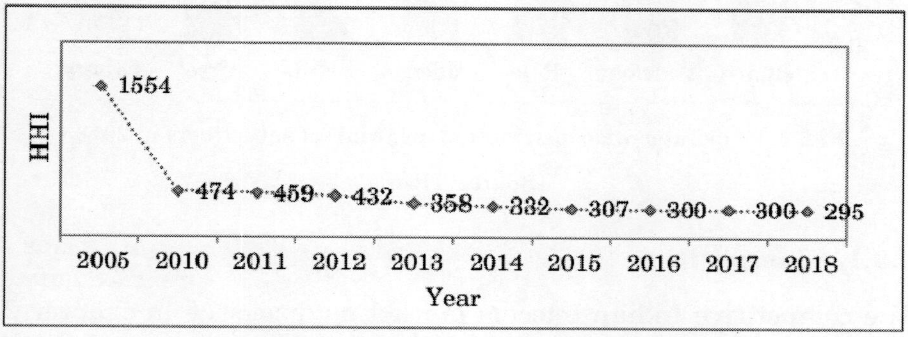

Fig. 3.3: Rural-urban divide index

Source: TRAI

3.3. MARKET STRUCTURE AND SIZE

The telecom service provision in India has changed over the years from government monopoly in early nineties to competitive market today. This was made possible due to favourable regulatory environment, changes in technology, availability of mobile phone and high economic growth of the country over the years. At present,5 major operators are competing with one-another at all India basis with presence of total 10 operators in the country (annexure). The competitive telecom market has helped accessibility of mobile phone services to rural and remote areas at affordable rate. In March, 2018, the average number of operators in the telecom market was 10. However, the top four operators have captured more than 78 per cent and top six, 94 per cent of the market. Bharti Airtel (25.7 per cent) was the leading operator in the market followed by Vodafone (18.6 per cent), Idea (17.8 per cent), RJio (15.8 per cent), Aircel (6.3 per cent), Telenor (3.2 per cent) and Tata(2.6 per cent) in March, 2018. The top four players have an all-India presence, while others are regional players. Public sector operator, BSNL (9.4 per cent) also maintained its position in top five mobile phone operators in the country as shown in Fig. 3.4.

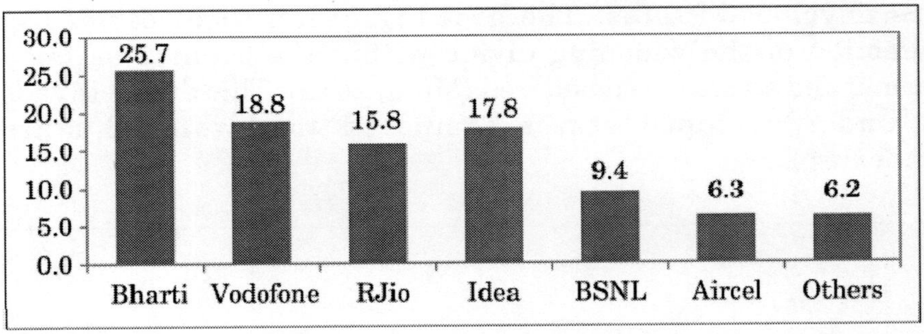

Fig. 3.4: Operator-wise distribution (per cent) of subscribers in 2018

Source: TRAI

3.3.1. Competition

The competitive Indian telecom market as discussed in chapter 2 allowed a range of prices and quality options for customers, which a monopoly service provider would have never considered. Indian telecom sector was monopolised by public sector operator before the privatisation in 1994. However, the market was not competitive till 1999 with only two telecom operators per circle. New Telecom Policy, 1999 ended the duopoly market and allowed the third operator, Mahanagar Telephone Nigam Limited (MTNL) to start its mobile phone service in two metros, Mumbai and Delhi, and Bharat Sanchar Nigam Limited (BSNL) in the rest of the country. The fourth operator entry was allowed in 2002 to make the telecom market competitive. Initially, these steps affected the incumbent operators' revenues and profitability, but over a period of time, these operators found themselves largely compensated by the significant growth in mobile phone subscribers' base and increase in minutes of usage.

The government removed cap of number of players in a circle and allowed entry of multiple operators,' and also auctioned and granted 122 new licenses on first come first serve basis at 2001 prices to the operators in 2008. This resulted from average 10 to 14 operators per circle, which considered intense-competitiveness in the telecom market (PwC, 2011). However, the Supreme Court (SC) had cancelled these licences citing allotted on the basis of faulty process as a result few small operators quit from the market[32]. But there are still around on an average 10 mobile

[32] STel and Telenor

operators, who are currently providing telecom services in the country. In general, four to five operators in the telecom market in a country are considered enough for a competitive market according to the world standard prevalent in most of the developed and developing countries (TRAI, 2012). It is argued that the government decision in 2008 of issuing multiple new licences had created intense-competition in Indian telecom market with highest operators per circle in the world[33]. Similarly, the government decision to allow entry of RJio into the market by providing initially free services for two quarters and services at low prices afterwards has turned telecom sector into intense competitive market again with price war.

3.3.2. Market Concentration

The mobile phone market is still dominated by only a few players. Fig. 3.5 shows that HHI[34]declined continuously from 2000 (1989) to lowest in 2012 (1350) and improved in 2015(1476), 2016(1544), and 2018(1060), which means Mobile Telecom Market transition from high concentrated (monopoly) market to competitive market. However, after the entry of RJio, there has been a consolidation wave that has swept the industry due to escalated levels of competition. This has been so intense that scale has become a necessary prerequisite. In fact, to quantify the increase in market concentration, we have calculated the (HHI) for the telecom market before and after the entry of Jio using TRAI data. The HHI increased by almost 1,000 points from 1,543 to 2,490 during the same period shows highly concentrated market. However, when we consider the recently merged operators (Bharti, Tata, Telenor), (Vodafone, idea) as a single operators, the HHI increased upto 2718, which means the oligopolistic telecom market (less competitive) with only three- four dominant players.

[33] The world's major developed and developing countries like USA (5), UK (4), Japan (3), Russia (3), China (3) and Brazil (5) had far less average telecom operators in the market than India in 2011 (TRAI, 2012).

[34] Note: Highly Competitive (Market where there are no dominant operators)- HHI below 1000; Competitive Market (High number of operators competing with each other)- HHI between 1000 and 1800; HHI above 1800- Duopoly or Monopoly Market (Market where there are one or more dominant competitors in this market).

This rise in HHI has been a result of a spate of mergers that have taken place since RJio's entry. Bharti Airtel has acquired the telecommunication services of Tata, Telenor and Videocon, while Vodafone merged with Idea and RCom exited from voice market. After the merger, Airtel has lost its two-decade-long held position as the industry leader since the Vodafone-Idea combine highest subscribers as compared to Airtel. At last count, RJio's subscriber base stood at 167.1 million in March, 2018. Considering that it had started from scratch and half year ago, the figure is simply gargantuan and presents the incumbents with effective competition and takes the industry towards maturity and emergence of an oligopolistic industry structure with only larger and relatively stronger players in the market.

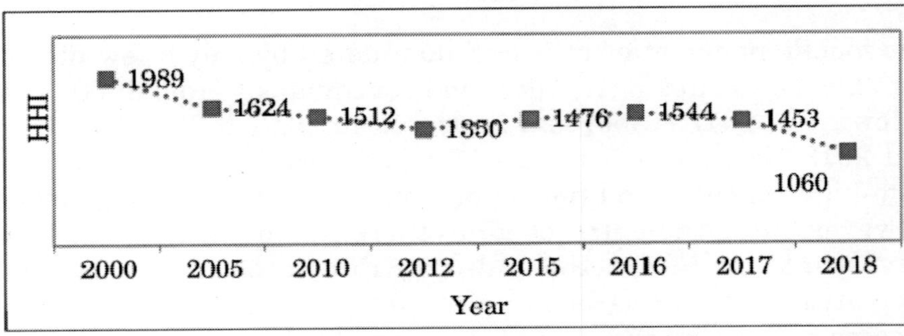

Fig. 3.5: Concentration of mobile telecom market (HHI Index), from 2000 to 2018

Source: TRAI

The first thing is to understand its impact on electromagnetic spectrum[35], which is the most essential input for the growth of wireless services. In India, spectrum is considered as a scarce natural resource and shared among Defence, Railways and other government departments and the telecom sector. In India, the DoT conducts auctions of licenses for spectrum. As mentioned in previous chapter, the government first issued licenses of GSM standards to two operators per service area for offering cellular services after competitive bidding for a 10-year period, extendable

[35] "According to the DoT, (2010), Radio Frequency Spectrum is the entire range of wavelengths of electromagnetic radiation which is used as carrier of wireless transmission and thus a basic requirement for providing wireless services. It is a finite but non-consumable global natural resource and commands high economic value in the telecommunication sector".

by five years. Further, third operator (DoT/MTNL) in 1999 and fourth operator provided licences through multistage auction in 2001.

In order to prioritise spectrum allocation among competing bidders, DoT introduced a subscriber linked spectrum allocation process in 2002, which provided for a maximum allotment of 12.5 MHz of spectrum per operator in each circle. The initial allotment of spectrum along with the licence was 4.4 MHz for GSM and 2.5 MHz for CDMA. This was further increased up to 6.2 MHz for GSM and 5 MHz for CDMA operators depending on availability and the operator's ability to justify the need for it. However, this criteria was not used anywhere in the World and the fixed amount of spectrum given to the operators in the country was also far below compared to the International average of 17.18 MHz (TRAI, 2012). The subscriber growth is being driven by wireless technologies, which made spectrum a valuable and often scarce resource. It gets fragmented if a large number of operators are present in the market. The average frequency allotted to an Indian mobile operator is 6.2 MHz, compared to the world average of 17.2 MHz (Malik, 2010). Such fragmentation leads not only to inefficient use of the spectrum but also increases the cost of providing services to consumers and due to more expenditure on infrastructure development. At present spectrum per subscribers' shows that India has just 0.2 MHz spectrum per subscriber compared to 7.9 MHz in UK, 2.1 MHz in USA, 3.3 MHz in Japan and 0.5 MHz in China.

Subscribers per MHz spectrum show that only few mobile phone operators are able to use their allotted spectrum efficiently. Average utilisation rate varies among large private operators in 2017 was Bharti (4.1 lakh), Voda (4.6 lakh), Idea (4.7 lakh) and Rjio (3.0 lakh) and others (1.9 lakh). This reveals that rest of the operators' are not able to use their available spectrum efficiently. This has created artificial scarcity of spectrum in the market. In addition, the allocated spectrum was fragmented and not harmonised, which was hampering the efficiency of mobile phone services and its quality of services (Brookings, 2015). The available spectrum in India is not harmonized and fragmented, which is very crucial for 5G that provides users with much faster data speeds with efficient use of spectrum. The high demand for data services in recent years has made spectrum availability and utilisation the key aspects of the industry.

The spectrum trading and sharing policy in 2015, spectrum re-farming in 2016 and spectrum auction have improved the efficiency conditions. Large mobile operators made trading/merger deals and purchase more spectrums through auctions as discussed in the previous chapter. Spectrum trading/sharing and business mergers allowed the spectrum holding of the operators to get better aligned to its utilisation, thereby leading to greater efficiency. The trading allows smaller operators also to monetize their underutilized spectrum holdings, and the larger operators to attain spectrum outside the auctions. Thus the trend of consolidation of spectrum holdings of the operators is expected to continue in the medium term and benefit the services.

If we take the current status of merger/consolidation, Airtel's acquisitions and Idea-Vodafone merger are primarily aimed at adding more spectrum to their portfolio. It was more gradual in the case of Airtel. The Vodafone-Idea merger was a reaction to the damage caused by RJio. The merged Idea-Vodafone entity will hold about 1850 MHz spectrum across different bands, including about 1645 MHz of liberalised spectrum. In comparison to Airtel's spectrum holding of 1692 MHz and RJio has 1301 MHz. The pooling of spectrum holdings - as is the case with Vodafone and Idea - leads to higher network capacity, which in turn means that the operators can use airwaves more efficiently than they were doing independently. For instance, spectrum needed to deliver voice services to the existing Idea and Vodafone customers will reduce to 400 MHz from 600 MHz now. The freed 200MHz can be deployed for data services. This allows the combined operators to accommodate over 15 times more data volumes than currently, and thus match with RJio's data offerings, and similar case with Airtel-Telenor-Tata. This shows that now not only market is moving towards consolidation but also becoming more efficient in terms of spectrum.

3.4. QUALITY OF SERVICES

The introduction of MNP appears to poise for a paradigm shift. The reasons for seeking the introduction of MNP are compelling to promote competition among mobile service operators so that service levels can improve further and to provide users the right to change operators at minimal cost and with minimal inconvenience. The introduction of MNP, mobile service providers are likely to face higher competitive pressures, especially in the initial phase as subscribers scout for better wireless deals, thereby raising the costs of subscriber acquisition and retention. As customers get a wider choice and are able to switch between service providers easily, mobile service providers would need to offer more competitive pricing plans. Loss of subscribers is measured by 'churn', which is the ratio of subscribers leaving the network to the current subscriber base. This leads to a drop in revenues and an increase in costs, which in turn would weaken their competitive position. The porting request by customers has been growing over the years from 0.8 cumulative per cent in 2011 to 31.4 per cent of the total in 2018 (Table 3.1). This clearly indicates that mobile phone operators are in continuous pressure to enhance its quality of services due to competitive market. If one operator is not able to provide the requisite quality services, the customer has the option to change to other available operators in the market.

Table 3.1: Porting request by the subscribers (in millions)

Year	*2011*	*2012*	*2013*	*2014*	*2015*	*2016*	*2017*	*2018*
Subscribers	812	868	868	905	970	1034	1170	1183
Porting Request	6	42	90	117	154	239	273	371
(per cent)	0.8	4.8	10.3	12.9	15.9	23.1	23.3	31.4

Source: TRAI

In recent year, the call dropping cases reported very high across the industry. The average rate of call drop in India stands at 4.7 per cent against the global standard of 3 per cent, which is much higher than the acceptable call-drops norms of 2 per cent prescribed by regulator Telecom Regulatory Authority of India (TRAI). This again raised the question on whether mobile operators are not investing enough in infrastructure development and technology to maintain quality services due to insufficient capital and higher payment of debt taken for financing spectrum and rollout services.

3.5. INDEBTEDNESS

The government raised large amounts of revenue through recent spectrum auctions. In 2010, 3G spectrum auctions generated INR 677 billion and the last two auctions held in 2014, 2015 and 2016 led to state revenues of INR 61.2 billion, INR 110 billion and 65.8 billion respectively. Mobile operators complained that the government auction raised prices to unreasonable levels and forced them to take on high debt levels. As the operators took a large amount of loan for investments to purchase spectrum and also need to invest in network building for rolling out services. Their debt and Debt/EBITDA (Earnings Before Interest, Taxes, Depreciation and Amortization) ratio has increased over the years as shown in Table 3.2. In general, once Debt-EBITDA ratios exceed 3.0, it becomes difficult for operators to satisfy credit worthiness to banks for further lending (PwC, 2013). Including domestic and external debt, the Debt-EBITDA ratio of Indian telecom sector has increased over two times between 2010 and 2018. This high indebtedness led to slower expansion of mobile phone networks in rural areas as well as rollout of 4G/5G across India. The additional amount required for spectrum could be largely funded by debt, which may increase the additional debt-burden on the sector.

Table 3.2: Debt (in Billion INR) and Debt-EBIDTA ratio from 2009 to 2015

	2008-09	*2010-11*	*2011-12*	*2012-13*	*2014-15*	*2015-16*	*2016-17*	*2017-18*
Debt	8,27	15,00	18,57	25,00	30,00	42,50	45,00	47,00
Ratio	3.0	5.3	4.9	6.0	7.0	6.0	6.5	8.5

Source: TRAI

Indian mobile phone operators are also burdened by multiple duties and levies, which include annual licence fees, spectrum usage fees, Universal Service Obligation (USO) charges, and service tax with additional taxes/duties such as Value Added Tax (VAT), stamp duty, and levies on towers etc. The total taxes come up around 30 per cent of revenue earned by telecom companies compared to around only 5 per cent in other APAC countries. This must have created not only revenue loss but also investment problem for further rollout of services.

3.6. INVESTMENT

The two main sources of investments or capital expenditure in telecom market are own resources of mobile phone operators and foreign investment in the sector, which provide opening for advanced technological skills and availability of huge amount of funds for infrastructure development in the market. The mobile phone operators' own investment or capital expenditure has gone up from INR 263 billion in 2007 to 521 billion 2010 and but declined to INR 477 billion in 2013 (TRAI, 2015). In recent years, Bharti Airtel, Idea Cellular and Vodafone contribute on an average around 70 per cent of the total Indian mobile phone capex. The average Capex/Revenue percentage of these three operators was 17.2 per cent in 2014 and 13.6 per cent in 2015 as compared to global average of 22.2 per cent and 20.6 per cent during the same years.

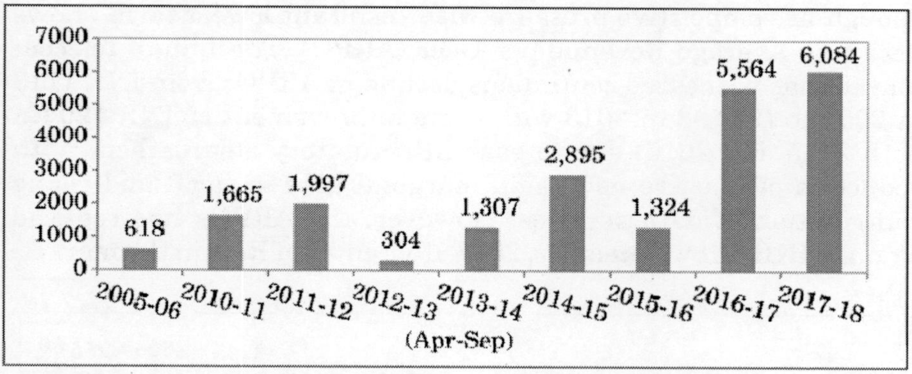

Fig.3.6: FDI inflow (in billion US$)

Source: BSNL, 2018

On the other hand, FDI inflow increased more than 3 times from 2005 (618 million US$) to 2011 (1997 million US$), which reduced drastically to 304 million US$ in 2013 (Fig. 3.6). This recovered after 2013 and reached highest level in 2017 and 2018 due to government announcement to raise FDI limit to 100 per cent from earlier 74 per cent to attract more investment (DoT, 2015). The reduction in FDI inflow during 2012-13 occurred due to uncertain regulatory environment in the country at a time when the sector required maximum capital to expand networks and to meet third generation (4G) roll-out challenges. Operators had put of their expansion plans at the back and failed to meet roll-out obligations in many circles. This confirms that the investment in the sector was badly affected by the poor regulatory environment, which improved after government eased the investment limit in 2013. In recent years, FDI inflow have made huge jump, which definitely will have a huge impact on infrastructure development for the industry.

3.7. REVENUE

The competition in telecom market lead to decline of cost of mobile services called as tariff from INR 7.3 per minutes in 2001 to INR 0.3 to 2010, which marginally increased to INR 0.5 in 2016 and again reduced to INR 0.3 in 2017. The current mobile tariff in India is among the lowest in the world resulted in substantial increase in minute of usage per month per subscribers of mobile services from 197 in 2001 to 441 in 2017 for GSM services (TRAI, 2018). However, this high use of minute of use of mobile services is not enough as competitive pressure with resultant lowest tariff shows declining Average Revenue per User (ARPU). The Indian telecom market has witnessed continuous decline in ARPUs from INR 1113 in 2001 to INR 98 in 2013 with some improvement at INR 120 (in both 2015 and 2016) due to ease in regulatory environment with reduction of inactive users and marginal hike in tariff and rising contribution of data services. However, the ARPUs has reduced again to INR 81 by December, 2017 after entry of RJio in the market.

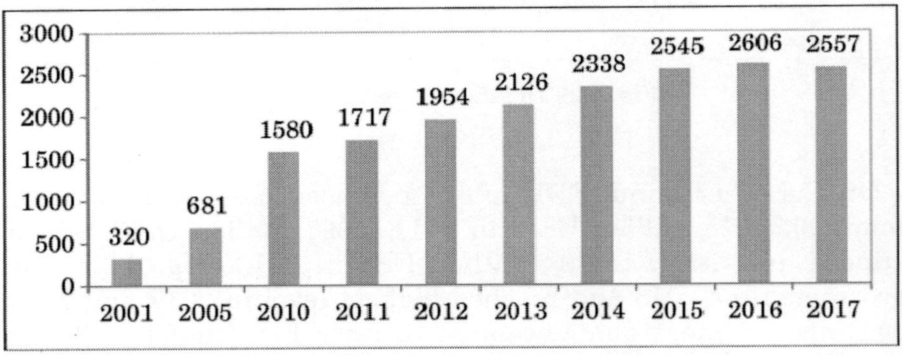

Fig. 3.7: Gross revenue at current prices (in billions)

Source: TRAI

The sector gross revenue grew at a double digit (21.5 per cent) compound annual growth rate during 2001 to 2009. This increase in revenue was attributed to cheaper mobile handsets, reduction in tariffs, and increase in mobile penetration and adoption of Value Added Services (VAS). However, the sector's revenue growth rate had declined substantially at 8.7 per cent per annum during 2010 to 2016. The reduction in revenue growth was largely attributed to poor regulatory and business environment in the sector (PwC, 2011, CARE, 2013). This uncertainty has reduced with some positive policy decisions after 2012 and FDI policy in 2013. But, the sector's revenue growth turned negative during 2017 and 2018, which dropped at the rate of 8.5 per cent during calendar year 2016 (2796 billion INR) to 2017 (2557 billion) at current prices.

3.8. FINANCIAL PERFORMANCE OF MOBILE OPERATORS

Top five operators in Indian Telecom market captured around 85 per cent share of the total mobile revenue. These five operators are Bharti Airtel, Vodafone, Idea, BSNL, Rjio. Other operators had contributed just only 15 per cent to the total revenue indicating that new operators or small operators are really struggling in the market. The other operators are Tata, Aircel, Reliance, MTNL and Telenor, while Quadrant and Videocon have stopped their services.

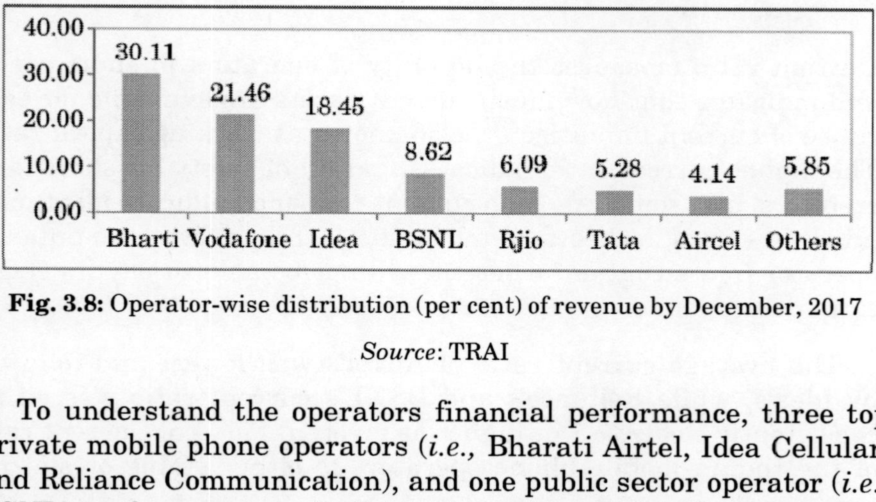

Fig. 3.8: Operator-wise distribution (per cent) of revenue by December, 2017

Source: TRAI

To understand the operators financial performance, three top private mobile phone operators (*i.e.,* Bharati Airtel, Idea Cellular, and Reliance Communication), and one public sector operator (*i.e.,* BSNL) performance analysis has been done in detail. Vodafone, a UK based mobile phone operator and RJio have been left-out from the analysis because their financial data is not complete. The annual financial data of these mobile operators has been collected from their annual reports. Some of the data for most of the operators is not available for latest years, so the comparison has been done upto 2017 only.

In addition, the discussion on entry after Jio in telecom market has been done separately in the last section of the chapter to understand its impact on the market. The performance of four

Indian mobile phone operators has been done by using financial ratio, partial productivity and data envelopment analysis. The period 2007 to 2016 has been taken for the analysis because financial data of the mobile operators is readily available for the period.

The three different approaches namely (i) Ratios analysis, (ii) Partial Factor Productivity (PFP) and (iii) Data Envelopment Analysis (DEA) have been used to compare the performance-efficiency and productivity of the operators have been used. These concepts are discussed in detail in the annexure. The data on subscribers was collected from TRAI, revenue and other financial variables from annual reports and annual financial statement[36] of the operators available at moneycontrol.com.

3.8.1. Ratio Analysis

Current ratio

Current ratio measures the liquidity of operators in short period and indicates that how much current assets are available for each rupee of current liabilities[37], also known as working capital ratio. The higher current ratio indicates margin of safety for short-term creditors, but, sometime high current ratio may indicate idle funds, piled up stocks, locked amount in debt, while a low ratio puts the operator in a situation, where it will not be able to pay its short-term debt in time.

The average current ratio of Airtel's was lowest and followed by Idea's, while Reliance's and BSNL's current ratio was either consistently closer to 1 or higher as given in Fig. 4.5. Current ratio of the Indian mobile phone operators is either stable or slowing

---

[36] There is mandatory requirement for all registered companies to file annual balance sheet, statement annually to company law board.

[37] Current Assets include cash and those assets which can be converted into cash within a year. Current assets will therefore include cash, cash in bank, stock (raw material, work in progress and finished goods), bill receivable, marketable securities, prepaid expenses, short term loans and advances and accrued incomes' and 'Current liabilities include all those liabilities maturing within one year. Current liabilities include creditors, bills payable, outstanding expenses, income received in advance, bank overdraft, short-term loans provision for tax, proposed dividend and unclaimed dividend' definition taken from Sharma E, (2011).

down since 2009. This trend of current ratios reflects slowing revenue of the operators with less liquid or cash in hand for the short term investment. Overall, current ratios of the Indian mobile phone operators either remained stable or declined since 2009 with some fluctuation in recent year. Overall results reveal the bad liquidly conditions of most operators in the Indian market.

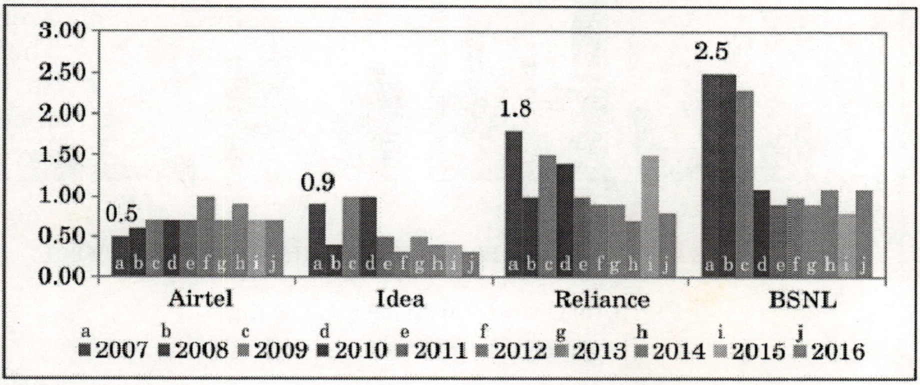

Fig. 3.9: Operator-wise current ratios

Source: Operators annual reports and moneycontrol.com

Debt equity ratio

The debt equity ratio is calculated by dividing total amount of debt by shareholders equity to judge the long term financial soundness of the mobile phone operator. Its low value reflects more security in long run as in the capital structure with less debt and more equity is considered favourable, and it reduces the chances of bankruptcy. On the other hand, high debt equity ratio is considered risky as it may put the operator in difficulty in meeting its long term obligations.

The average debt equity ratio was the lowest for BSNL, followed by Airtel, Reliance, and the highest for Idea. Airtel's debt equity ratio is almost consistent but increased due to investment in spectrum purchase and other infrastructure in recent year as shown in Fig. 4.5. Other private mobile phone operators, Idea's and Reliance's debt equity ratio is relatively higher than Airtel and also rising in recent years. On the other hand, public sector operator BSNL's debt equity ratio is lowest and stable. Overall, the debt equity ratio of the Indian mobile phone operators has either increased or stagnated after 2009, which reflects increasing operating cost and debt in recent period.

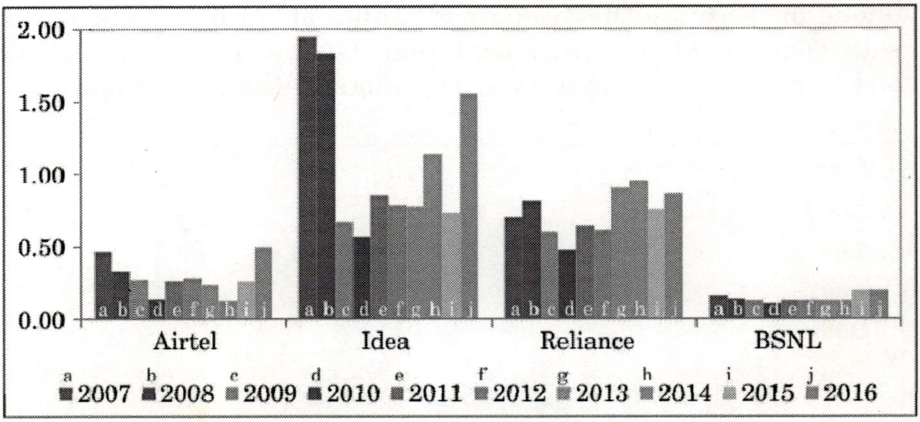

Fig. 3.10: Operator-wise debt equity ratio
Source: Same as Fig. 3.9.

Earnings per share

Earnings per Share (EPS) indicate the profitability of mobile phone operator on their per share basis. This is very important indicator from investors' point of view, which helps in making comparison with other operators to ascertain its capacity to pay dividend. Airtel's average EPS is highest followed by Idea, while Reliance and BSNL's EPS turne.d negative as shown in Fig. 4.7.

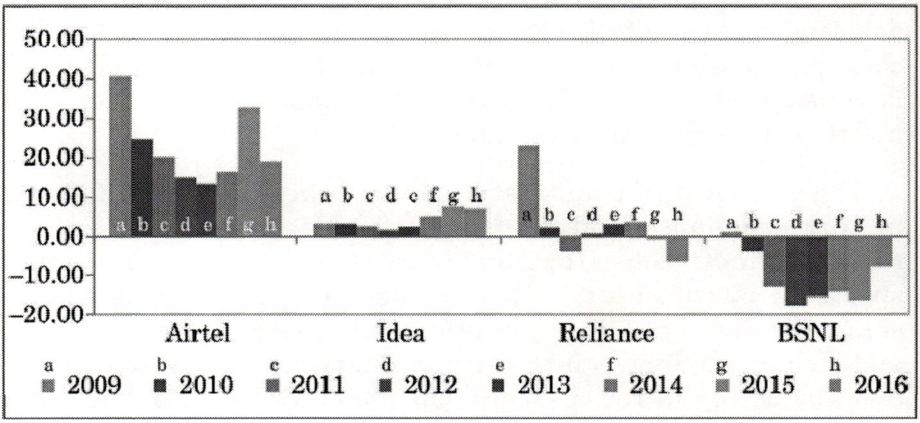

Fig. 3.11: Operator-wise Earnings per Share (EPS)
Source: Same as Fig. 3.9.

Overall, the value of earning per share of the Indian mobile phone operators has been declining since 2009, which may be attributed to slowing down of their revenue and profit margin as discussed above. However, Airtel's and Idea's share are still considered to be an attractive investment option by investors, because of its long term stability and high value in the market.

Earnings before tax, depreciation and amortization margin

The earning before tax, depreciation and amortization (EBITDA) in true sense is the indicator of the company's actual operating efficiency. The earning before tax, depreciation and amortization margin is represented in percentage by dividing value of EBIDTA by total sales or revenue. The average EBITDA margin of Airtel was the highest followed by Idea, Reliance and BSNL. EBITDA margin of Airtel, Reliance and Idea was consistently positive as shown in Fig. 4.8. However, EBIDTA margin of public sector BSNL became negative due to its continuous fall in profit margin and higher operating cost.

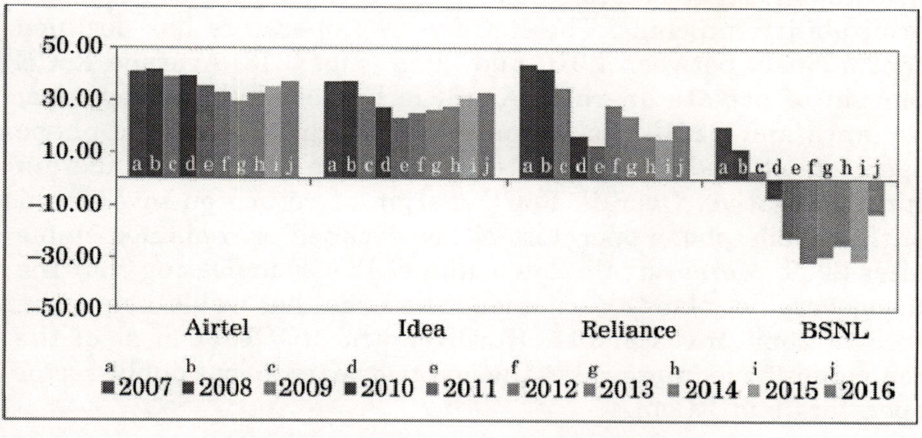

Fig. 3.12: Operator-wise EBITDA margin
Source: Same as Fig. 3.9.

It was argued that Indian private mobile phone operators showed high EBITDA margins by adopting various cost-cutting measures such as outsourcing of network and IT operation, passive infrastructure sharing, encouragement of consumers to use self-service and maintaining low subscriber acquisition and retention costs. These mobile phone operators also offered low-value recharge vouchers to attract low income pre-paid consumers, which increased mobile phone adoption (Capgemini, 2010). On the other hand, the increasing operating cost of BSNL, which includes salary of huge manpower and maintenance of unused assets and technological challenges were responsible for its negative EBITDA margins. Overall, the EBIDTA margin of the Indian mobile phone operators was declining with Airtel and Idea performing relatively better than others through efficient use of their assets and better operational mechanism like cost cutting measures as discussed above.

Return on capital employed

The efficiency of an enterprise is judged by the amount of profits but it depends upon the investment made in assets or capital employed in the business. The efficiency of an enterprise is judged by the amount of profits but it depends upon the investment made in assets or capital employed in the business. This expresses the relationship between profit and capital employed and calculated in percentage by dividing the net-profit by capital employed or investment. Therefore, RoCE margin[38] is considered an important profitability indicator. The RoCE of top operators has declined continuously between 2010 and 2013 (Fig. 3.13).Average RoCE margin of private operator Airtel is highest followed by Idea, Reliance and BSNL. RoCE margin of the private mobile phone operators started declining after 2009, while BSNL RoCE margin turned negative. Overall, RoCE margin or return on investment of the mobile phone operators either declined or remained stable after 2009. Moreover, the low value of ROCE indicating that the firms were not able to earn enough returns that would help them recover their investments. However, the ROCE of most of the companies have improved in the last two years except public sector operators and RCom.

Net profit margin

The revenue of most of the mobile operators has slowed down substantially in recent years. It is argued that the net profit or

[38] Return on capital employed (RoCE) margin expresses the relationship between profit and capital employed and calculated in percentage by dividing the net-profit by capital employed or investment.

return indicates more realistic picture of the mobile phone operators' financial health in the market. The increasing operating expenditure and higher debt have attributed to declining profit ratio or return of the operators in recent period as discussed in the previous chapters. Most of the mobile operators' net profit has either turned negative or slowed down particularly between 2010 and 2013 and started recovering after it.

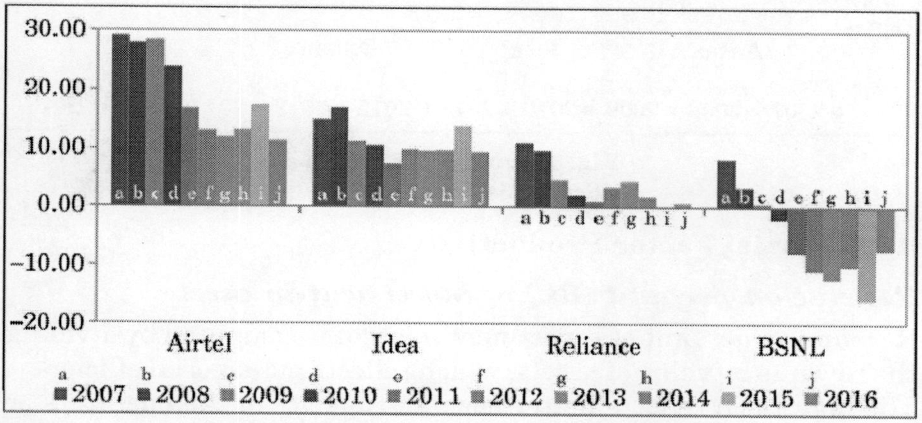

Fig. 3.13: Operator-wise capital employed margin

Source: Same as Fig. 3.9.

Deterioration of operating parameters due to hyper-competition and interest payments associated with high level of indebtedness that also severely impacted the net profit margins of operators. This can be seen from their declining net profit margin (NPM). The NPM of top operators have deteriorated over the past few years and in fact, majority of them exhibit significant losses in particular between 2010 and 2013 (Fig. 3.14). However, NPM of the operators is on the way of recovery in the last three years but public sector operators and reliance still suffering losses.

This declining value of RoCE and NPM coupled with high debt levels do not augur well for the industry. It is likely that many operators might have to curtail their expansion plans as they are not confident of recovering their investments in light of the poor financial performance. Interestingly, in the current revenue share regime, the government levy of 19-28 per cent is more than the NPM margins of the most efficient operators in the telecom sector.

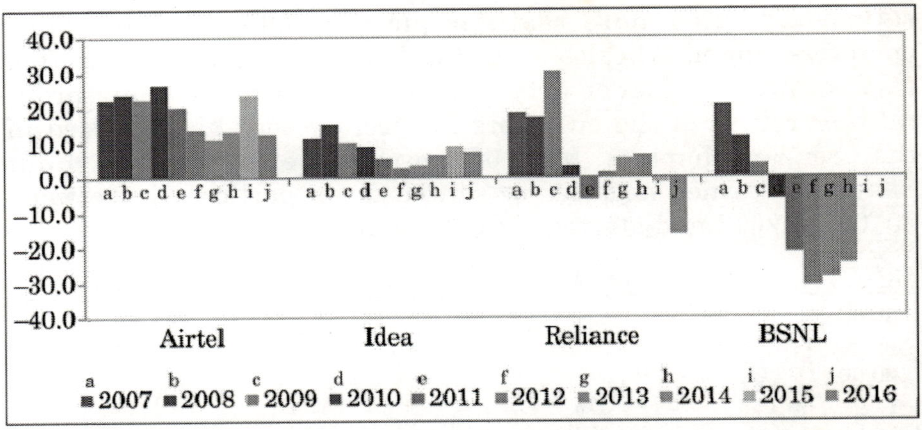

Fig. 3.14: Net profit margin
Source: Same as Fig. 3.9.

3.8.2. Partial Factor Productivity

Revenue on per unit (Rs.) of investment in asset

Revenue on per unit of Investment in asset is computed by dividing the revenue by value of assets, which reflects managerial efficiency. The high ratio reflects better earning capacity of the operators or *vice versa*. The average revenue per unit of investment in asset of Airtel is highest followed by Idea, BSNL and Reliance as shown in Fig. 3.15. Revenue on per unit of investment in asset of Indian mobile phone operators have either declined or remained stable. The revenue per unit of investment in asset of Idea and Airtel was relatively higher than other operators, which may be due to their better investment planning in assets by applying revenue model (more investment in high revenue generating circles) for market expansion (Mehta, 2013).

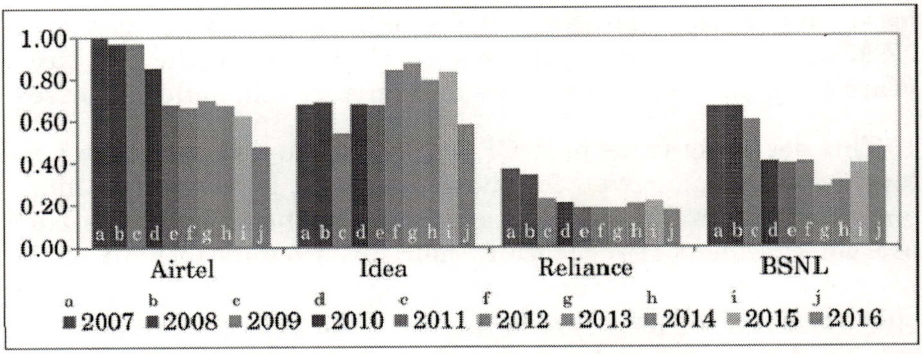

Fig. 3.15: Operator-wise revenue on per Rs of investment in asset
Source: Same as Fig. 3.9.

Revenue on per unit (Rs.) of expenditure

Revenue per unit of expenditure is an indicator of how much revenue an operator can generate on per unit of expenditure. More than one ratio of revenue per unit of expenditure means operator's performance is satisfactory, and its higher value indicate stronger profit margin of the operator. The average revenue per unit of expenditure of Airtel is highest followed by Idea, Reliance and BSNL as shown in Fig. 3.16. Airtel's and Idea's revenue per unit of expenditure is consistently higher than other operators. These private mobile operators are continuously investing in expansion of their network, which also reflected from their positive (more than one) revenue per unit of expenditure). On the other hand, BSNL's revenue per unit of expenditure was continuously unsatisfactory, *i.e.,* below 1 after, 2009 and slightly improved in 2016.

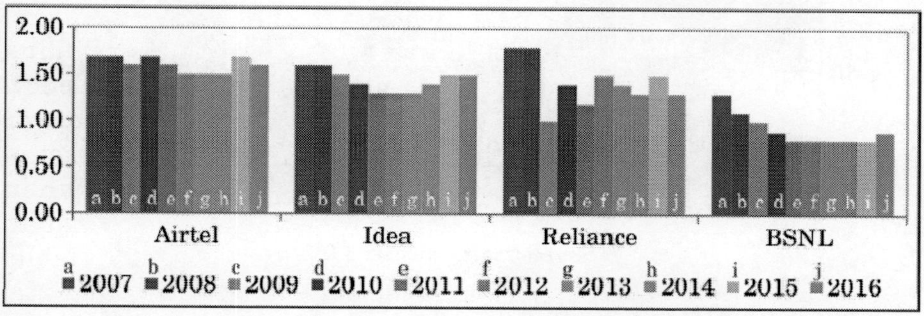

Fig. 3.16: Operator-wise revenue on per Rs of expenditure

Source: Same as Fig. 3.9.

Average revenue per user

Average revenue per user expresses the quantity of revenue generated per user. However, the active users are still comparatively lower than subscribers due to holding of multiple SIM cards. TRAI started collecting active users' data from operators and asked them to remove the inactive users after 2011. Hence, comparison of average revenue per user has its limitations for earlier period.

The average revenue per user (at real 2011-12 prices) is highest for Airtel followed by Idea, BSNL and Reliance as given in Fig. 3.17.Revenue per user of mobile phone operators is declining continuously over the years, which may be due to increasing competition in the market and declining tariff. However, Airtel is still able to maintain its lead in the market by adopting innovative strategies such as outsourcing Information Technology related service and maintenance to IBM, and tower and other infrastructural maintenance to Indus Infrastructure Company. The innovative strategies of Airtel subsequently followed by other private operators such as Idea and Reliance to get the market edge. On the other hand, BSNL's higher revenue per user may reflect its large wireline subscribers as the data of wireless and wireline revenue is not available separately.

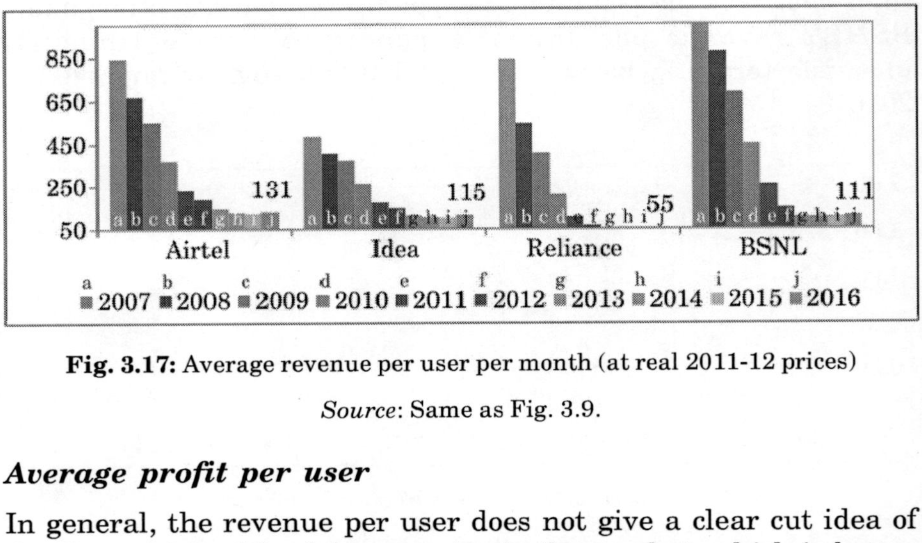

Fig. 3.17: Average revenue per user per month (at real 2011-12 prices)

Source: Same as Fig. 3.9.

Average profit per user

In general, the revenue per user does not give a clear cut idea of the financial health of the operator in the market, which is better reflected by the average net profit per user. The average net profit per user of BSNL was highest followed by Airtel, Reliance and Idea (Fig. 3.18). Over the years, net profit per user of the private mobile operators is declining continuously, while for public sector operator, BSNL it has remained negative since 2009.

3.8.3. Efficiency Analysis

Data Envelopment and Sensitivity analysis used to measure the relative efficiency of operators. In the DEA, assets[39] and

[39] Assets is defined as all assets owned by the company, including current assets, fixed assets, intangible assets and deferred tax assets.

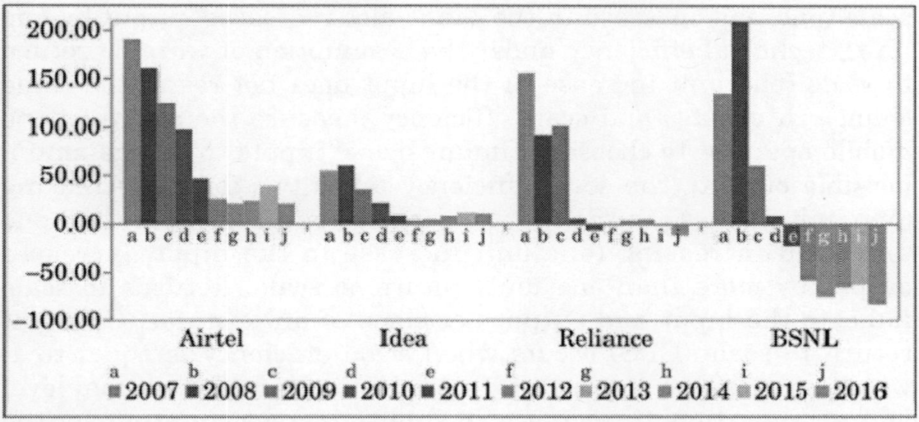

Fig. 3.18: Net profit per user per month

Source: Same as Fig. 3.9.

expenditures[40] have been used as input variables and revenue[41] as output variables. The best-practice or most efficient telecom operators can be found by comparing their respective operational efficiencies. In addition, Sensitivity analysis is also used, which ascertain the extent of sensitiveness of data variations in DEA. It reflects the stability of technical efficiency scores by omitting or deleting one input variable at a time from the DEA analysis. Sensitivity analysis compares stability of efficient operators *versus* inefficient under different input variables.

Data envelopment analysis (DEA)

The DEA has been used to measure the relative efficiency of mobile phone operators for the period from 2007 to 2016. Charnes, Cooper and Rhodes (CCR) model[42*] for each operator is used to measure the overall efficiency (OE), which is decomposed into technical efficiency (TE) and scale efficiency (SE). The efficiency score measures the use of inputs to achieve maximum possible output as performed by comparative mobile phone operators. It is known as overall efficiency under the assumption of constant return to

[40] Expenditure includes, infrastructure development cost, access charges, licence fees and payments to employees, non-executive directors and sales and general administration expenses.

[41] Revenue is defined as operating revenue earned from charge for telecommunication services, including voice and other services.

scale (one unit increase in the input also increases output by one unit), technical efficiency under the assumption of variable return to scale (one unit increase in the input does not result the same change in output) and scale efficiency measure the ability of the mobile operator to choose optimum size of inputs to get maximum possible output. The scale efficiency takes two forms decreasing (one unit increase in the input, decreases output by less than one unit) and increasing (one unit increase in the input, increases output by more than one unit) return to scale. Returns to scale indicate the input and output decisions of an operator. Constant return to scale (CRS) occurs when scale efficiency is equal to 1, which implies that the operator's production is under optimal level and a proportionate increase in inputs increases output by the same proportion (Liao Chun-Hsiung *et al.*, 2007).

A number of factors including imperfect competition or regulations may cause suboptimal production and inefficiency. If scale efficiency is less than one there is scale inefficiency due to increasing return to scale or decreasing return to scale. When the inefficiency is due to increasing return to scale, if inputs are increased appropriately, the mobile operator can move into constant returns to scale zone. For decreasing return to scale, if inputs are reduced appropriately, the operators can move into the constant return to scale zone (Liao Chun-Hsiung *et al.*, 2007).

Frequency of occurrence refers to the frequencies with which the fully efficient operators appear in the reference sets of the remaining mobile operators. These fully efficient operators could be considered as benchmarks and are good examples for inefficient ones. Using DEA model, overall efficiency, technical efficiency and the scale efficiency measures for four mobile phone operators for ten years, from 2007 to 2016 has been analysed.

Overall and scale efficiency of Airtel from 2007 to 2016 (Table 3.3) results indicate that Airtel achieved optimal production scale means increase in one unit of its input resulting one unit of output. The average partial factor productivity and financial ratios of the Airtel as discussed earlier also showed better and satisfactory results compared to other operators. Airtel occurred as reference category for others and continuously show optimum scale efficiency with constant return to scale. It is benchmark operator due to its proper management of input variable such as asset and expenditure to get optimum revenue, which can be a useful example for other inefficient operators in the market.

Table 3.3: Efficiency measures of airtel

Year	*Overall efficiency*	*Technical efficiency*	*Scale efficiency*	*Return to Scale*	*Reference category*
2007	1.00	0.82	0.82	Increasing	0
2008	1.00	1.00	1.00	Constant	2
2009	1.00	1.00	1.00	Constant	2
2010	1.00	1.00	1.00	Constant	2
2011	1.00	1.00	1.00	Constant	2
2012	1.00	1.00	1.00	Constant	3
2013	1.00	1.00	1.00	Constant	3
2014	1.00	1.00	1.00	Constant	3
2015	1.00	1.00	1.00	Constant	2
2016	1.00	1.00	1.00	Constant	3

Source: Same as Fig. 3.9.

Idea's overall efficiency is fluctuating over the entire period of analysis (Table 3.4), while scale efficiency has fluctuated over the years and achieved optimal production scale only after 2013, which may be due to following the Airtel's practice of proper investment in assets and management of its expenditure. Idea also occurred as a reference operator for others after 2013, which showed its increasing presence and optimum efficiency level with increasing return to scale in the mobile telecom market after continuous inefficiency between 2009 and 2012.

Table 3.4: Efficiency measures of Idea

Year	*Overall efficiency*	*Technical efficiency*	*Scale efficiency*	*Return to Scale*	*Reference category*
2007	1.00	1.00	1.00	Constant	1
2008	1.00	1.00	1.00	Constant	1
2009	0.97	0.90	0.93	Increasing	0
2010	1.00	0.86	0.86	Increasing	0
2011	1.00	0.86	0.86	Increasing	0
2012	1.00	0.99	0.99	Increasing	0
2013	1.00	1.00	1.00	Constant	3
2014	1.00	1.00	1.00	Constant	3
2015	1.00	1.00	1.00	Constant	3
2016	1.00	1.00	1.00	Constant	3

Source: Same as Fig. 3.9.

Reliance was efficient till 2012, but became inefficient after it (Table 3.5). The operator's scale efficiency score has reduced after 2012 with increasing return to scale means that it needs more investment in assets and proper management of expenditure to improve its efficiency level. This can also be seen from its poor financial ratios and partial factor productivity as discussed earlier. It occurred as a reference category in 2009, when operator scale efficiency results indicated constant return to scale.

Table 3.5: Efficiency measures of reliance

Year	*Overall efficiency*	*Technical efficiency*	*Scale efficiency*	*Return to Scale*	*Reference category*
2008	1.00	1.00	1.00	Constant	0
2009	1.00	1.00	1.00	Constant	1
2010	0.83	0.80	0.94	Increasing	0
2011	0.86	0.80	0.95	Increasing	0
2012	0.87	0.81	0.96	Increasing	0
2013	0.83	0.85	0.97	Increasing	0
2014	0.82	0.80	0.98	Increasing	0
2015	1.00	0.98	0.98	Increasing	0
2016	0.90	1.00	0.90	Increasing	0

Source: Same as Fig. 3.9.

BSNL was efficient till 2010, and became inefficient after it with substantial decline in overall efficiency score (Table 3.6). BSNL was efficient till 2010 by decreasing return to scale. This means that operator was not under optimal production scale and reduced its investment and expenditure level to get into scale efficiency zone. The operator showed either increasing or decreasing return to scale between 2011 and 2016 but turned into inefficient operator after 2011.

Overall results indicate that Airtel is efficient operator, while Idea, Reliance and BSNL became inefficient in terms of input variable asset and expenditure and output variable revenue after 2010. This reflects these other operators need to take a lesson from the benchmark operator, Airtel, which Idea has been started following with positive results by outsourcing its operational activities, sharing towers and other infrastructures to reduce its operating cost.

Table 3.6: Efficiency measures of BSNL

Year	*Overall efficiency*	*Technical efficiency*	*Scale efficiency*	*Return to Scale*	*Reference category*
2007	1.00	0.95	0.95	Decreasing	0
2008	1.00	0.79	0.79	Decreasing	0
2009	1.00	0.80	0.80	Decreasing	0
2010	1.00	0.74	0.74	Decreasing	0
2011	0.54	0.50	0.80	Increasing	0
2012	0.55	0.51	0.85	Increasing	0
2013	0.57	0.57	0.95	Increasing	0
2014	0.52	0.50	0.91	Decreasing	0
2015	0.50	0.44	0.87	Decreasing	0
2016	0.41	0.45	0.91	Decreasing	0

Source: Same as Fig. 3.9.

Sensitivity analysis

The sensitiveness of the input variables is used in data envelopment analysis. It evaluates the stability or variation in overall efficiency scores of DEA output by deleting or changing one input variable at a time. This shows the sensitivity and stability of efficient and inefficient operators under different range of input data variations. There are two input variables used in the analysis, asset and expenditure. The results reveal sensitivity or change in overall efficiency by removing one input variable at a time, either expenditure (only asset) or asset (only expenditure) from DEA analysis. This analysis is focus mainly between 2007-09 and 2010-13 to understand the sensitive second period compared to earlier one.

The result shows that Airtel was efficient till 2011 (Table 3.7), but turned inefficient from 2014, when the input variable expenditure was removed from the analysis. It was inefficient till 2012, and turned efficient afterwards in case of removing of asset input variable from the analysis. This indicates that Airtel needs to curb its extra expenditure to remain operationally efficient as the operator has invested huge amount in spectrum purchase and expanding business not only within India but also overseas in recent years.

Table 3.7: Sensitivity analysis of Airtel

Year	*Overall efficiency*	*Expenditure removed*		*Asset removed*	
		Overall efficiency	*(per cent)*	*Overall efficiency*	*(per cent)*
2007	1.00	0.01	99.00	0.81	19.00
2008	1.00	1.00	0.00	0.97	3.00
2009	1.00	1.00	0.00	0.24	76.00
2010	1.00	1.00	0.00	0.94	6.00
2011	1.00	1.00	0.00	0.97	3.00
2012	1.00	1.00	0.00	0.84	16.00
2013	1.00	1.00	0.00	1.00	0.00
2014	1.00	1.00	0.00	1.00	0.00
2015	1.00	0.80	20.00	1.00	0.00
2016	1.00	0.80	20.00	1.00	0.00

Source: Same as Fig. 3.9.

Idea's cellular efficiency has decreased when input variable, either expenditure or asset was removed from the analysis (Table 3.8).

Table 3.8: Sensitivity analysis of idea cellular

Year	*Overall efficiency*	*Expenditure removed*		*Asset removed*	
		Overall efficiency	*(per cent)*	*Overall efficiency*	*(per cent)*
2007	1.00	0.64	36.00	0.89	11.00
2008	1.00	0.71	29.00	0.92	8.00
2009	0.97	0.56	42.27	0.78	19.59
2010	1.00	0.80	20.00	0.86	14.00
2011	1.00	0.99	1.00	0.85	15.00
2012	1.00	1.00	0.00	0.88	12.00
2013	1.00	1.00	0.00	0.81	11.00
2014	1.00	1.00	0.00	0.79	10.00
2015	1.00	1.00	0.00	0.72	7.00
2016	1.00	1.00	0.00	0.68	5.00

Source: Same as Fig. 3.9.

However, operator has turned efficient or almost efficient, after removing the input variable expenditure from the analysis after 2011. This reflects that mobile phone operator was able to control its operating expenditure by outsourcing its operation, sharing towers and investing properly in assets to get into efficient zone.

Reliance efficiency has decreased, when input variable expenditure was removed throughout the period of analysis (Table 3.9). But marginally decline in efficiency level has observed, while deleting asset input variable from the analysis during 2012 and 2016. The percentage decrease in efficiency is higher, when input variable expenditure has removed from the analysis compared to asset. Therefore, reliance has to manage its expenditure, which has affected more to its efficiency level.

Table 3.9: Sensitivity analysis of reliance communication

Year	*Overall efficiency*	*Expenditure removed*		*Asset removed*	
		Overall efficiency	*(per cent)*	*Overall efficiency*	*(per cent)*
2007	1.00	0.35	65.00	1.00	0.00
2008	1.00	0.35	65.00	1.00	0.00
2009	1.00	0.24	76.00	1.00	0.00
2010	0.88	0.25	71.59	0.85	3.41
2011	0.82	0.27	67.07	0.80	2.44
2012	1.00	0.21	79.00	0.98	2.00
2013	0.90	0.20	77.78	0.90	0.00
2014	1.00	0.21	79.00	0.98	2.00
2015	0.90	0.20	78.58	0.92	0.00
2016	0.90	0.20	78.88	0.95	0.00

Source: Same as Fig. 3.9.

The efficiency of public sector operator (BSNL) has decreased, when input variable either expenditure or asset is removed from the analysis with few exceptions in case of expenditure (Table 3.10). Over the years, both asset and expenditure has played equally an important role in overall efficiency score of the operators. So, the operator has to manage both its assets and expenditure properly to get into efficient zone.

Input variables, asset and expenditure both were affecting the efficiency score of operators as shown in Fig. 3.19. It fluctuated over the years for the operators. Input variable expenditure influenced the efficiency of Reliance, while, expenditure as well as asset affected the overall efficiency of Airtel, Idea and BSNL. However, the results of two period (2007-9) and 2011-13) shows that expenditure affected overall efficiency of Airtel's and Reliance's relatively more compared to expenditure, while asset influenced more than expenditure of BSNL's and Idea's overall efficiency. Overall, the efficiency of three out of the four mobile phone operators declined when expenditure was not included as an input variable. This means that mobile operators overall efficiency was affected by expenditure, which means they need to manage their expenditure properly to get into the optimal efficiency zones.

Table 3.10: Sensitivity Analysis of BSNL

Year	*Overall efficiency*	*Expenditure removed*		*Asset removed*	
		Overall efficiency	*(per cent)*	*Overall efficiency*	*(per cent)*
2007	1.00	0.61	39.00	0.70	30.00
2008	1.00	0.69	31.00	0.64	36.00
2009	1.00	0.63	37.00	0.53	47.00
2010	0.57	0.47	17.54	0.57	0.00
2011	0.57	0.57	0.00	0.53	7.02
2012	0.50	0.44	12.00	0.05	90.00
2013	0.41	0.25	39.02	0.41	0.00
2014	0.41	0.24	39.01	0.40	0.00
2015	0.42	0.28	39.00	0.40	0.00
2016	0.43	0.29	41.02	0.45	0.00

Source: Same as Fig. 3.9.

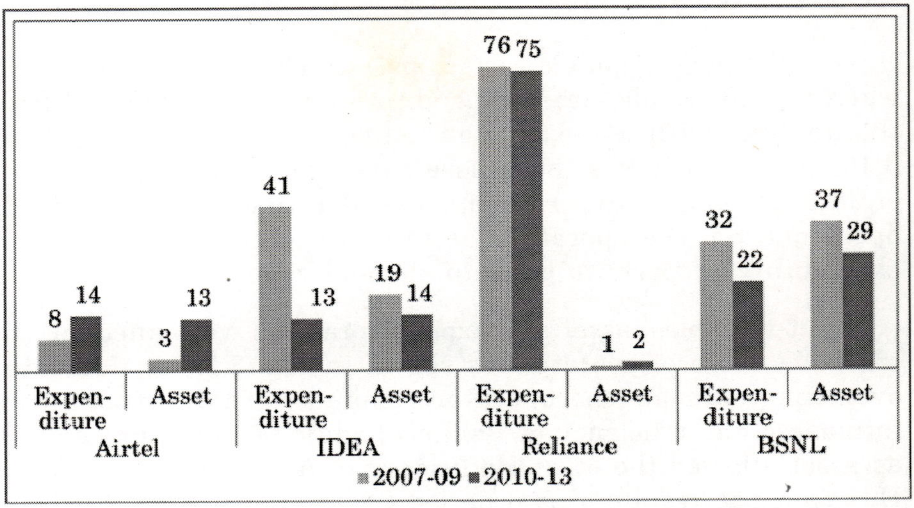

Fig. 3.19: Average percentage change in overall efficiency after removing input variable expenditure/asset

Source: Same as Fig. 3.9.

Performance compared to the benchmark mobile phone operator

The performance of benchmark mobile phone operator (Airtel) has been compared with other operators for the last three years (average from 2011 to 2016) by making Airtel as benchmark operator to examine their level of efficiency. Idea, Reliance and BSNL had high debt, low returns on their investment and expenditure, which resulted in lower efficiency compared to Airtel as shown in Fig. 3.20. Reliance needs to increase its efficiency by increasing investment in asset and rollout of the mobile phone services. Idea reached at constant return to scale in terms of investment in assets and expenditure by adopting innovative strategies like Airtel.

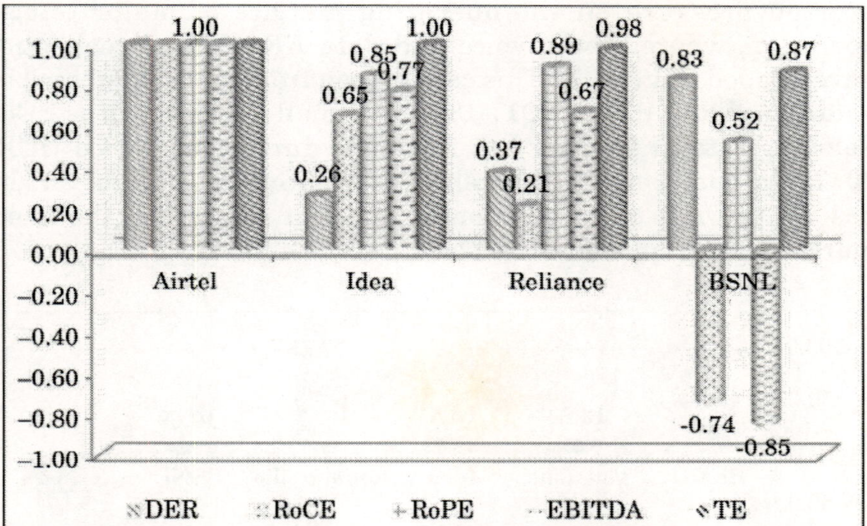

Fig. 3.20: Performance of Indian operators compared to benchmark operator, *i.e.,* Airtel

Note: DER:Debt Equity Ratio;RoCE:Return on Capital Employed; EBITDA: Earning Before Interest Depreciation and Amortisation and TE:Overall Efficiency

Source: Same as Fig. 3.9.

3.9. RECENT DEVELOPMENT

In the last two years, the telecom sector has witnessed favourable events such as approved spectrum trading and sharing norms, eased merger and acquisitions guidelines, reduced spectrum usage charges (SUC) from 5 per cent to 3 per cent, approved active infrastructure sharing, spectrum auctions held to enhance operators spectrum portfolio, and the most talked one is entry of Reliance Jio (RJio) in September, 2016. The RJio offered free unlimited data and a bouquet of mobile applications free as a part of the inaugural offer till December 31, 2016 by setting a target to acquire 100 million customers in shortest time and further extended it till March 31, 2017. It crossed the target of 100 million by Feb, 15, 2017.

This situation continued even after the free period was over, the tariffs introduced by the RJio since April, 2017 was significantly lower. The other operators were virtually forced to reduce their data tariff charges and in the process of either merger or spectrum trading and sharing talk with other operators. It has exerted pressure on the operating metrics of major telecom operators, wherein both voice and data ARPUs and realisations have slipped (Fig. 3.21). This can be seen from highest subscribers' addition by RJio during 2017-18, while small players such as RCom, Telenor, Tata and Aircel lost the same during the period (ICRA, 2017). In addition, the RJio showed negative revenue in 2016-17 has jumped into third position in terms of revenue in the mobile market by last quarter of 2017-18.

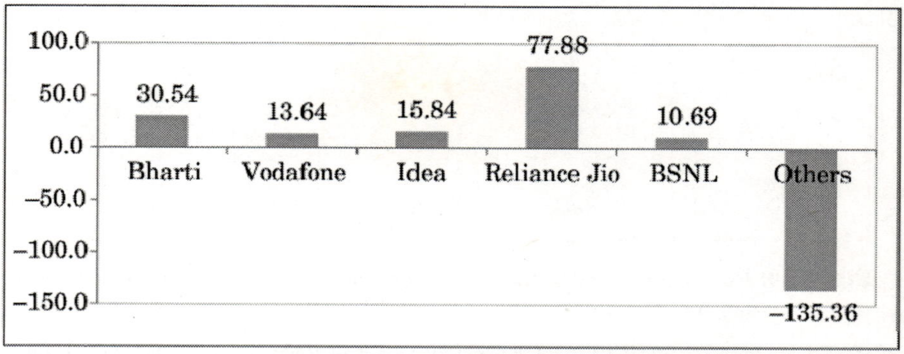

Fig. 3.21: Subscribers additions by operators (March, 2017 to March, 2018)

Source: TRAI

3.10. CHAPTER SUMMARY

This chapter discusses phenomenon success of mobile phone sector in the last one and half decade. The spectrum trading and sharing norms, easing merger and acquisitions guidelines and hiking FDI limits are welcome sign for the industry. There are challenges such as hyper competition, spectrum efficiency, quality of services and disruption by entry of RJio. Operators' current ratio is declining, debt equity ratio is increasing and earnings per share have reduced in recent years. This indicates operators' bad liquidity position or insufficient cash reserve for investment in short term and their recent investment is largely funded by debt.

The earnings before interest, depreciation and amortization and return on capital investment of the operators has either declined or stagnated over the years. Partial productivity of the operators in terms of average revenue per asset, average revenue per unit of expenditure and the average revenue per user has also either declined or stagnated over the years. Airtel is still performing well and invested more than other operators for expansion of their operation due to adoption of innovative practices, *i.e.,* outsourcing model (IT related services to IBM, tower and other infrastructural maintenance to Indus) and revenue model (focusing more on high revenue generating circles), while public sector, BSNL turned into loss making entity due to high operating cost. Airtel is fully efficient operator in terms of proper management of assets and expenditure with constant return to scale efficiency, whereas Reliance with increasing return to scale and Idea with constant return to scale was nearly efficient till 2017, and BSNL turned as inefficient with decreasing return to scale. The sensitivity analysis reveals that at average level, expenditure has affected the efficiency of Reliance and Idea, and expenditure as well as investment in assets plays an important role in Airtel efficiency and of BSNL inefficiency.

RJio initially offered free data and voice services in 2016, and later low tariff to attract new customers and penetrate into the market. These developments are good for the expansion of telecom sector and consumers also benefitted. In particular, the internet data service has increased substantially during the last years mainly due to RJio. However, this type of strategy may be good for operator and customer initially for short term but disruptive for longer period. This predatory pricing to have market share and grab customer is always questionable (Ghuha Tahakurta, 2017; Bhatia and Rao, 2017). The sign of disrupted has seen in terms of consolidation wave by mergers and acquisitions in the market with operators declining subscribers additions and revenue. The likely scenario is similar to most of the developed countries four to five large operators' would remain in each telecom circle of India. But cartelization amongst the operators is a genuine fear in time to come. It is for the competition commission of India has to ensure that it does not happen.

4

Economic Contribution of Mobile Phone Sector

4.1. BACKGROUND

This chapter focuses on the impact of the mobile phone sector on Indian economy in terms of direct and indirect contribution. It ranges from the direct contribution on Gross Domestic Product (GDP) and Employment to indirect contribution on the same. Globally mobile industry contributes to the GDP (3.6 trillion $) in 2017. By 2022, this contribution will reach $4.6 trillion, or 5 per cent of GDP, as countries around the globe increasingly benefit from the improvements in productivity and efficiency brought about by increased take-up of mobile services and Machine to Machine (M2M)/Internet of Things (IoT) solutions. In 2017, the wider mobile ecosystem also supported a total of 29 million jobs (directly and indirectly) and made a substantial contribution to the funding of the public sector, with almost $500 billion raised through general taxation and $25 billion through mobile spectrum auctions.

A number of studies in the past have established relationship between mobile phone services and economic growth. All studies shows that there is a positive relationship between GDP per capita and telephone density indicators. The magnitude of the impact, however, varies by the level of development in the country or region as well as by the extent of prevailing tele-density. The scatter plot between GDP per capita and tele-density shows the points tightly clustered within a small band along a straight line (NCAER, 2009). The discovery of high correlation between telecom penetration and growth means that telecommunications could play in accelerating growth and economic development. The notion that telecommunication infrastructure creates an *externality*[42] also exists in much of the available research. GDP is higher and growth is faster in countries with more advanced telecom networks. The value of telecom infrastructure including internet, thus, confers greater benefits on a society as compared to private benefits.

The relationship between GDP and telecommunications sector especially wireless phone in India has been widely examined. Mobile services industry generated an annual GDP contribution of Rs 313 billion in mid-2000s by one estimate. Another study tested the impact of telecommunications, especially wireless phone, on GDP for India. McKinsey (2006) analyses that there is both direct and indirect impact, "direct impact from mobile operators, indirect impact from other companies in the wireless business system (hardware and software vendors, handset vendors, and so on), and a second form of indirect impact: the surplus enjoyed by end users. It finds that the economic impact of wireless phones in India in 2005 ranged from 1.3 to 1.9 per cent of GDP. It also finds that increasing the mobile penetration ratio by 10 per cent would produce end-user value of $10 billion, equivalent to 0.61 per cent of GDP.

Using Indian state level data for mobile phones, one study finds that a 10 per cent increase in tele-density will increase Gross State Domestic Product (GSDP) by 1.12 per cent, keeping everything else constant. Similarly they find that a 1 per cent increase in GSDP per capita or income by 10 per cent will increase tele-density by 24.5 per cent, keeping everything else constant. Mason studied the potential impact of wireless broadband and found that a 1 per cent increase in wireless broadband penetration will contribute 0.11 per cent (Rs 162 billion) to Indian GDP in 2015.

In addition studies find that mobile phone sector has generated both direct and indirect jobs to people. Not only mobile operators,

[42] An 'externality' is said to exist when the social benefit is greater than private benefit and, hence, classical economics would support a policy of subsidy to infrastructure rollout.

but others who are associated sectors in the value chain such as handset manufacturing, assemblies, mobile content and application generators, retail sales and other infrastructure related sector also generate a large number of jobs.

In this context, this chapter studies the economic contribution of mobile phone sector in terms of value added to GDP, public funding and jobs. The attempts also made to understand the relationship between per capita growth and growth of mobile phone sector with its current position and future trend of these aspects.

4.2. CONTRIBUTION TO NATIONAL INCOME

India has done well to stay ahead of the curve in the technological revolution. The country's telecom sector has led to the revolution from the front. The Indian mobile phone sector has performed yeoman service to the Indian economy and social fabric since the very inception of economic liberalization. The sector is one of the largest contributors to the economy. Its contribution to the economy is rising over the years from 17th position in the 1980s and 1990s, it has moved up to 13th position in the 1990s, gradually climbed to 8th position in 2007-08 and has retained the position after it (NCAER, 2017).

The mobile phone sector is one of the fastest growing sectors of the economy. In fact, according to Reserve Bank of India data, the sectoral change in productivity has been the highest in the telecom sector since the reforms of 1991, growing by over 10 percent. On the other hand, no other sector has had a productivity growth of above five percent during the same period. It is no wonder that it has also been one of the fastest-growing sectors of the Indian economy, growing at over seven percent in the last decade itself. ICRIER estimated that a 10 per cent increase in rate of mobile penetration delivers on average of 1.5 per cent increase in rate of GDP growth.

The government data showed that communication sector (only services part) contribution to GDP has been rising in India. Its contribution increased from below 1 per cent in 2000 to 1.5 per cent in 2011-12, and further wentup to 1.94 per cent in 2015-16 (Fig. 4.1). In value terms, it has increased to almost 1.5 times from

INR 48,023 in 2011-12 to INR 72,107 in 2015-16. Although, this value excludes manufacturing and other indirect contribution, which is estimated about 5 per cent in 2016.

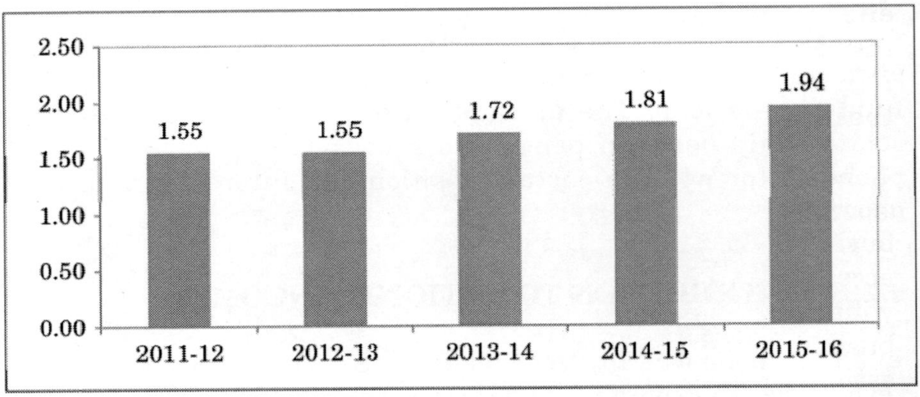

Fig. 4.1: Contribution of communication sector (services) to GDP (in %)

Source: Central Statistical Organisation, GoI, 2018

According to GSMA report, the mobile phone sector contribution to GDP was around 6.5 per cent in 2016 with contribution amount of more than INR 9.3 trillion of gross value added. The value accounts for both direct economic activity generated by mobile operators and the other related activities in India, and broader knock-on effects on the rest of the economy, including the indirect impact on the economy and the productivity enhancement from the use of mobile phone by individuals and firms. Productivity contribute maximum followed by direct and indirect contribution to the gross value product (Fig. 4.2).

The direct economic contribution to GDP of mobile network operators, infrastructure providers, handset manufacturers, mobile content and application generators, distributors in the mobile ecosystem is calculated as the value added generated by companies operating in the mobile phone market in India. The total value added generated by the mobile phone sector directly was INR 2.4 trillion (2 per cent of GDP).

The mobile operators purchase inputs and services from their providers in the supply chain, a multiplier effect on other Indian businesses is produced, generating sales and economic value added in other sectors and industries. For example, distribution and transport companies draw part of their revenues from supporting the operations of tower companies when upgrading and expanding their mobile internet networks. The same effect can be observed in many other sectors of the economy, including energy, retail and professional services such as finance or insurance. The conservative estimate of value added of around INR 0.5 trillion (0.4 per cent of GDP) was generated through these indirect impacts.

Mobile phone has transformed the way economic activity is carried out in many sectors of the economy, easing ways of doing business and allowing more efficient ways to communicate and access information. The productivity impacts brought about by the widespread adoption and use of mobile phone by individuals, businesses and governments generated about INR 6.2 trillion, an estimated 4.3 per cent of India's GDP.

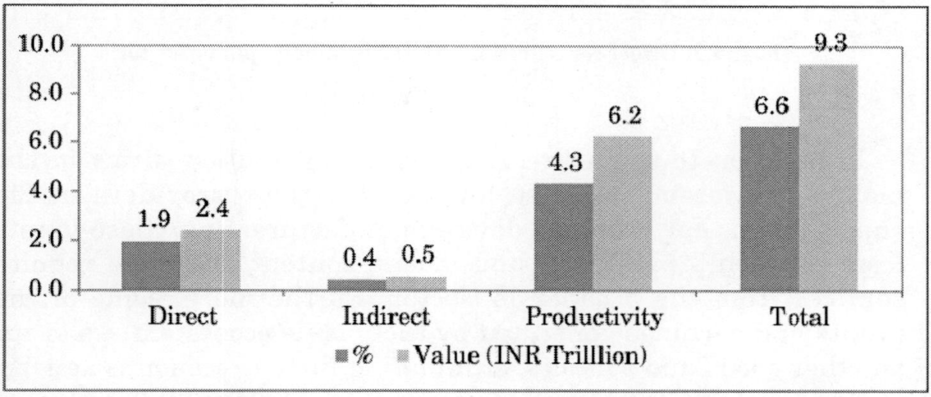

Fig. 4.2: Telecom sector contribution to GDP (in %)

Source: GSMA, 2018

In the direct contribution to GDP, the greatest economic contribution among all mobile ecosystem players coming from mobile operators, with a total direct impact of INR 1.3 trillion, or around 1 per cent of GDP (Fig. 4.3). Beyond mobile network operators, India has a solid and vibrant mobile ecosystem, with all the four ecosystem industries considered in our analysis generating significant economic activity. The fast-growing mobile content and apps services sector generated nearly INR 0.1 trillion (0.1 per cent to GDP). The largely established and consolidated

Indian mobile towers and infrastructure sector generated around INR 0.3 trillion; the Indian handset manufacturing sector generated INR 0.2 trillion (0.1 per cent to GDP); the mobile retail sector generated around INR 0.7 trillion (0.7 per cent to GDP).

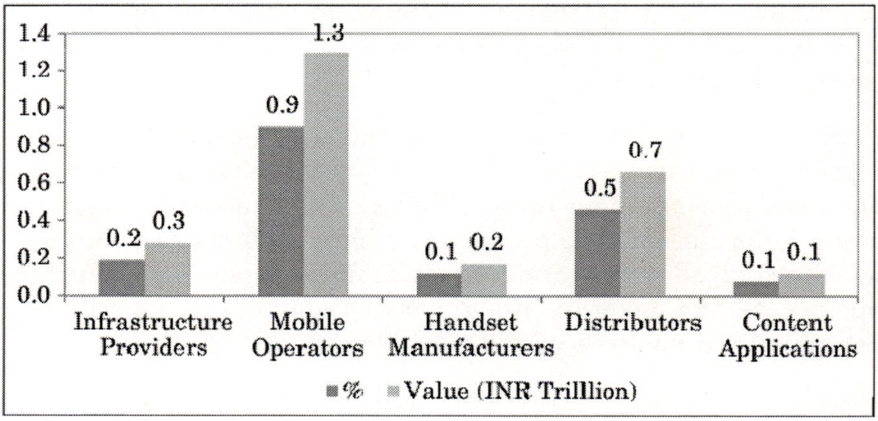

Fig. 4.3: Direct contribution to GDP by mobile phone sector

Source: GSMA, 2018

In addition to their direct economic contribution, firms in the mobile ecosystem purchase inputs from their providers in the supply chain. For example, device manufacturers purchase inputs from microchip providers, and mobile content providers require services from the broader IT sector. Furthermore, some of the profits and earnings generated by the mobile ecosystem are spent on other goods and services, stimulating further economic activity in those sectors. This additional economic activity will boost value added further. The use of mobile technology also drives improvements in productivity and efficiency for workers and firms. Different types of mobile technology have their own impact on the productivity of the global economy. Mobile voice and text services allow workers and firms to communicate more efficiently and effectively (by reducing unproductive travel time, for example). 3G and 4G technology allow workers and firms to use mobile data and internet services. This improves access to information and services, which in turn drives efficiency in business processes across many industries, including finance and health.

The impact of mobile internet is particularly significant in developing countries, where fixed infrastructure is poor and mostly confined to large cities and business/industrial districts. Machine to Machine (M2M) and Internet of Things (IoT) allow for the digitisation of services and improvement of industrial processes. As these technologies would increasingly adopted, we expect them to create significant benefits by driving cost savings and operational efficiency gains in areas such as manufacturing, logistics and retail and generated higher value added in coming years. Overall, taking into account the direct, indirect and productivity impacts, the mobile industry made a total contribution of about 9.5 per cent to GDP.

According to GSMA research, the contribution of mobile phone sector is expected to go up to 9.6 per cent and in value term 14 Trillion INR by 2020. This increased contribution reflects the fact that the mobile phone sector will experience faster growth than the rest of the economy.

In addition, most of this growth will be driven by the boost to business productivity and economic output resulting from previously unconnected citizens becoming first time internet users, with virtually all of this additional connectivity provided through mobile networks. Internet connectivity is directly linked to greater productivity and economic growth, and the large increase in the number of internet users will be the key driver of the transformation in the productivity of the Indian economy.

4.3. CONTRIBUTION TO EMPLOYMENT

India's employment data shows that the share of employment of the transport, storage and communication went up from 3.7 per cent in 1999–2000 to 3.8 per cent in 2004–05, further upto 7 per cent in 2011-12 and 9 per cent in 2015-16. According to the GSMA report, the total employment in mobile phone sector in 2016-17 was 4 million. This was divided into three segment, formal sector (0.3 million), informal sector (1.9 million) and other related economic activities (1.8 million) as presented in Fig. 4.4. The total number of jobs directly supported by the mobile will also grow significantly in the period to 2020 to approximately 3 million, with an additional 2 million indirect jobs also supported by 2020.

The formal employment is provided directly by mobile operators and the ecosystem. The informal employment is those employed in retail and distribution of mobile phone, primarily mobile handsets. In addition to this, economic activity in the ecosystem generated jobs in other sectors. Firms that provide goods and services as production inputs for the mobile phone (for example, microchips or transport services) employ more workers as a result of the demand generated by the mobile sector. Furthermore, the wages, public funding contributions and profits paid by the mobile industry are spent in other sectors, which provide additional jobs.

Further to the employment that is directly sustained within the ecosystem, additional jobs were indirectly supported in other industries, as the ecosystem generated demand and jobs in other sectors that benefit from the activity of the mobile industry, particularly in the direct supply chain.

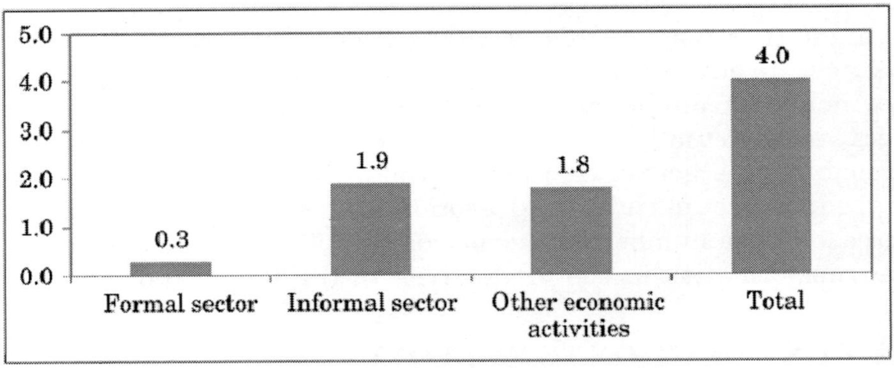

Fig. 4.4: Employment (in million)

Source: GSMA, 2018

The largest formal employment provider in the mobile phone sector was operators, (100 thousands), followed by the content, applications and services sector (85 thousands), handset manufacturers (50 thousands), distributors and formal retail such as large retailers, small chains and increasingly also general retailers (45 thousands) and infrastructure providers (15 thousands) as given in Fig. 4.5. However, a large number of jobs in this sector are on a part-time or self-employed basis. A number of mobile manufacturers have reported plans to open or strengthen their presence in India, while the formal retail sector is also growing and expanding faster than traditional retailing.

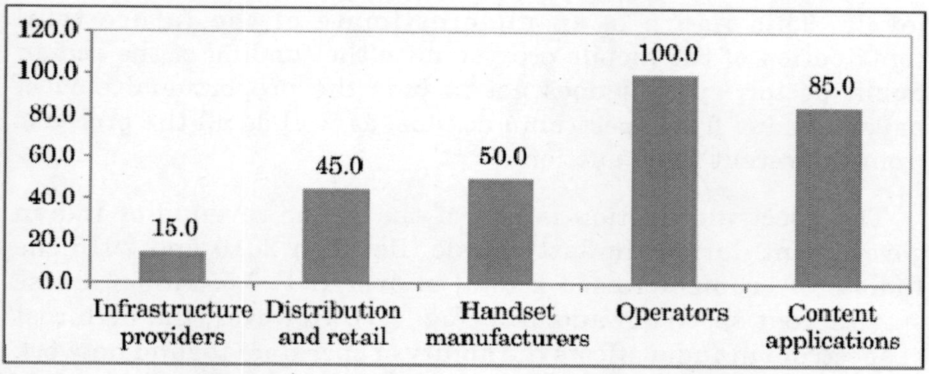

Fig. 4.5: Formal employment (in INR 000)

Source: GSMA, 2018

4.4. CONTRIBUTION TO PUBLIC FUNDING

The mobile ecosystem also makes a highly significant contribution to the funding of the Indian public sector, with approximately INR 1.3 trillion (Fig. 4.6). This contribution comprised INR 0.67 trillion in general taxation, INR 0.38 trillion in mobile specific taxation, and payments of approximately INR 0.34 trillion for the licencing of spectrum acquired as a result of the multi-band spectrum auctions (800 MHz, 900 MHz, 1800 MHz and 2100 MHz). The public funding contribution of the mobile ecosystem in the form of general and mobile specific taxes will reach INR 1.45 trillion by 2020 in real terms if tax rates and regulatory fee rates remain at current

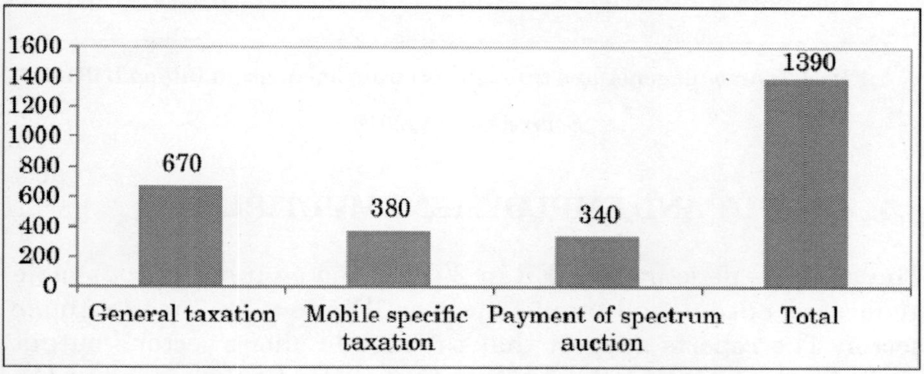

Fig. 4.6: Contribution to public funding (in Billion INR)

Source: GSMA, 2018

levels. This figure is an underestimate of the future total contribution of the mobile ecosystem to the funding of the Indian public sector, since it does not include the proportional part of payments due from spectrum auctions, as well as all the proceeds from the recent 2016 auction.

The spectrum auction is one of the major revenue of Indian government during the last decade. Between 2010 and 2016 the Indian government raised a total of over INR 3.5 trillion across six different spectrum auctions (Fig. 4.7). However, the high cost of spectrum in India affects the ability of operators to fund network investments. Spectrum auctions in the past have contributed to sizeable debt on the books of the industry estimated at 4.6 INR trillion as on March 31, 2017. Out of this, 2.8 INR trillion pertains to non-spectrum debt while 1.8 INR trillion is the deferred spectrum payout related debt. This debt estimated around 4.8 INR trillion by March 2018. Hence, the annual repayment obligations for the spectrum debt remain high at around 0.28 trillion in 2018 and around 0.35 trillion per year from 2019 to 2025.

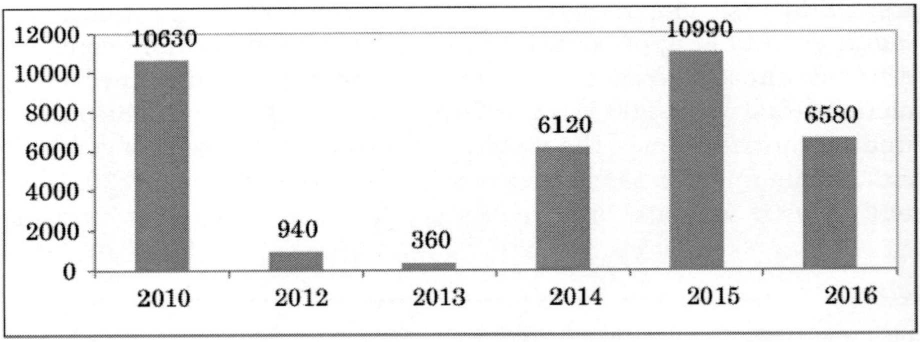

Fig. 4.7: Amount generated through spectrum auctions (in Billion INR)

Source: GSMA, 2018

4.5. OUTPUT AND EMPLOYMENT MULTIPLIER

The analysis done by NCAER in 2010 based on input-output table generated output and employment multipliers for mobile phone sector. The reports suggest that the mobile phone sector's output multiplier stands at 2.2, implying that if the final demand of the communication sector increases by, say, Rs 1,00,000, then the total output of the economy will increase by 2.2 times, that is Rs 1,00,000, of investment will result in an output of Rs 2,20,000. This is because of the direct as well indirect relationship that the communication sector has with other sectors of the economy. Also, this would lead to the creation of 37,200 new jobs, as the employment multiplier of this sector is 0.3720.This is because of the direct as well indirect relationship that the mobile phone sector has with other sectors of the economy.

On obtaining these multipliers, various simulations can be carried out to study the impact of, say, an increased demand in the mobile phone sector on other sectors due to its inter-linkages with them. The impact could be analysed on both output and the employment of these sectors. Inevitably, industries with strong backward and forward linkages with the mobile phone sector will have high impact but others which are indirectly linked, also get impacted. In a simulation, the impact of increase in the final demand component of the mobile phone sector in future years was worked out by assuming that the sector growth will remain same. The final demand component for the mobile phone sector for the year 2019-20, the value of output will reach up to Rs 19,03,122 crore due to its strong linkages with Electronic Equipment and Business services sectors, their value of output also shows hefty growth. Similarly, if the mobile phone sector continues to grow at this pace, the sector will employ 27.7 million people by 2019-20 due to its direct impact. As a result of its linkages with other sectors of the economy, there will be a total of 69.8 million jobs created.

4.6. NATIONAL INCOME AND MOBILE PHONE GROWTH

The relationship between growth of national domestic product and mobile penetration show a linear relationship. This reveals that the growth of the economy is associated with growth of mobile sector in India (Fig. 4.8). However, there are many other factors that also play an important role such as government relation, investment and other related factors.

Hence, the causality analysis has been done to understand the growth factors in detail. For the analysis quarterly data (2007-17) of six indicators: (i) per capita gross national product (PCGNP) which indicates consumer income or purchasing power; (ii) mobile subscriber per 100 inhabitants or density (SUB) represents penetration level; (iii) government effectiveness index (GOV) which signifies mobile telecom policy and regulatory environment; (iv) foreign direct investment (FDI) which specifies the investment level; (v) internet density (INT) which denotes internet or data services penetration, and (vi) revenue of mobile phone services (REV), which shows that industry's financial health have been used for the regression exercise (see Annexure for detail).

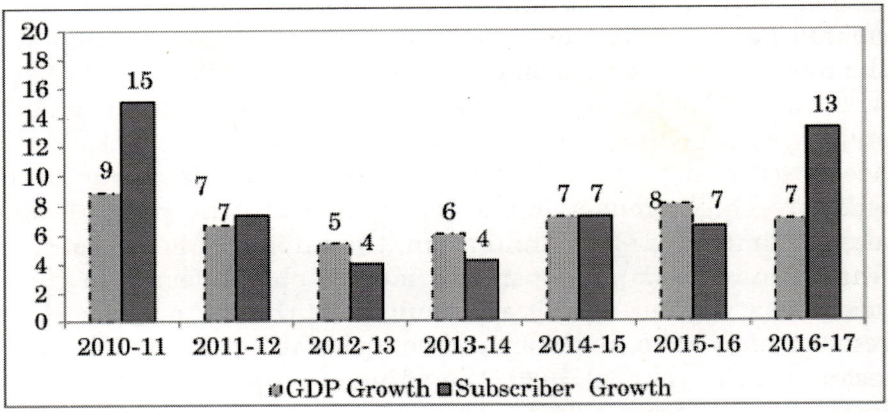

Fig. 4.8: Relationship of growth of GDP and mobile subscribers

Source: CSO and TRAI

The result shows that growth of per capita gross national product is bi-directionally related to mobile phone revenue and mobile phone subscribers (Table 4.1). This explains that national income or income level or purchasing power of the people and penetration of mobile phone are positively associated to the growth of mobile phone sector revenue. On the other hand, revenue or growth of mobile phone sector also associated to the rise in national income or income level of people and mobile phone penetration rate. However, foreign direct investment, government effectiveness index and internet penetration relates uni-directionally to mobile sector growth or revenue, this means that these variables are associated to the growth of mobile phone sector but opposite is not true. The state policies and investment can help in rolling out mobile phone and internet services, which may result in growth of mobile phone sector revenue or growth of the sector.

Table 4.1: Pair wise granger causality test results

Hypothesis (both ways)	***Probability***	***Null Hypothesis***
ΔlnREV does not Granger cause ΔlnPCGNP	0.018	Reject
ΔlnPCGNP does not Granger cause ΔlnREV	0.065	Reject
ΔlnREV does not Granger cause ΔLnSUB	0.042	Reject
ΔLnSUB does not Granger cause ΔlnREV	0.000	Reject
Hypothesis (one-way)		Reject
ΔlnFDI does not Granger cause ΔlnREV	0.003	Reject
ΔlnGOV does not Granger cause ΔlnREV	0.002	Reject
ΔLnINT does not Granger cause ΔlnREV	0.070	Reject

4.7. CHAPTER SUMMARY

India's telecom revolution has been the driving force of the economy since the turn of the century and it has done well to evolve with the times and climb the data bandwagon. It has largely gone unnoticed, but now India has also become the highest mobile data user in the world with monthly usage exceeding a billion GB. An econometric analysis for the Indian economy showed that the 15 percent increase in internet penetration due and the spill-over effects it creates will raise the per capita levels of the country's GDP by 5.9 per cent, provided all else remains constant. So, it is clear from the above analysis that the mobile sector is contributing to the Indian economy both directly and indirectly. It has larger indirect economic contribution than direct, and the contribution is rising over the years. This makes the mobile phone sector as a sun shine sector of Indian economy. But there are some challenges also emerging in recent years like reduction in government revenue due to disruption in the market with deteriorating financial conditions of some major operators. Hence, the government needs to take some positive steps to take the sector out of it.

One of the major challenges witnessed is loss of jobs in the FY2018 due to consolidation of the market. Some estimates show that during FY2018 the sector has lost around 40,000 jobs and the trend is likely to continue for the next year, with the total figure expected to reach 80,000-90,000. Mobile phone services contribute revenue to the government in the form of licence fees and spectrum charges including earning from spectrum auction. The government revenue from the sector has been declining due to declining profitability of mobile operators in FY2018. Not only licence fee, which is collected on the basis of adjusted gross revenue, the spectrum usage charges have also declined during the last year. It is also argued that there is shortfall in revenue from the sector primarily because no auction took place in the current financial year and competitive pressure from Reliance Jio. The commercial launch of Reliance Jio forced incumbent operators to drastically lower their voice and data charges, which has taken a toll on their payment of licence fee and spectrum usage charges.

With the consolidation happening in the mobile phone market there seems no need for incremental spectrum, though the government will get amount that is due for earlier auctions. There is need to thrust on rural population that will have a spin off effect on the sector as it would increase rural spending power. The focus on electrification of rural areas will give a push to installation of cell towers. This suggests that financial stress in the debt-laden mobile phone sector is a matter of grave concern that cannot be ignored. Revenues are falling, and debt is piling up. According to data from the RBI, the telecom sector is India's largest debtor, with 4.6 trillion INR payable as discussed in chapter 3. Even the Economic Survey, 2017-18 has declared the telecom sector is in a 'severe crisis'.

The Government has taken numerous measures to lift the sector out of its crisis but its efforts have not been fruitful. For instance, it formulated the Inter-Ministerial Group to suggest solutions. The body made a number of suggestions, such as slashing the spectrum charges and license fees as well as other levies. For decades now, there have been demands for rationalization of various duties, fees, spectrum charges, and taxes by industry, as well as recommendations for the same by organisations with stakes in the sector. But the license fees and spectrum charges have not been cut. This shows that the government is well-aware of the problems that are ailing the sector but is not serious about acting. The reason behind this may be that the telecom sector is the highest revenue generator for the government. Also, Digital India is entirely based on providing cheap internet services to the electorate.

Government is aware of current employment situation in the mobile phone sector, and taking some positive steps. According to the secretary telecom, "we are assisting in re-employment of those who have lost their jobs. The government is working in three layers, first proving assistances to those who work at lower level such as at service centre and retail outlets. Then we provide new job opportunities by re-training in public Wi-Fi and Bharatnet.

This important sector needs government support, because it plays a critical role in the growth of the economy, employment generation and contributes to the government's key programmes. The upcoming new telecom policy, 2018 has high hopes for revival of the sector and its future growth by addressing these current challenges.

5

Socio-Economic Impact on Mobile Phone Consumers – A Case of Rural Bihar

5.1. BACKGROUND

Mobile has provided best solution for people's socio-economic empowerment in recent years. In particular, to people from backward or geographically remote areas who hitherto were not able to access the information. Mobile phone has provided access to information on agriculture, education, health, marketing, banking, governance and empowering women, poor people and people from rural areas. It is contributing in digital literacy to unconnected people, delivering financial access to the unbanked population and delivering innovative services and applications.

The impact of mobile phone has been documented globally. Its importance in socio-economic empowerment of people has been articulated best in the paper by Jensen (2007). The 'Law of One Price' (that is the price of a good should not differ between any two markets by more than the transportation cost between them) did not work in countries like India characterised by incomplete information. Similarly, Veeraraghavan *et al.*(2009) discussed an experiment in rural Maharashtra where they replaced a PC-based system with an SMS-based mobile phone system and found the latter to be more successful with the farmers in terms of convenience, popularity and expense. However, the SMS-based mobile phone system had its limitations in the sense that it took a long time to enter long strings of information. Mittal *et al.*(2010) finds that "the final leg of delivering connectivity from a communications provider to a customer" is served better by a mobile phone than a personal computer for fishermen especially the ones out at sea because of its "low cost, real-time delivery and expanded reach".

Sood (2006), in his comprehensive study across various regions and occupations, finds that mobile phones helped in various ways including accessing market information, coordinating travel and transport, increasing paying work days and managing remote activities. The ease of use, portability and comfort level of the mobile phone has made it the vehicle of choice for delivery of development programmes. Mehta (2012) also finds that mobile phone helped in the empowerment of rural women. The above studies emphasise the importance of mobile phone in socio-economic development of people.

In this context, the chapter six discusses impact of mobile phone on its consumers. The chapter also highlights the problem faced by consumers at remote and rural areas. It is based on mobile phone consumers survey conducted in rural Bihar, which is the most underdeveloped state with lowest tele-density in the country. The rural area of state (see annexure) is selected for the study to understand the impact of mobile phone and to understand the digital divide. It was assumed that people from underdeveloped area might face more difficulties in accessing mobile phone due to their poor socio economic conditions and infrastructure, which helps in understanding the impact of mobile phone better.

The consumer ssurvey in rural area of Bihar was conducted in six districts namely, Nalanda, Rohtas, Gopalganj, Gaya, Madhubani and Purnea in 2015. In total, 394 mobile phone users were selected for survey by using systematic circular random sampling[43*]from the census survey list of Rodgers *et al.*(2011) study in Bihar (see annexure). A structured questionnaire was prepared for the survey in Bihar, which included one section on 'demography' and 'ownership of and access to mobile phones'. The second section pertained to the usage of mobile phones, with major sub-sections on activities, information sources and the benefits or impact of their usage. The third section focused on innovative uses of mobile phones and constraints faced with respect to their usage.

5.2. PROFILE OF RESPONDENTS

Profile of Mobile Phone Users

In Bihar, 394 mobile phone users were interviewed in 6 districts namely Gaya, Nalanda, Rohtas, Gopalganj, Madhubani and Purnea. The distribution of mobile phone users across the districts, according to the Census of India, 2011 and sample survey is given in Table 5.1. The sample mobile phone users across districts are almost representing the households having mobile phone according to the census of India, 2011. The percentage of households having mobile phone has gone up in a years' time with almost in similar pattern across districts with Purnea showing the least and Gopalganj the highest.

Table 5.1: Distribution of mobile phone users households

	Census, 2011	*Survey, 2015*	*Sample number*
Gaya	48.6	62.8	39
Gopalganj	70.3	80.4	30
Madhubani	50.0	65.7	146
Nalanda	50.0	71.8	40
Purnea	37.5	61.1	101
Rohtas	63.2	74.5	38
Bihar	50.1	66.4	394

Source: Census of India, 2011 and Field Survey, 2015

Table 5.2 shows the profile of mobile phone user on the basis of their economic background. On the basis of ration cards, around 28 per cent of respondents belonged to Below the Poverty Line (BPL) families and 16 per cent were from very poor families. Around 40 per cent of respondents belonged to households with migrants[43] and more than 80 per cent households comprised of marginal landholders and the landless. As large number of marginal landholders and landless families migrate out because of poor economic conditions and lack of jobs or income opportunities in their native towns. Therefore, the incidence of out-migration is very high

[43] At least one member of the household is a migrant.

in rural Bihar. The members of these migrant families remain in touch with each other through the mobile phone.

Table 5.2: Household economic, migration and landholding status of mobile phone users (in per cent)

Criterion	***Sub-group***	*%*
Economic status	Very poor	15.6
	BPL	28.2
	Above Poverty Line (APL)	56.2
Residential Status	Households without any migrant(s)	59.7
	Households with migrant(s)	40.3
Landholding	Landless	34.7
	Marginal	47.3
	Small	10.5
	Medium	4.9
	Big	2.6
Total		100.0

Source: Field Survey, 2015

Note: Four major categories of landholding are marginal (below 1 ha), small (1-2 ha), medium (2-10 ha) and large/big (10 ha and above).

A little more than one-fourth of respondents were female. These were predominantly middle-aged (between 30 and 59 years of age), married and literate as presented in Table 5.3.

Table 5.3: Gender, marital status, age group and educational status of mobile phone (in per cent)

Criterion	***Sub-group***	*%*
Gender	Male	71.8
	Female	28.2
Marital status	Unmarried	28.2
	Married	87.0
	Widow/widower	4.7
Age group	15-29	8.4
	30-59	65.3
	59+	16.3
Educational status	Illiterate	6.1
	Below primary	37.1
	Secondary & higher secondary	38.5
	Graduate	18.4
Total		100.0

Source: Field Survey, 2015

About two-fifth of the respondents were self-employed and engaged in the farming and non-farming sectors, reflecting dependence on agriculture and small trading activities for their livelihood as presented in Fig. 5.1. A substantial proportion of them (22 per cent) were involved in household activities, particularly women, who took care of domestic chores like preparing food, washing utensils and taking care of the children and elderly members of the family. Regular and casual workers constituted one-tenth and one-fifth of the respondents.

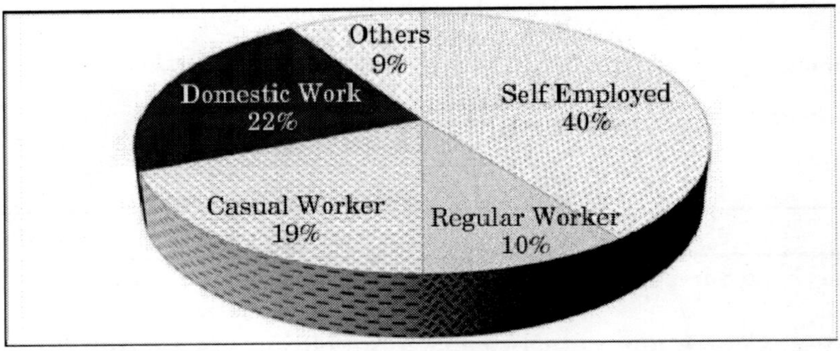

Fig. 5.1: Occupational profile of mobile phone users (in percentage)

Source: Field Survey, 2012

The individual characteristics of the mobile phone users survey revealed that the early mobile users in the underdeveloped areas belonged to the dominant social class. This mainly included male, literate, working and married, and young to middle-aged people.

Mobile phone ownership and access

Most of the respondents owned mobile phone sets and 6 out of 10 had purchased them as shown in Table 5.4. The rest got them from their family members, primarily from their children and parents. This phenomenon was observed to be higher among women, who got their mobile phone sets from their spouses and parents. Those who did not have mobile phones used devices belonging to their neighbours, relatives/friends and family members.

The differences were also found in the average number of outgoing and incoming calls per week. The average outgoing calls were lower when compared with the average number of incoming calls per week as given in Table 5.5. This is because substantial number of people in rural areas use their mobile phones only to receive calls from their migrant family members. A missed call to their migrant family members was used as a signal for a return call. The average expenditure per month on mobile phones by males was higher as compared with that by the female. As mentioned earlier, rural women keep mobile phones largely to receive calls from their family members. In addition, the surveyed area had very low level of mobile penetration as presented by low level of tele-density (20.9 per cent).

Table 5.4: Mobile phone ownership and access pattern of mobile phone users (in per cent)

Ownership/Access	*Male*	*Female*	*Total*
Ownership Purchased:			
Self	61.8	49.6	58.3
Parents	4.6	10.8	6.3
Brother/sister	2.8	0.0	2.0
Spouse	4.9	14.4	7.6
Son/daughter	22.8	21.6	22.5
Relatives	3.2	3.6	3.3
If no, access:			
Family members	16.7	0.0	11.8
Relatives/friends	16.7	30.0	20.6
Co-workers	8.3	0.0	5.9
Neighbor's	58.3	70.0	61.8
Total (Col %)	100	100	100
N (Row %)	283(71.8)	111(28.2)	394(100)

Source: Field survey, 2015

Table 5.5: Average calls per week, expenditure per week, density of mobile phone

Call patterns	*Male*	*Female*	*Total*
Outgoing per week (N.)	29	25	27
Incoming per week (N.)	35	30	34
Monthly expense (Rs.)	176	152	169
Tele-density*(mobile phone per 100 population)		20.9 per cent	

Source: Field survey, 2015

5.3. USE AND IMPACT OF MOBILE PHONE

The survey results show that almost every single respondent used the mobile phone for keeping in touch with friends and family members (social networking) as shown in Fig.5.2. One-fifth of respondents were found to be using mobile phones for economic purposes like securing information on agriculture, employment, trading and credit. One-tenth of respondents mentioned that they used mobile phones for improving their livelihood skills through education and securing information on healthcare. Around 7 per cent of respondents revealed that they used mobile phones for entertainment and contacting others during emergencies.

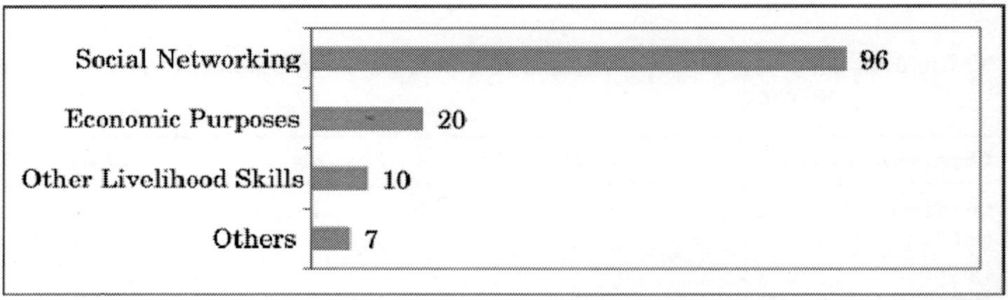

Fig. 5.2: Type of mobile phone usages (in per cent)

Note: Percentage do not add to hundred because of multiple responses.

Source: Field survey, 2015

Mobile Phones and Agriculture Sector

Agriculture contributes between 10 per cent and 35 per cent of GDP in developing countries (World Bank, 2016). As global food demand is rising, the vast majority of agribusinesses, including major corporations in the food and beverage industries, directly procure from smallholder farmers, who supply the majority of the food production consumed worldwide. However, agribusinesses face business inefficiencies when sourcing from smallholder farmers, primarily related to the challenges of operating in cash. In addition, those agribusinesses procuring cash and export crops from smallholders are under pressure to ensure not only that supply chains are reliable and efficient but also that the produce they source is adherent to international standards and, increasingly, traceable.

Digitising the last mile offers significant opportunities to address these challenges. Use of mobile-enabled digital tools in the last mile allows agribusinesses to optimise procurement and business performance and promotes smallholder farmers' financial inclusion, empowerment through transaction transparency and better agricultural practices. Agriculture is the largest employer in India and most of its states. Mobile phone can provide important information to improve the conditions of agriculture and its allied activities. The GSMA estimates show that there could be 45 million potential agricultural value-added services (VASs) users in India by 2020. This would help in government target of doubling farmer income by 2022.

The survey findings show that respondents involved in farming activities collected information through their mobile phones at various stages of the agricultural cycle, and for vegetable and dairy farming purposes. One-tenth of respondents collected information on agriculture through their mobile phones. They mainly collected information at initial stages pertaining to cultivation (64 per cent) like on seeds and fertilisers, as depicted in Fig. 5.3. Some of them also said that they collected information pertaining to the growing (13 per cent), harvesting (8 per cent) and trading stages (15 per cent). They mostly sell their produce to middlemen, who buy the produce from the villages. Very few of them directly go to the *mandi* (wholesale markets).

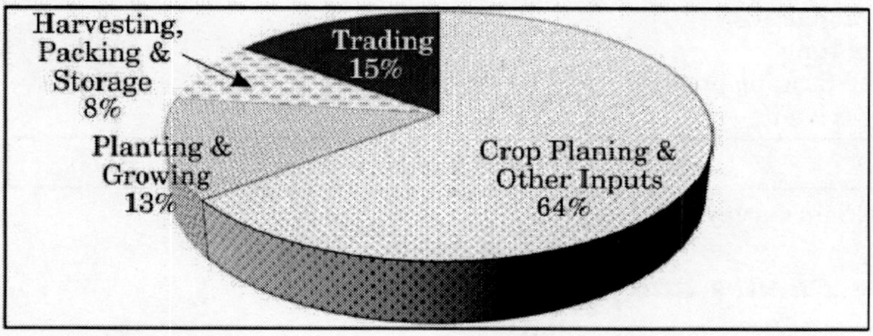

Fig. 5.3: Usage of mobile phones in the agriculture production (in per cent)

Source: Field survey, 2015

The major sources of information to collect agricultural related information were traders/middlemen (42 per cent) followed by other farmers (22 per cent) and input dealers (13 per cent) as presented in Fig. 5.4. Some of them also contacted the state farmer call centre (10 per cent) directly to receive important information.

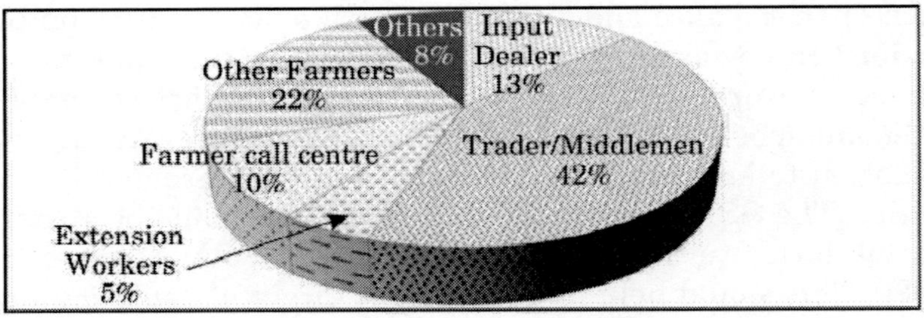

Fig. 5.4: Sources of agriculture information (in per cent)

Source: Field survey, 2015

Those found to use mobile phones for farming purposes, though small in number, had saved their time (62.5 per cent), improved farming techniques as well as productivity (12.5 per cent), reduced production costs (12.5 per cent) and struck better bargains with middlemen and traders (6.3 per cent) resulted in higher profits as shown in Table 5.6.

Table 5.6: Most important benefits in the agriculture production by use of mobile phone (in per cent)

Benefits	*No.*	*%*
Reduction production cost	4	12.5
Higher productivity	2	6.3
Saving of time	20	62.5
Improved farming practice	2	12.5
Timely decision	2	6.3
Total	32	100.0

Source: Field survey, 2015

Mobile Phones and Vegetable Farming

Mobile phones have also helped in a great deal of increasing both productivity and income in the field of vegetable farming. Vegetable-growing farmers sell their vegetables at the local market situated within a radius of 10-15 km from the villages. They enquire about the prices of vegetables from other markets situated in a radius of around 100-200 km through their mobile phones and accordingly decide the appropriate sale price of their vegetables at the local market. This has helped them secure better prices (37.5 per cent), reduce wastage (12.5 per cent), provide timely service (12.5 per cent), and ensure easier access to buyers (12.5 per cent) as given in Table 5.7.

Table 5.7: Most important benefit in vegetable selling by mobile phone use (in per cent)

Benefits	*No.*	*%*
Reduction in wastage	5	12.5
Availability of additional time to provide services	5	12.5
Reduction in procurement cost	10	25.0
Higher returns	15	37.5
Access to buyers	5	12.5
Total	40	100.0

Source: Field survey, 2015

Mobile Phones and Dairy Farming

Mobile phones used in dairy farming were not commonly used as respondents revealed that they sold milk only locally to their regular customers within the villages or to consumers in nearby places. Some of the farmers, however, reported using the mobile phone to contact veterinary doctors rather than making personal visits. Mobile phones were also used to receive information on the market rate for the sale and purchase of cattle.

Mobile Phones and Education/Skills Development

The enhancement of education/skills development is considered a priority as they help improve livelihood skills. The concept of m-learning (the use of mobile devices to deliver education anytime anywhere) could be a boon for India's education sector, especially in the field of adult learning. The government has already taken some initiatives to popularise m-learning in India like the distribution of Aakash tablets to college students. However, these initiatives should be accelerated to ensure that the benefits of m-learning penetrate across the length and breadth of India and not only the student population. Mobile operators are also working to support students and teachers in integrating mobile technologies into the classroom. Mobile enables access to greater learning opportunities for youth in urban hubs and remote locations.

In the survey, respondents revealed that they gathered information relating to opportunities for higher education through relatives or friends and employees of educational institutions and through websites. There have been instances where the use of mobile phones has helped in obtaining information about educational institutes, admission procedures and examination results. However, most respondents claimed they still preferred visiting educational institutes directly to obtain detailed information. Information was also sourced from relatives/friends and family members and by contacting the institutions directly.

Around 10 per cent of the responded reported accessing the internet on their mobile phones. However, the use of education-related websites was common among students and highly educated people only. Some respondents also mentioned use of SMS and whatsapp to know about examination results and other related information. They revealed that mobile phones had transformed the education landscape by providing timely information, as well as helped them in cutting down travel expenses. One such respondent revealed as:

I enquired about the admission procedure for engineering colleges in Delhi and nearby Delhi from one of my relatives residing in Delhi. I got a few contact numbers and spoke to the college administration staff directly. This helped my son to secure a seat in an engineering college near Delhi' (respondent in rural Bihar)

Mobile Phones and Health Services

Developing countries continue to face poor healthcare funding, which affects access, quality of service, cost and key health outcomes. Some 400 million people do not have access to essential healthcare services, mostly in Africa and South Asia, and the shortage of health professionals and facilities is significant. Seven of the 10 most populous low- and middle-income countries have maternal mortality rates above 70 per 100,000 live births– India, Indonesia, Pakistan, Nigeria, Bangladesh, Philippines and Ethiopia. While digital health in developing countries is still in its infancy, recent initiatives show how last-mile digital solutions in the health sector can help expand coverage (access), enhance services (quality) and optimise resources (cost).

Several public-private partnerships (PPPs) have been launched over the last few years to address key health challenges faced by developing countries, including high maternal mortality. These partnerships involve governments (who play the role of funders or payers), health tech companies (providers of healthcare solutions, content, software) and mobile operators (ICT partners), and increasingly represent a viable business model to share resources, capabilities, opportunities and risks among stakeholders.

This is one of the important areas where mobile phone can make an impact. In particular, the use of telemedicine delivered by broadband. Medical advice, monitoring, diagnosis and training delivered through broadband can help a great deal to overcome the heath gaps. Training of professionals in all sectors can also be imparted through broadband video and other applications. Mobile operators are engaging in digital heath in developing countries by providing – directly or through partnerships – business-to-government (B2G), business-to-business (B2B) and business to-consumer (B2C) services throughout most of the value chain. These range from digitisation of healthcare professionals to digitisation of health centres, supply chains and patient data, and integrated digital platforms for information, booking, payments and complementary services.

In India the health sector is facing a number of challenges when it comes to obtaining information on health services or developing healthcare infrastructure. In the survey the respondents mentioned that they sourced information on health services through mobile phone either to their relatives/friends or by contacting doctors directly. While traditional healers in the village could be called within minutes in case of emergencies, ambulance services were also made available at a call. People also call ambulances or private vehicles during an emergency. Mobile phones have ensured they are made available within minutes bringing in the necessary medical attention.

To illustrate, World Health Partners, a Bill & Melinda Gates Foundation project being implemented along with the Idea Foundation, has established a regional medical centre at Patna in Bihar. A team of doctors at the centre ask their patients or medical personnel to describe the symptoms of their illness over the mobile phone and accordingly dispense remedies. This has helped the rural population to cut down travel and medical expenses and also obtain professional advice rather than being solely dependent on touts/healers and paramedics. Sub-centres established at the block level in every district have trained rural health workers, who provide basic and primary healthcare services to rural patients with the help of doctors based in Patna. These centres have been established primarily for rural patients who do not have access to doctors or medical facilities, and are situated in remote locations. Doctors or counsellors at the regional centre also provide medical information and conduct referrals for their patients in the rural areas. Thus, with mobile phones now easily available in most places, rural India has easier and better access to medical care.

In some places, pregnant women and women nursing their infants are informed about impending health check-ups and vaccinations through text messages. Rural healthcare workers use mobile phones for consulting doctors in urban hospitals for serious cases. A list of the mobile phone numbers of doctors has been made available by the government to all rural healthcare workers for consultation purposes and emergencies, and in complicated medical cases. In case of the latter, mobile phones also facilitate direct referral to other hospitals. Easier and cheaper access to medical services with the use of mobile phones has thus led to a change in the healthcare sector there and has also helped in saving lives.

Mobile Phones and the Labour Market

Mobile phones also play an important role in accessing labour market information. Respondents said there were two major sources of labour market information: migrant members (who could be family members, relatives and friends) and employers. Both these sources provide information through mobile phones. Employers and casual labourers contact each other for construction and agricultural work, both within and outside the state. Mobile phone usage has reportedly reduced the control of middlemen or contractors in casual labour outsourcing processes and also led to better working conditions for labourers. Earlier, contractors or middlemen used to exploit workers, which resulted in low wages and poor working conditions. Few such respondents describe:

My friends are working in private companies in Delhi and they call me whenever there is a vacancy in their companies' (educated unemployed respondent in rural Bihar).

'I used to go to Punjab during the harvest season. Earlier, we had to either contact local contractors or visit Punjab and stay unemployed for a few days before getting work. Now, we are able to save time and money, apart from bargaining for higher wages and better working conditions' (respondent working as a casual labourer in rural Bihar).

Mobile Phones and Finance and Credit

In recent years, the government initiated several schemes such as Jan DhanYojana and also cashless initiatives such as use of mobile money, Paytm and BHIM App for the financial inclusion and digital banking. Today around 65 per cent of Indian adults have an account with a financial institution, and there is significant room to leverage mobile technology to increase use of financial services.

The mobile phones use for credit or cash transfer by family members is gaining popularity in underdeveloped areas. In the survey, only around 15 per cent respondents said they are using mobile application for money transfer. Mobile phones enable families to learn about the amount transferred and other bank transactions detail through SMS or Whatsapp from their migrant family members or other family members transfer money. Apart from the formal banking system, the informal money transfer system is still popular through the usage of mobile phones. Few such respondents revealed that:

I have an account in the local State Bank of India branch where my husband deposits money every month in my account from Delhi. Details of the deposit are then conveyed over phone. I withdraw money from the ATM machine in the local market' (female respondent in rural Bihar).

'My son deposits money into my neighbour's account and gives the details over phone. My neighbour withdraws the money and hands it over to me the same day. Earlier, I used to get money only once in every six or twelve months from my son, depending on his visits' (senior citizen in rural Bihar).

In the formal banking system, processes of money transfers through internet banking or cash deposits in the accounts of family members are gaining popularity. Money is transferred in two ways:

when family members from rural areas deposit money in the accounts of their children and other family members, and exchange details about these transactions over the mobile phone; and when migrant family members deposit money regularly into the accounts of their family members in their native villages and communicate details of these transfers over the phone. Some also mentioned that they used the bank accounts of other people to receive or deposit money for their relatives back home. The respondents from Bihar said:

'I prefer to take loans from the local trader or moneylender as no paperwork is require and is also easily available' (respondent in rural Bihar).

'I regularly send money via mobile phone to my mother in Purnea district in Bihar. It's very easy and stress-free as the money reaches my mother quickly' (respondent in rural Bihar).

In addition, Vodafone India in association with ICICI bank has started the unique money transfer and payment service "M-Pesa" in Bihar and Jharkhand where banking network and financial penetration is in rural areas. M-Pesa' service is available across 32 districts and 250 tehsils in Bihar at present. The innovative use of mobile technology makes it possible for customers to enjoy a fast, simple and secure way to transfer money and make payments. Using their M-Pesa account, customers can at their convenience avail facilities of deposit and withdraw cash from designated outlets, transfer money through any mobile phone in the country, make payment to recharge mobile, clear utility bills and for DTH service subscription and shop at select shops among others. The service is available across Bihar through over 2800 specially trained authorised agents.

The use of mobile phones for obtaining formal bank loans is, however, still not popular in rural areas. Given the low literacy rate, people often prefer seeking loans from relatives, friends and local traders or moneylenders. Only a few people hold formal bank accounts in rural areas, which is why they mostly depend on the informal credit system. The respondent revealed that digital transfer of money *via* mobile phones has helped greatly in cutting down travel time, thereby reducing costs, besides making access to information easier.

Mobile Phones and Social Capital

Mobile phones have proved to be a boon in rural areas, as they have brought about a sense of social security, connectivity and safety among the people there. Mobile connectivity has made it possible for people to get emotional and financial support during emergencies. Mobile phone users have been benefited by broadening their social network. In particular, there is widespread use of Whatsapp and facebook among the women and youth. It has enabled easy communication with family members (40.6 per cent to spouse, 21.9 per cent to parents) and relative/friends (95.6 per cent), particularly for women whose spouses are working in far-off places. Women added that mobiles had actually helped in maintaining and strengthening their familial and social bonds as presented in Table 5.8.

Table 5.8: Use of mobile phone in connectivity and social security (in per cent)

Connectivity	*Male*	*Female*	*Total*
Spouse	34.7	55.4	40.6
Parents	20.5	25.6	21.9
Other family members	38.6	40.5	39.2
Relatives/friends	95.5	95.9	95.6
Total	100.0	100.0	100.0

Note: Percentage do not add to hundred because of multiple responses.
Source: Field survey, 2015.

Overall, the social impact of mobile phones was observed in the form of enhanced social capital for mobile phone users, which in turn resulted in improved personal well-being and satisfaction, and in saving time.

Mobile Phone and Governance

The use of mobile phone for accessing government welfare schemes has increased in recent years. In particular, the people are using mobile phone to access information on MGNREGS, government health schemes, and information such as scholarship etc. The information about schemes and other transaction details are directly send to the beneficiary. Around 30 per cent of the respondents reported use of mobile phone for accessing information on government welfare schemes. They also said approaching to government officials through mobile phone such as kishan call centres, health centre etc. The officials also informed them through mobile phone regarding several government initiatives launched in the state. The government of Bihar has introduced SMS and mobile application-based monitoring system in 2009 to track the status of government schemes. This monitoring system has helped in promoting transparency and accountability to check officials' laxity.

Mobile Phone and Value Added Services

Mobile phone and value added services (MVAS) are slowly gaining popularity among rural people. About one-tenth of total respondents mentioned using SMS during festivals and important occasions like birthdays and New Year celebrations for sending congratulatory messages. A higher percentage of female respondents (9.9 per cent) were found to be listening to music as compared to their male counterparts (8.8 per cent) as shown in Table 5.9. On the other hand, male (15.2 per cent) downloaded films more than female (5.2 per cent), while only a few of them (6.8 per cent) mentioned accessing the internet through mobile phones in rural areas. Approximately one-tenth of total male users added that they also used mobile phones to download ring tones, music and games. This facility was availed by people who were relatively wealthier and more educated.

Table 5.9: Use of MVAS by mobile phone users (in per cent)

		Male	*Female*	*Total*
Use of	SMS	8.4	4.1	7.2
	Internet	7.5	5.0	6.8
	Music	8.8	9.9	9.1
Downloading of	Ring tone	13.3	13.2	13.3
	Music	14.3	10.7	13.3
	Gamesfilm	10.715.2	10.75.2	10.710.2

Source: Field survey, 2015

In general, mobile handsets were used as much for 'entertainment' as they were for communication. Many of the respondents mentioned that people, especially youngsters, had started using mobile phones for only listening to the music in rural areas.

Impacts on Livelihood

There are numerous livelihood impacts of mobile phones uses. There has been improved access to knowledge in agriculture, including non-grain products, such as vegetables and milk production. Besides knowledge, information about market prices secured through mobile phones enabled farmers to choose wholesale markets in which to sell their products or even the harvesting of vegetables. The farmers, who use mobile phone for seeking information has reported improved marketing because of better price information. Increasing access to price information would seem to improve the functioning of markets, reducing the spread between prices in different locations. Cost savings were realized by both farmers and petty traders. Farmers could reduce spoilage by harvesting when prices in the market were better. Small traders could fine-tune their supplies according to customers' needs, conveyed over mobile phones.

One area in which mobile phones have had a clear impact is in reducing the role of intermediaries in market relations. Small farmers, who earlier sold to intermediary traders in the village, could not find out prices in wholesale markets and take their produce to these markets. The mobile phone has developed strong linkage with labour-absorbing (Punjab, Haryana, Delhi and others area) and labour-supplying regions (Bihar, Uttar Pradesh). Intermediaries had an important role in bringing employers and workers together obviously they had a cut for their intermediation services. With the mobile phone, employers and workers could be in direct contact with each other. Wage rates are easily known and contracts and timing of work negotiated over the phone.

The role and costs of being an intermediary are reduced but some new form of intermediaries also arises. Locally landowners contact leaders of worker gangs, who then gather together the required groups of workers. Search cost is reduced on both employer and worker sides. Economic networks become denser, with multiple interactions between employers and workers. Market functioning has become more efficient, with a reduction in search-related transaction costs.

Remittance is one of the main reasons for migration from rural to urban cities or metros. Mobile phone-based remittances, whether through formal channels or informal networks, have become cheap and safe. Remittances are made regularly and do not have to be made just during a home visit. Returning migrants were known to be carrying money and thus were easy targets for robbery. Mobile phone-cum-ATM-based remittances have eliminated this risk and thus increased the real returns from migration.

The most important impact this study found is that in networking, a topic that has been neglected in the study of the impact of mobile phones in India. Networks are both economic and social, the latter usually based on familial and kinship relations. Economic networks are connected to improve market functioning. There are now greater connections between buyers and sellers, whether in product or factor (labour) markets. The mobile phone, enables both direct connections and larger numbers of intermediaries, and could reduce the margin that intermediaries get. The mobile phone is particularly important in sustaining familial relations in multi-locational households with at least one migrant. Mobile phone has made it possible for migrants and their families to remain in regular touch.

Being allowed to keep or use a mobile phone has become a matter of struggle for young women in rural area. Many village councils have banned unmarried women for having or using phones. Traditional social norms prohibit pre-marital contact between young women and men, and certainly those between members of different castes. In conjunction with educational institutions, which bring together young people of various castes, the spread of mobile phones has also made it easier for young women and men to develop relations that go against traditional and caste-based norms. The mobile phone enables a privacy of communication otherwise quite absent in rural India (Jeffrey and Doron, 2013). It has helped to disrupt traditional social relations.

5.4. INNOVATIVE USES OF MOBILE PHONES

In the surveyed areas many stakeholder and mobile phone customer have come up with innovative methods of using the technology. These are as follows:

- In general, the use of the 'missed call' was very common among migrant family members/friends, serving as an indication for them to return the call. Women and senior citizens in particular benefited from this practice.

- The courier facility: This basically meant using the mobile phone for money transfers and credit facilities in rural areas.
- Members of poor families used a single mobile phone set with multiple SIM cards. A member could then insert his/her SIM card in the phone to make a call. Understanding this pattern of saving on fixed costs, mobile phone manufacturers came out with instruments that could hold multiple SIM cards.
- In one of the surveyed village in Bihar, a local shop had installed solar panels and was charging Rs. 4 to recharge a mobile phone.
- As can be seen from the above list, a number of these innovations have been carried out not by phone companies but by users. These examples reaffirm the role of users in carrying out innovations in poor areas to use the new technology.

5.5. CONSTRAINTS IN ACCESSING MOBILE PHONE

People were also found to face a number of constraints, while using mobile phones like the lack of electricity for charging (59.8 per cent), voice/internet rates (58.6 per cent), mobile phone handset (30.5 per cent), lack of knowledge of MVAS (31.6 per cent) as given in Table 5.10 and others such as poor signals, non-functional base stations or mobile towers in the absence of electricity and finally fraudulent money deduction by operators.

Table 5.10: Constraints in accessing mobile phone (in per cent)

Difficulties	*Male*	*Female*	*Total*
High cost of handset	28.8	35.7	30.5
High voice/internet rate	56.1	66.7	58.6
Difficulty in mobile phone operation	33.3	52.4	37.9
Difficulty in Power (Electric) Charging	58.3	64.3	59.8
Inadequate VAS knowledge	32.6	28.6	31.6
Others	3.0	0.0	2.3
Respondents (number)	100 (132)	100 (42)	100 (174)

Note: Percentage do not add to hundred because of multiple responses.
Source: Fields Survey, 2015

One of the most common problems is charging of mobile phones, where electric supply is erratic and load shedding occurs for long hours. Some people were found to walk more than 10 km a day just to charge their phones because their villages did not have electricity. They also had to pay more for mobile battery charges than services recharges at local shops (that demanded a price of Rs 5-10 per charge). Problems were also found to be in terms of call quality and receptivity (as generators were not switched on during power failures in rural areas necessary for the functioning of mobile towers).

The revenue of mobile operators in rural areas was found to be low and in order to overcome this they resorted to money deduction even if a call was not made. The call also gets dropped regularly due to distance and non-functional mobile towers. This entailed additional expenditure and pressure on the consumers in rural areas. It was also found that a large number of people still did not trust mobile phones because it enabled debtors to lie about their whereabouts; creditors therefore preferred making personal visits.

Mobile phones were also found to have certain negative outcomes in traditional, rural societies. Local vendors were found to be earning substantial revenue by selling obscene movie clips (local and other), film songs and MMS, which had gained popularity among the rural teens and youth. Though vendors earned a substantial amount in the process, the use of mobile phones did have a negative impact on 'traditional values' in society particularly girls and women according to some respondents. As discussed earlier some village council have banned unmarried women from using mobile phones. These village council members feel that cell phones helped in the elopement of young couples and also receive prank calls frequently besides this also distracts them from their studies. Concerns were also raised regarding offensive SMS and MMS being circulated to women.

In general, additional expenditure on monthly household budgets due to unnecessary charges and deduction by mobile operators were also found to create lot of tension and pressure. Children in rural areas played games and listened to songs on mobile phones which had a negative impact on their studies. Unnecessary advertisement calls and others messages also proved to be major distractions.

5.6. CHAPTER SUMMARY

The rural consumer survey revealed that mobile phone has reduced the cost of accessing information, as the search is carried out over the phone. The mobile phone enables rural people to access knowledge about crop and livestock rearing. The phone also enables small producers to reduce their transportation and wastage costs by making deliveries more in line with the demands of consumers. The access to market information through mobile phone has reduced transportation and transaction costs, and enhanced interaction between buyers and sellers. In the fields of education and health too, mobile phones have increased rural access.

The mobile phones helped migrant households to keep in touch and remit money in safe and secure ways. Mobile phones enable the development of social relations in non-traditional ways, although conservative sections of rural society often oppose their use by young women. The issues of changes in networks and social relations enabled by mobile phones come out in this study as quite prominent effects of mobile phones.

The survey shows that an urgent attention is required in rural areas regarding consumer awareness on mobile value added services, high cost of mobile phone, non-existent/erratic power supply, non-functional towers in absence of electricity and money deduction by operators without any call for their profit. The study showed that mobile internet access is spreading among only few educated youth.

6

Growth Drivers of the Mobile Phone Sector

6.1. BACKGROUND

The mobile phone technology is the most successful technologies – from the radio to the radar, from the steam engine to the fitness band –undergo a period of rapid progression before reaching an inexorable plateau. The mobile phone sector is one of the important sector, which has huge future growth potential in India. There are several factors, which are considered as future growth drivers for the sector. These are ranging from rising per capita income, rural areas, data and internet services, value added services, mobile commerce, manufacturing services, smart phones, internet of things, and other government efforts such as digital India etc.

6.2. RISING INCOME LEVEL

The rising income level of people is one of the key drivers of telecom growth in India, which fuel demand for more mobile phone services. Per capita income in India has increased at a fast pace and will continue to increase given the country's strong economic prospects. GDP per capita (US$) is expected to grow at an annual compound growth rate of 7.5 per cent from US$1482 in 2012 to US$3274 in 2023(IBEF, 2018). The emergence of affluent and middle income group is triggering demand for the mobile and internet segments. The affluent (3 per cent to 6.4 per cent) increased more than twice and middle income group (8 per cent to 20 per cent) during the last decade (IBEF, 2018). This can be seen from Figure 6.1 that with rising GDP per capita income level of people, the mobile penetration in the country is rising. During 20011-12 to 2017-18, the per capita GDP has increased from 72 thousand annual to 96 thousand, and telecom penetration rate from 79 per hundred population to 96 per hundred population. This reveals that the rising level of income of people will make higher demand of telecom services.

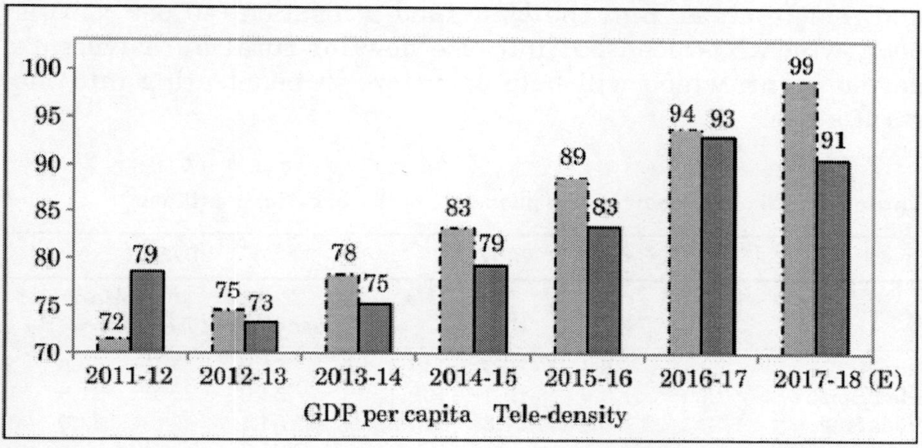

Fig. 6.1: GDP per capita (in 000 INR) and telecom density relation.
Source: TRAI and CSO; E: Estimated

6.3. UNTAPPED RURAL MARKET

The increase in income level also experienced by rural areas with its growing youth population is aiding increasing demand for smart phones. However, the rural tele-density reached at 57.4 per cent by March, 2018, growing from 43.05 per cent as of March 2016. Rural wireless tele-density in the country increased to 57.4 per cent by March 2018 from 50.9 per cent as of March 2016. Around 43 per cent of rural market is yet to be covered by the mobile phone services and huge opportunity still remains. It is argued that private operators were less interested in serving low revenue rural areas due to high operational cost, low population density, lack of commercial activity and low affordability.

However, the subscriber's share of major five operators including private operators in rural area has gone up to twice during 2007 to 2018 (Table 6.1). As of December 2017, the rural subscriber base accounted for 42.7 per cent of the total subscriber base, thereby fuelling growth across the sector. The two factors may have contributed to this growth, one is the saturation of mobile services in urban areas and, another one being significant reduction in tariffs, which made services affordable for rural consumers (Mani, 2012). In addition, like most of the countries in the world, the government of India has made rural rollout mandatory and also put in place the USO to encourage telecom services in rural and remote areas. But, the USO fund utilisation (40 per cent) is poor, which has been put into use now for rural infrastructure development, which will help operators in penetrating into the rural areas.

Table 6.1: Penetration of mobile phone in rural areas (No. in Millions)

	2007		*2018**		
	No.	*%*	*No.*	*Rural Subscribers (%)*	*Market share (%)*
Bharti	8.1	19.0	147.9	51.0	29.6
Idea/Spice	3.7	19.1	106.1	54.0	21.3
Vodafone	8.4	27.3	114.9	54.1	23.0
Reliance Jio	-	-	41.1	25.7	8.2
% Rural	20.7	21.2	499.0	42.7	100.0

*Upto December, 2017
Source: TRAI

There are still close to 55,669 villages in India which are devoid of telecom services. The objective, under the NTP12, includes improving the rural tele density to 70 per cent by 2017, which stood at 57 per cent in 2017. Hence, there is still huge untapped market in rural India for the mobile operators.

6.4. GROWING INTERNET/BROADBAND SERVICES

Worldwide, voice revenue is declining while data revenue is increasing. In India too, data revenue has been increasing the profitability of the operators. The kind of exponential growth is expected out of data and the mobile phone is supposed to be the largest platform to facilitate the same. The Indian telecom industry has seen a paradigm shift from a voice centric market to a data-centric market. While voice business still contributes a large chunk towards operator revenues, data revenues have shown an exponential growth trajectory over the last few years particularly during the year 2016 and 2017. The share of revenue from data grew from 12.5 per cent to 15.7 per cent mainly due to entry of RJio, who is leading at market with 36 per cent share of total data subscribers by the end of 2017.

This is also evident from drastic reduction in data prices that has not only brought the internet within the reach of larger proportion of the Indian population but has also allowed newer segments of society to use and experience it for the first time. Since the monthly saving of an average internet user came out to be INR 142 per month (taking a conservative estimate that the consumer is still using 1 GB of data each month) and there are about 450 million mobile internet users in the country, the yearly financial savings for the entire country comes out to be INR 600 billion (Indian Express, 2017).Therefore, mere savings by the consumer on data has been at astonishing proportions. Now, this data has been used for services that have brought to life a thriving app economy within the country. So, the second level of impact has been in the redressal of a variety of consumer needs — ranging from education, health and entertainment to banking. For instance, students in remote areas can now access online course-ware and small businesses can access newer markets. Information asymmetry has been considerably reduced.

India currently has over 446 million internet subscribers, making it the second largest internet users in the world, ranked only behind China. Over the last few years, increase in internet penetration has been driven mostly by availability of cheaper smart phones. Internet penetration is expected to grow steadily and is likely to be bolstered by government policy. The number of internet subscribers in the country increased at a CAGR of 41.62 per cent, with the number reaching 446 million in December, 2017 from 8.6 million in 2006. The number of internet subscribers in the country is expected to double by 2021 to 829 million. As per Internet and Mobile Association of India (IAMAI) estimates mobile internet users in India has estimated to touch 478 million by June 2018. This attributes to cheaper smartphones, faster connectivity, and affordable services.

Overall IP traffic is expected to grow 4-fold at a CAGR of 30 per cent by 2021. Wired broadband subscriptions in the country witnessed an increase at a CAGR of 17.5 per cent during FY07-17

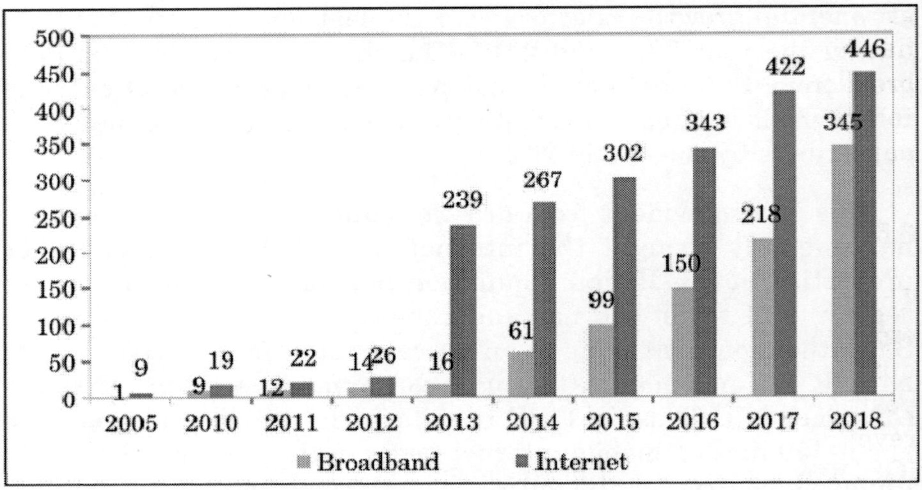

Fig. 6.2: Internet and wireless broadband subscribers (in Million)
Source: TRAI

to reach 18.2 million. Wired broadband subscriptions stood at 18 million and total number of broadband subscriptions at stood at 345 million. More than 92 per cent of rural users and 77 per cent urban users have been using mobile as primary device for accessing internet through cellular data connections. This rise in internet penetration has distinct positive effects on economic growth of a country. These effects arise not merely from the creation of an internet economy, but also due to the synergy effects it generates. Information becomes more accessible and communication a lot easier. Businesses find it easier to operate and access consumers. Education and health services become available in inaccessible locations and labour working in cities has to make less frequent trips home and becomes more productive as a result. Multiple avenues open up for knowledge and skill enhancement (Indian Express, 2017).

However, the overall internet penetration is still low at 34.4 per cent, skewed in favour of urban India, which has 77 per cent of internet penetration. Rural India is still underpenetrated with only 15 per cent penetration and clearly the next area of growth.

The rising affluence of households will lead to an increased demand for consumer goods, entertainment systems etc. which will further drive demand for internet services. Hence these untapped households will represent the next wave for internet growth particularly wireless internet in India. The Government has placed considerable emphasis on growth of internet and broadband in the country as part of its Digital India campaign and recently announced to provide free Wi-fi to more than 1000 gram panchayats to encourage mobile internet and m-cash.

6.5. GROWING MOBILE APPS MARKET AND MVAS

The mobile application market is growing globally and India has emerged the world's fastest growing market for mobile Apps during the last few years. India overtook USA to reach the second position in terms of number of app downloads in 2017. Mobile app revenues in India shot up in FY 2018 across both – Android and iOS platforms. Market insights from data analysis firm App Annie show that India's app market grew 41 percent year-on-year FY2018, and 250 per cent from 2016. The number of app downloads in the country has gone up more than twice during the last 3 years. Number of App downloads were 3.5 billion in 2015 increased to 7.7 billion in 2017 and expected to go up by 20.1 billion 2020. This segment's growth is expected to be driven by increasing mobile connections and availability of low range smartphones.

Over 100 million apps are downloaded every month from different platforms such as iOS, Blackberry, Nokia and Android. Total time spent by Indians on mobile applications increased to 50 billion hours during Oct-Dec 2017. In recent times, video streaming apps such as JioTV, AirtelTV, and Hotstar have emerged three of the top ten apps downloaded in India. With the rise of cheap internet services and low-cost phones, the mobile app market is expected to see an exponential growth in coming years. As far as the content streaming market is concerned, the rural population is slightly catching up the urban internet population. An average user in India has nearly 80 apps and accesses over 40 of them in a month. In addition, the banks are now using mobile banking services for their customers.

The government is ambitious about its Digital India program and the country's mobile operators are confronting and competing against the most aggressive strategy witnessed thus far in the history of its sector – in the voice-over-LTE service offerings (4G VoLTE) provided by Reliance Jio. India in a similar situation as China – a bulk of India's population has come online for the first time *via* the medium of mobile internet. As mobile internet gets easier to access and becomes cheaper in India, its app economy is certain to lunge forward into a much more profitable future. Mobile phone now is not just used to be in touch, but also to express themselves, their attitude, feelings and interests. From playing games and listening to music, to keeping a tab on astrology and checking their bank balance, to reading news headlines and surfing the internet, the Indian mobile user has created a platform of boundless growth for mobile Value Added Services (MVAS)[1] in the market. The revenue from MVAS in India in past half a decade has grown substantially. The (MVAS) industry is expected to reach US$ 23.8 billion by 2020.The MVAS also cover utility services and opportunities are available in this area, specifically encompassing m-commerce, m-health, m-education, m-governance etc. This segment has huge future potential for generating revenue for the sector.

6.6. EMERGING INTERNET OF THINGS

The Internet of Things (IoT).is next great revolution in technology. A world where every object we use has a sensor, enabling it to connect to the internet so it can communicate with each other. It describes the coordination of multiple machines, devices and applications connected to the internet by multiple networks. Mobile is expected to be a key enabling technology for IoT, acting as an aggregator or hub to connect a range of devices and offering wide-area connectivity. Experts estimate that the IoT market could be worth as much as $1.7 trillion by 2020, with more than 50 billion devices connecting to the IoT by that time.

The government is pushing the potential of the Internet of Things in India. Collaboration between the Department of Electronics and Information Technology and the Ministry of Urban Development has resulted in an emphasis in programs designed to expand the capabilities of the country in using the IoT. Some of these initiatives include the support of smart cities (or cities that use IoT devices to manage traffic, utilities, and other aspects),

[1] Entertainment (Ringtones, Caller Ring-back tones, Games), M-Commerce (Services allowing transactions on mobile phones, *e.g.*, Fees deposition, Booking Air Tickets and Information (Bank Balance Enquiry, Air/Train Ticket Status, News Alerts, Stock Prices.

healthcare IoT sensors for monitoring health, and Indian Railways. In the Indian Railways example, IoT devices on the trains communicate through the cloud to indicate fuel consumption. This information can be used to increase efficiency on India's railroads. These projects are a good indication of how important India's government views the IoT.

However, there are many challenges such as internet accessibility among the general population. Many people in India still cannot get the internet on a consistent basis, with reliability problems plaguing many areas. Even when internet performance is consistent, bandwidth becomes a serious issue, and since the IoT needs plenty of bandwidth to function properly, this may hinder widespread prevalence of the IoT. The cost of IoT devices is another major hurdle in mainstream acceptance. Some existing devices, such as wearable health bands, have failed to take off among Indian customers, mainly due to price. India also deals with plenty of challenges regarding its infrastructure. To make the IoT function well, more work first needs to be done to set up support for smart grids, traffic systems, and technologies that can handle increased data demands, like flash storage (SSD).

Despite these challenges in consumer acceptance of the IoT, the outlook is more optimistic and by 2020, a quarter of a billion vehicles will become internet enabled and giving a push to automated driving. In the next five years, the Government of India plans to create a $15 billion IoT market in the country, equivalent to 5–6 per cent of the overall global IoT industry. Forecasts from Machina suggest that the total number of connected IoT devices in India, using a range of different technologies, could reach more than 1 billion by 2020. This is expected to be led by the utilities, automotive, transport & logistics and financial services sectors. There is also likely to be an important role in improving access to government services.

The Indian Government is planning to develop 100 smart city projects, where IoT would play a vital role in development of those cities. Reliance Jio has partnered with Samsung Electronics to set up a nationwide Internet of Things (IoT) network. As of May 2018, trials for the service have already begun at a few locations. Consumption of video content is also forecasted to be 75 per cent of India's mobile data traffic by 2021, compared to 49 per cent in 2016. Advancements in innovative IoT technologies, like health monitors, smart transport, smart meters among others, is projected to result in 21 per cent increase in M2M services. These advances will result in a significant growth of mobile data, and as the telecom sector moves to newer technologies. Operators will need to identify innovative avenues to monetise this data opportunity.

6.7. UPCOMING FIFTH GENERATION (5G) TECHNOLOGY

India was far behind when comes to adoption of mobile technology, but today it has emerged as a second largest internet user in the world. In recent years, the internet data users have gone up by multiple times (12 million in 2010 to 345 million in 2018), and further increase needs technology up-gradation. Hence, the Indian regulator has a target to high speed data 5G launch in India by 2020. Now, the race to 5G is on, as technology companies and mobile phone operators push to lead in the next generation of wireless. Today, a 4G mobile phone offers typical data download speeds of 5 Mbps (megabytes per second) while 5G aspires to reach speeds as high as 10 Gbps (gigabytes per second) and support up to 100 times as many connected devices, mostly machines or "things". Extremely reliable 5G networks will provide for better remote health care, virtual reality, tactile internet, autonomous-connected cars and other applications.

This massive leap in connectivity will deliver a new world of benefits to consumers and huge growth opportunities to businesses and government bodies that depend on wireless technologies. However, the benefits of 5G cannot be realized if the infrastructure isn't ready – and in India, where the focus remains on making the move from 2G/3G to 4G, network operators need to take proactive steps right now in order to future-proof their networks and prepare for the next wave of wireless technology.

As massive investment is required to multiple input multiple output - 5G plug-in technology, cloud radio access network, network virtualisation, to evolve its existing 4G networks to 5G which significantly improves spectrum efficiency. In addition, there will be new requirements around 5G, as a wide range of Internet of Things (IoT) devices – from sensors, to self-driving cars, to vending machines – which depend on the new generation of networks to stay connected.

Operators also need to contend with radical changes in the architecture of the network and moving from a centralised system into a more cloud-like architecture. Developed countries such as USA and few Asian countries like Korea and Japan have started testing high-speed 5G networks. Operators in India should also start preparing now for the future of 5G, even as they continue to upgrade 4G capabilities. By taking early steps to bring in technology and expertise around the move to 5G, operators can position their business to capture future benefits such as transforming their cost base and enabling new revenue streams by enhancing fibre networks and bringing in the next generation of virtualization technologies.

6.8. OTHER GROWTH DRIVERS

The other future growth drivers are increasing use of mobile commerce, mobile payment or banking, smartphones use, telecom manufacturing, government positive steps and policies.

Rising M-Commerce or M-Payment/Banking

Mobile commerce has changed the face of the Indian online commerce industry in the past few years. The increasing online commerce market in India has seen significant growth in recent years, with growth fuelled by rising disposable income levels as well as increasing internet access. The various payment mobile payment options available to consumers are increasingly using their mobile devices to transact. Lack of available cash will no longer deter the people to buy anything even on the road as they have the option to transact money electronically. Cashless economy is fuelling the rise of m-commerce in India with cashless payment options like Paytm becoming popular with smaller merchants. In addition, various options are available now Ola and Uber taxis available throughout the country, and people pay and book cabs from their mobile phones. In addition, the transaction of money, transfer of money or any on-line shopping is possible from the Smartphone with the use of mobile applications.

Digital transactions reached an all-time high of 1.11 billion in January 2018 with mobile banking transactions reaching 102.6 million. In March 2017, the government set a target of achieving 25 billion digital transactions for banks. As of May 2018, nearly

400 banks have been permitted to provide mobile banking services in India. The Indian digital payments industry is poised to grow to $500 billion by 2020.

More Adoption of SmartPhones

The use of smartphone is rising with most of the mobile related services can be done through it. This is required for e-commerce activities, value added services, accessing your mails, social networking and accessing any other information. The reduction of prices of smartphones in recent years has increased its adoption substantially even in rural India. The fair pricing of mobile connections and the introduction of cheap Chinese and local smartphones into Indian market has been resulting in increasingly adoption of smartphones. The aggressive marketing of smartphones by the mobile manufacturing companies and government efforts has also transformed the smartphone from a luxury to a necessity.

India today has become the second largest smartphone market in the world, trailing China and overtaking the US with about 250 million smartphone users. India currently has around 300-400 million smartphone users and is expected to lead the smartphone growth reaching 810 million by 2021. There is still huge rural and urban divide. However, the scenario will change soon with the increasing availability of affordable telecom services and handsets in the market and the numerous Government initiatives to connect the unconnected. Smartphones are also empowering people and students by accessing education, health and other services. The adoption of smartphone will increase further in the future with rising income level of people and expansion of its use for multiple purposes.

Growing Manufacturing

The domestic handset manufacturing market is growing over the years, which is one of the reasons for dropping the prices of smart phones. India is now the world's second largest smartphone market, overtaking the US in 2016. As the 'Make in India' campaign gathers pace, more than 25 vendors are now manufacturing cheaper smartphones locally in India. To boost telecom manufacturing companies government provided exemption from basic customs duty, countervailing duty and special additional duty has been withdrawn on chargers, adapters, battery, wired headsets and speakers for mobile phones. This will help the local manufacturers by making imports costlier. Correspondingly, to encourage local manufacturing, import duties on inputs that contribute into making of such parts and components have been removed.

Over two-thirds of the smartphones shipped were assembled within the country. Many global majors are also eyeing the significant opportunity that 4G adoption will create in the market. In May 2017, the central government announced the Phased Manufacturing Programme (PMP) to promote domestic production of mobile handsets. This will help in building a robust indigenous mobile manufacturing ecosystem in India, and incentivise large scale manufacturing.

Government's Other Positive Initiatives

Government of India (GoI) has launched ambitious scheme of the 'Digital India' initiative focussed on converting more than 100 towns and cities into 'Smart Cities' across India and implementing 'BharatNet' which involves roll out of 'National Optical Fibre Network (NOFN) across India. More than three-fourth (77 per cent) of urban users and 92 per cent of rural users consider mobile as the primary device for accessing the Internet. Under 'BharatNet', government has deployment target of high-speed optical fiber cables to connect 258 thousand Gram Panchayat across the country.

Under Digital India programme, every Indian will have a smartphone by 2019 programme implemented India's smartphone shipments grew 14 per cent year-on-year to a total of 124 million units in 2017. The fiberized of the sites has implemented in phases, with more than 100,000 gram panchayats connected under phase-I as of July 201710 and states like Kerala, Karnataka, Chhattisgarh, Haryana, Uttar Pradesh and Madhya Pradesh neared 100 per cent completion.

The government provide financial support through USOF, which is expected to extend financial support to operators providing services in rural areas and encourage active infrastructure sharing among operators. The government in 2018 revised cap on spectrum holding from 25 per cent to 35 per cent for encouraging consolidation in the market and for availability of enough spectrum with operators. In order to overcome the cash related problems being faced by people Paytm launched a service through which consumers and merchants can pay and receive money instantly, without an internet connection. This has enabled non-smartphone users to go cashless.

The government has doubled its allocation for the Digital India programme to INR 30.73 billion in 2018-19. The money will be invested in research, training and skilling in robotics, AI, digital manufacturing, Big Data analysis, quantum communication and Internet of Things. The Government also proposes to invest INR 100 billion in 2018-19 for creation and augmentation of Telecom infrastructure, and set up five lakh Wi-Fi rural hotspots to provide broadband access to fifty million rural citizens. To harness the benefit of emerging new technology, the Department of Telecommunications is to support establishment of an indigenous 5G Test Bed at IIT Chennai. This will provide the desired growth momentum to the telecom sector in the future.

6.9. CHAPTER SUMMARY

This chapter highlighted future growth drivers of India's mobile phone sector with challenges and opportunities. The analysis shows that growth of the sector will depend upon economic growth, rise in income level of people, financial and physical conditions of operators to adopt emerging new technologies. The Jio's entry has hugely impacted the rising Internet and data accessibility in recent years. As data accessibility of Indian consumers increases, it creates a multitude of opportunities for the individuals and government to reach out and enable social progress by providing services that were previously not feasible. It, however, added that there have been some silver linings for mobile operators such as expedited consolidation and increased data stickiness.

These factors would lead to gradual restoration in pricing power of the remaining operators, which should translate into improvement in financial position in FY-2019. The larger operators continue to seek higher market share, especially from the smaller or exiting ones, to achieve improved visibility of returns. The role of the government is considered important because it can provide the much needed push through positive policies and other infrastructural support.

7

Evaluation of Telecom Regulatory Environment

7.1. BACKGROUND

The present chapter is devoted to understand the effectiveness of present telecom regulatory and policy environment in the country.

The regulatory and policy environment has been given an important place in the success of any industry. It is argued that the political institutions and economic conditions of a country have an impact on the regulatory and policy processes of a sector or industry. It may be possible for regulatory actions to be "good" or optimal but sectoral performance can be poor due to the negating influence of the larger political or policy climate in a country (Levy and Spiller, 1994). A good regulatory policy includes clarity of functions assigned, regulatory autonomy, accountability and transparency (NERA, 1998; Stern and Holder, 1999; Stern and Cubbin, 2005).

Historically, the regulatory system of network infrastructure industries such as telecom has always been debated. To encourage the private sector and ensure consumer welfare, certain characteristics of telecom services such as extensive economies of scale and scope, large sunk costs[1], and necessary provision of services have necessitated and justified regulatory action. An efficient national telecom policy and regulatory environment

[1] A cost that has already been incurred and thus cannot be recovered like cost on network buildings like towers, cables, space etc.,

(TPRE) facilitates economic growth, more investment, technological advancement, affordability and availability of services (Kessides, 2004).

Telecom is a dynamic (active) sector, where technology changes very fast and requires regular updating of regulations and policies. Given the importance of regulations and policies in the telecom sector, only few studies are available (Samarajiva and Dokeniya, 2005; Payal, 2008, 2009) to measure the impact of existing TRPE of India. This dynamic sector in India needs regular assessment of the TRPE to understand the nature and problem of the sector. Berg (2009) analyzes different approaches to evaluate diverse regulatory systems including TPRE. In this approach, respondents were asked to evaluate TPRE. It was a survey of stakeholders' opinions. Instead of surveying the opinions of regulators, it surveys the opinion of those directly or indirectly impacted by regulatory actions. This provides a better assessment of a country's telecom regulatory environment. Several scholars in the past used TPRE approach to evaluate Asian and Indian telecom sector (Samarajiva and Dokeniya, 2005; Malik, 2008, 2010).

In this study, the regulatory and policy effectiveness have been measured on seven selected dimensions by interviewing stakeholders comprising of operators, telecom consultants, users groups and former regulators. The six dimensions are based on the GATS (General Agreement for the Trade in Services) reference paper on telecom that has widest consensus globally on what constitutes "good regulation" and is adopted by over 80 countries (Malik, 2009). An additional dimension of NTP12 has been also included to understand the opinion of telecom policy. The seven issues includes, (i) market entry and competitive behavior, (ii) allocation of scarce resources (iii) interconnection regulation (iv) tariff regulation (v) universal service obligations (vi) quality of service and (vii) national telecom policy, 2012. The stakeholders interviewed are classified into three categories (Malik, 2008, 2010):

- ***Type 1*:** Those involved directly in the sector such as operators and industry associations
- ***Type 2*:** Those involved indirectly in the sector or those studying and observing the sector with broader interest such as consultants working for financial institutions and law firms.

- ***Type 3*:** Those who represent the broader public interest such as academicians, journalists, and former member of regulatory and other government agencies.

The government telecom officials were not interviewed in the survey because the objective is not to do a self-evaluation, but to evaluate how the present policies and regulations are impacting. The interview was conducted with stakeholders, who were well informed about the present regulatory and policy environment in the country. Therefore, the interviews were conducted with senior level people in various organizations. In order to minimize biasness, at least a minimum number of stakeholders were interviewed. A minimum of 30 respondents from each group were interviewed using snowball sampling technique. This is a non-random sample technique that relies on reference or referral methods from the respondents. For the collection of data a semi-structured interview questionnaire containing both close and open ended questions related to the objectives was canvassed (see annexure).

The stakeholder interview was administered through multiple modes: *via* the mail, telephonic interview and personal meetings. The purpose of survey and description of questions were explained to respondent before conducting the survey. The respondents were asked to rate the quality of the regulatory environment for each dimension on a Likert scale ranging from 1 (highly ineffective) to 5 (highly effective).

Interviews were conducted in Delhi and the National Capital Region (Noida, Gurgoan, Faridabad and Ghaziabad). The interviews with different stakeholders were conducted in 2015. Ninety (90) stakeholders were interviewed in the survey, 30 from each type of stakeholder: as type 1 (those involved directly in the sector such as operators and industry associations), type 2 (those involved indirectly in the sector or those studying and observing the sector with broader interest such as consultants working for financial institutions and law firms) and type 3 (those who represent the broader public interest such as academicians, journalists, and former members of regulatory and other government agencies). The respondents were asked to rate the quality of telecom regulatory policy environment in the country on each dimension (see annexure) on a Likert scale ranging from 1 (highly ineffective) to 5 (highly effective).

7.2. SURVEY RESULTS

7.2.1. Market Entry and Competition

Market Entry regulation reflects stakeholder perceptions about the conditions for entry and operating conditions in the telecom market. This includes transparency, ease of licensing provision procedure and barriers to access the market. As discussed earlier, the government allowed one private operator entry in the market after opening the sector in 1994. The New Telecom Policy, 1999 ended the duopoly market and allowed the third operator, Mahanagar Telephone Nigam Limited (MTNL) to start its mobile phone service in two metros, Mumbai and Delhi, and Bharat Sanchar Nigam Limited (BSNL) in the rest of the country. Subsequently, with the entry of the fourth operator and Code Division Multiple Access (CDMA) technology based operators in 2002, the competition in the market increased significantly, leading operators to reduce telephone rentals and tariffs to maintain or increase their market share.

Initially, these steps affected the incumbent operators' revenues and profitability, but over a period of time, these operators found themselves largely compensated by the significant growth in domestic telecom service subscribers' base and increase in minutes of usage. But the multiple operators' entry in 2008 resulted in the presence of 10-12 operators in every circle, which is considered a highly competitive telecom market (PwC, 2011). This is reflected also from the stakeholders' survey as more than half of the respondents reported the ineffective regulatory environment of market entry and competition. In addition, they reported that cancellation of 2G licenses issued by government in 2008 by the Supreme Court in 2012 reflected the poor entry and competition policy.

After the exit of a few operators in 2012, there are still more than 10 mobile operators who are currently providing telecom services in India. However, the top five operators have captured more than 85 per cent of the subscriber market and top 6 operators have about 90 per cent of the revenue share. This indicates that despite having licenses for provisioning of telecom services, the majority of the operators are unable to penetrate into the market and it is still dominated by only a few players. It is a highly competitive market in the sense of spectrum as discussed earlier, which has fragmented the spectrum among a large number of mobile operators operating in the market. In general, four to five operators in the telecom market in a country are considered enough for a competitive market according to the world standard prevalent in most of the developed and developing countries (TRAI, 2012).

This also reflected from stakeholder responses. In particular, consultants (66.7 per cent) were more concerned about the existing environment than the public interest group (60 per cent) and operators (46.7 per cent) as shown in Table 7.1. They pointed out that excess competition in the market attributed to poor market entry regulation. The stakeholders' said that

> *"There is moderate competition in the telecom market with only the top six operators holding over 85 per cent market share and it is difficult for the new players to grab the pie."- Telecom Consultant (2015); and*
>
> *"Indian telecom sector is now consolidating and smaller operators will be either shutting or scaling down their business. This can ease the competition and operators can now correct the low tariff by hiking it"*
>
> *- Reliance Communication's Executive (2015).*

Table 7.1: Stakeholders perception on market entry and competition regulations (in per cent).

Rating	*Type 1*	*Type 2*	*Type 3*	*All*
Highly Ineffective	0.0	13.3	33.3	15.6
Ineffective	46.7	66.7	60.0	57.8
Neutral	46.7	13.3	6.7	22.2
Effective	6.6	6.7	0.0	4.4
Highly Effective	0.0	0.0	0.0	0.0
Total (N)	100(30)	100(30)	100(30)	100(90)

***Note*:** Type 1 (direct- operators); Type 2 (indirect-consultants) and Type 3 (public interest group - academician/former regulators)

Source: Field survey, 2015

7.2.2. Access to Scarce Resources

Though scarce resources are defined as spectrum, rights of way and numbering, it is likely that spectrum is foremost in the minds of stakeholders. The subscriber growth is being driven by wireless technologies, which made spectrum a valuable and often scarce resource. It gets fragmented if a large number of operators are present in the market. Such fragmentation leads not only to inefficient use of the spectrum but also increases the cost of providing services to consumers due to more expenditure on infrastructure development.

The average frequency allotted to an Indian mobile operator is 6.2 MHz, compared to the world average of 17.18 MHz (Malik, 2010). The lack of spectrum is affecting the quality of service offered to the customers. In order to ensure optimum utilization of the available spectrum and to bring down the cost of providing service, the government allowed passive infrastructure sharing (antenna, feeder cable, node, radio access network and transmission system) among the operators in April, 2008. In addition, the government proposed sharing of active infrastructure like spectrum sharing and trading in NTP12.

More than 66 per cent of the stakeholders revealed that there is ineffective regulation for access to scarce resources as presented in Table 7.2. Operators were more concerned about regulation of access to scarce resource compared to consultants and public interest groups. They expressed poor spectrum management and complicated process of right of way of laying optical fibre as areas of concern. The stakeholders raised their concerns as:

> *"It is unfortunate that we need to spend our capital just to keep up our services in place instead of spending it on 3G rollout. Almost more than 15 years after the telecom space was opened up, we are yet to have a comprehensive and technology-neutral spectrum policy to provide a clear growth path."-Idea Executive (2015)*
>
> *"The stage is set for the Government to milk the already bleeding Indian mobile industry. The decision of the additional charges for extra spectrum and re-auction of spectrum after re-farming in 2014 and additional spectrum usage charges suggests that the Indian mobile services will further get into trouble."-Airtel Executive (2015)*

Table 7.2: Stakeholders perception on regulation of access to scarce resources (in per cent)

Rating	*Type 1*	*Type 2*	*Type 3*	*All*
Highly Ineffective	46.7	0.0	0.0	15.6
Ineffective	53.3	46.7	53.3	51.1
Neutral	0.0	53.3	46.7	33.3
Effective	0.0	0.0	0.0	0.0
Highly Effective	0.0	0.0	0.0	0.0
Total	100(30)	100(30)	100(30)	100(90)

Source: Same as Table 7.1

The government is creating a nationwide optical fibre network and BSNL has been chosen to provide the optical fibre network under the National Broadband Plan. But a large amount of the network is lying unused due to BSNL's poor record of active infrastructure sharing. The merger/acquisition and trading/sharing of spectrum proposed in NTP12 can help in spectrum management in future.

7.2.3. Interconnection

One of the main operating expenditures for mobile phone operators is interconnection cost. Interconnection cost as discussed in the earlier chapter is the cost of operators interconnecting with other operators in the same telecom circle and different circles respectively. The interconnection arrangements are decided by the TRAI from time to time and the rates charged for carrying traffic through interconnecting networks have an impact on the business of the operators. The high termination charge gives a cost advantage to large operators over new and smaller operators. But high termination cost may lead to market distortions and lower cost may increase cost of services. Therefore, the cost should be just about the actual cost incurred (TRAI, 2012).

Mobile operators having operations in a large number of circles have better bargaining power with other operators, which can provide them advantage over operators/players operating in one or two circles. The large operators with an all-India present have the advantage of using their own network for interconnection, unlike small operators.

The regulatory agency TRAI has the power to decide about tariffs and interconnection regulations. After 2000, even the government would have no right to overrule its decision. With the TRAI powers clear on interconnection, the interconnection regime in India has been fairly stable since 2003, when the principal interconnection regulation was put in place by TRAI. Further amendments were made in 2008 and 2011. It has revised the ceiling for interconnect charges between operators by fixing the upper limit for annual per port fees for fixed line networks at INR 10,000 and for mobile phone networks at INR 4,000. Prior to this, operators had to pay port-in charges of as high as INR 39,000 to connect their subscribers to another operator's network. Further, TRAI monitors congestion at the points of interconnection between various service providers on a regular basis to ensure seamless interconnection. It has also appointed independent agencies to conduct surveys to assess customers' perception on services and has reviewed interconnection and port charges again in, 2012.

More than 62 per cent of the stakeholders interviewed reported an effective interconnection policy environment. According to the public interest group, regulations of interconnection are more effective compared to views of the financial consultant and operators. The public interest group and financial consultants also indicate an effective regulatory environment provided affordable tariff and good quality of services to the end-users.

> *"The reduction of termination charges would bring down operational expenses of operators by almost a fourth. New players are expected to benefit the most by this move as the majority of their calls are to the networks of incumbent operators, to whom they invariably end up paying high interconnect fees." -Telecom Expert (2015)*
>
> *"While incumbent operators may lose some revenues as a result of reduction in termination charges, this will have a marginal impact, if any, on subscriber tariffs," - Mahesh Uppal (Telecom Expert or Public Interest Group (2015).*
>
> *"BSNL, which was pushing for higher port charges from private players, stands to lose, but there will be no sizeable impact on others. While the move comes as a relief to us, tariffs are already very low and reducing them further would increase pressure on operators." - Rajan Matthews (DG), Cellular Operators Association of India (2015).*

Overall, all the stakeholders had a positive opinion about interconnection regulation as shown in Table 7.3. But some operators also raised concerns about the all-India free roaming provision of NTP12 and said that they have to pay the interconnection charges without any revenue from the services.

> *"The provision of free roaming as suggested in NTP12 virtually removes the interconnection charges. Removing national roaming charges proposed in new telecom policy is not a positive step. This will result in thousands of crores loss to the operators. I do not understand how the government thinks operators will willingly give up this revenue loss as they are already providing the lowest tariffs in the world. The government has to think before implementing such a policy" - Airtel Executive (2015)*

Table 7.3: Stakeholders perception on interconnection regulations (in per cent)

Rating	*Type 1*	*Type 2*	*Type 3*	*All*
Highly Ineffective	0.0	0.0	0.0	0.0
Effective	6.7	0.0	0.0	2.2
Neutral	53.3	46.7	6.7	35.6
Effective	40.0	53.3	66.7	53.3
Highly Effective	0.0	0.0	26.7	8.9
Total	100(30)	100(30)	100(30)	100(90)

Source: Same as Table 7.1

7.2.4. Tariff Regulation

Tariff regulation was initiated by the regulatory body TRAI in 1999. But the agency stated that emerging market forces could effectively regulate mobile tariffs and the regulator could therefore be set aside in 2002. Since then, TRAI forbearance is allowed in regulating the tariffs. Only integrated operators are required to seek prior approval for their tariffs. Despite early opposition from the policy maker and the government, the regulator has proved that the approach of forbearance was right: With the introduction of competition in the market mobile phone consumers' have one of the cheapest tariff systems in the world today.

Around half of the total stakeholders said mobile tariff regulations were effective as shown in Table 7.4. However, the results across the type of stakeholders show a contradictory pattern with operators rating tariff regulations ineffective and public interest group/consultants rating it effective. The public interest group and consultants pointed out the success of the regulator and welfare of consumers, but operators were concerned about their profitability. Some stakeholders raised their negative as well as positive concerns as follows:

> *"High inflation, high spectrum charges, interest to the banks and other services charges are putting pressure on operators' margins. This would mean the industry will have to force their hands to raise the tariffs to get the margins back." – A Telecom expert (2015)*
>
> *"The mobile operators currently have to pay termination and interconnection charges to complete a call for their consumers on the networks of other operators, which get added to the final cost of the call for the consumers. The government's proposal of free roaming all over the country will compel the operators to hike mobile tariff. This hike will equally affect both roaming and non-roaming consumers because of the one tariff plan" – A Telecom analyst (2015)*
>
> *"Free roaming will help to expand the overall market significantly. The growth of business would be rewarding for service providers as can be seen and confirmed by the international experience: In USA, free roaming boosts the overall business. Average revenue per user (ARPU) - a key gauge of profitability - and minutes of use in the American market began rising even as roaming revenues fell after the US did away with the concept of roaming in 1998 and consequently ARPU in the US market increased from $39 to $49 in five years from 1998"- A Reliance Communication' Executive (2015)*

Table 7.4: Stakeholders perception on tariff regulation (in per cent)

Rating	*Type 1*	*Type 2*	*Type 3*	*Total*
Highly Ineffective	6.7	0.0	0.0	2.2
Ineffective	73.3	0.0	0.0	24.4
Neutral	20.0	53.3	0.0	24.4
Effective	0.0	46.7	26.7	24.4
Highly Effective	0.0	0.0	73.3	24.4
Total	100(30)	100(30)	100(30)	100(90)

Source: Same as Table 7.1

Universal service obligations

The Universal Service Obligation Fund (USOF) was launched in 2002 with the objective of providing universal telecom services. It was proposed that USOF would be used to fill the rural-urban gap of telecom services, as mentioned in the earlier chapters.

More than three-fourth of the stakeholders expressed their concern about ineffective regulation for USOF as shown in Table 7.5. Until March 2007, only fixed line operators could qualify to receive funds from the USOF, even though mobile operators were being charged 5 per cent of their gross revenue as a contribution to the fund. The mobile operators were also eligible to receive the fund after 2008, and further broadband roll out has also been brought under the ambit of USO. However, a huge amount of USOF is lying unused. In spite of this, the TRAI and Ministry of Communications have not reduced the USO levy from the current 5 per cent. This huge un-utlised fund of USO has raised questions on its management.

Table 7.5: Stakeholders perception on regulation for universal service obligation (in per cent)

Rating	*Type 1*	*Type 2*	*Type 3*	*Total*
Highly Ineffective	33.3	0.0	0.0	11.1
Ineffective	66.7	46.7	93.3	68.9
Neutral	0.0	53.3	6.7	20.0
Effective	0.0	0.0	0.0	0.0
Highly Effective	0.0	0.0	0.0	0.0
Total	100(30)	100(30)	100(30)	100(90)

Source: Same as Table 7.1

This inefficiency clearly comes out from the various stakeholders responses. All the operators expressed the view that USO was ineffective, and more than 80 per cent of the public interest group revealed the same. Around half of the consultants were also dissatisfied with the USO implementation.

Quality of service

In India, the TRAI is responsible for monitoring the quality of telecom services in India. The quality of services in telecom includes frequent call drops, poor connectivity, unwarranted messages, telemarketing calls and absence of a consumer redressal cell, which are common to mobile phone consumers in the country. There are continuous efforts made over the years by both the regulatory agency and nearly 24 consumer advocacy groups, which regularly express concerns on quality of services by telecom operators.

The TRAI defined quality of services: "It is the main indicator of the performance of a telephone network, and of the degree to which the network conforms to the stipulated norms" (TRAI, 2012). The subscriber's perception of quality of services is determined by a number of performance factors specified by the telecom regulators as discussed above and particularly related to network congestion. TRAI has regulations for assuring quality service and looks at various other parameters to define quality of services by the operators. These include accessibility of call centres, response time to the customers, call drops, voice quality and network congestion.

In order to curb unsolicited commercial communications (UCC), regulations came into force from September, 2011. The response is positive and millions of customers have registered with the National Consumer Preference Register (NCPR) under various preferences. The number of unsolicited calls and SMSs has also reduced. Another attempt is the introduction of MNP (Mobile Number Portability) facility in 2011, which provides customers an option to switch operators without changing their number, if not satisfied by the services.

The Base Transceiver Station (BTSs)[2] installed on the towers are required to be connected to the rest of the mobile network through some kind of a telecom link called backhaul. Presently, point- to-point microwave links are used for this purpose. For increasing voice and possible data traffic in future, optical fibre seems to be more suitable for backhaul and quality internet

---

[2] "Base Transceiver Station (BTS) or cellular phone tower in mobile communications holds the radio transceivers that coordinate the radio-link protocols with the mobile device. BTS is the networking component of a mobile communications system from which all signals are sent and received. It is controlled by a base station controller. BTS is also called a base station (BS) and is commonly referred to as a "cell phone tower." definition accessed on 12 March, 2013 from http://www.indiatelecomonline.com/gsm-network-architechture

services. An extensive fibre optic network was proposed in the country in the national broadband plan in 2010 as a backhaul network, and the project was implemented throughout the country. Once this network is complete, it will provide backhaul connectivity for the BTSs and provide improved quality services of voice, internet, data, and TV on a single network.

The TRAI amended the quality of service regulations, 2013 and recommended an audit of the metering and billing system of mobile operators, to protect the interests of consumers. Mobile operators have to get their metering and billing systems audited annually for basic and cellular mobile phone service in each service area, through any one of the auditors from the panel notified by TRAI.

Table 7.6: Stakeholders perception on regulations for quality of services (in per cent)

Rating	***Type 1***	***Type 2***	***Type 3***	***All***
Highly Ineffective	0.0	0.0	0.0	0.0
Ineffective	0.0	53.3	86.7	46.7
Neutral	40.0	46.7	13.3	33.3
Effective	60.0	0.0	0.0	20.0
Highly Effective	0.0	0.0	0.0	0.0
Total (N)	100(30)	100(30)	100(30)	100(90)

Source: Same as Table 7.1

The respondents revealed that these efforts are still not fully satisfactory with only around one-fifth of them saying effective regulation exists for quality of services, as shown in Table 7.6. The results differ across type of stakeholders with operators finding regulation effective, while on the contrary, public interest group and consultants indicate ineffective regulation. The public interest group and consultants revealed that Quality of Service (QoS) was mostly affected by call drops, voice quality, internet speed and congestion. However, operators who provide the services apparently advocate for quality of service regulations. Some stakeholders expressed their concerned about quality of services as:

> *"MNP remains an important parameter for QoS for us to exhibit our strength in network, customer services, brand power and employee resilience." – An Idea Executive (2015)*

> *"The bigger future challenge lies in ensuring better quality of services in terms of data as compared to voice. With regard to data, while a customer could be connected, providing a good speed could be really difficult due to low network quality." – An Airtel Executive (2015)*
>
> *"Removing congestion and call drops, improving customer services and awareness among rural subscribers is necessary for better QoS." – A Telecom Consultant (2015)*
>
> *"If small operators have to stay in the market they have to compromise with quality of services due to high operating cost required to maintain the infrastructure and providing quality services to consumers."– A Telecom Consultant (2015)*

Telecom policy, 2012 (NTP12)

The highlights of National Telecom Policy, 2012 are: unified licences in future, delinking spectrum from licences; free national roaming; national MNP; providing affordable broadband and adequate availability of spectrum. Some targets set in the policy are to provide secure, affordable and high quality telecom services; increase rural tele-density from around 39 to 70 by 2017 and 100 by 2020, provide affordable broadband by 2015, and to achieve 175 million broadband connections by 2017 and 600 million by 2020.

The respondents' results presented in Table 7.7 show that only one-fifth of them were satisfied with this new telecom policy. Operators were highly optimistic about the new telecom policy and more than half of them said it is effective.

Table 7.7: Stakeholders perception on telecom policy, 2012 (in per cent)

Rating	*Type 1*	*Type 2*	*Type 3*	*All*
Highly Ineffective	0.0	0.0	0.0	0.0
Ineffective	0.0	26.7	23.3	16.7
Neutral	40.0	53.3	56.7	50.0
Effective	60.0	20.0	20.0	33.3
Highly Effective	0.0	0.0	0.0	0.0
Total (N)	100(30)	100(30)	100(30)	100(90)

Source: Same as Table 7.1

However, only one-fifth of the consultant and public interest group regarded this policy as effective. They revealed that the new policy promises a lot but without much clarity on spectrum re-farming, merger and acquisition, migrating to new licence regime and all-India roaming. Some of them expressed their opinion regarding new telecom policies are given below:

> *"NTP-12 mentioned delinking of spectrum from mobile services license. This is a laudable goal that would bring about more efficient utilisation of scarce spectrum resources at an industry level and provide additional impetus to data services delivery, including video" – An Executive of an Operator(2015)*
>
> *"The policy also addresses the issue of broadband penetration, recognising broadband access as a basic necessity. The policy emphasis is to form an institutional framework to coordinate between different Government departments for laying of optical fibre networks up to village panchayats. It also emphasises mobilisation of the Universal Service Obligation (USO) fund for this purpose."- A Telecom Expert (2015)*

Industry's concerns

The stakeholders' raised concerns for the industry in order of rank are as presented in Table 7.8, were: high cost of 3G services (46.7 per cent), intense competition in the market (40 per cent), policy uncertainly (38.9 per cent), absence of local content of mobile-application (31.1 per cent), high prices of smart phones (24.4 per cent), low penetration of data services (23.3 per cent), high spectrum scarcity (20 per cent), poor quality of services (20 per cent), low tariff (11.1 per cent), and high taxes/regulatory charges (6.7 per cent).

These issues differ across type of stakeholders as operators and consultants were concerned about intense market competition, policy uncertainty, spectrum scarcity, lower tariff and high taxes. Consultants and public interest groups pointed to high cost of 4G services and absence of local content mobile application for poor penetration of the 4G services. Operators were also concerned about low tariff and spectrum availability that affected their business and public interest groups were concerned with poor quality of services.

Table 7.8: Concerns on industry's present environment (in per cent)

Concerns	*Type 1*	*Type 2*	*Type 3*	*Total*
High cost of 4G services	0.0	53.3	86.7	46.7
Intense competition in the market	66.7	53.3	0.0	40.0
Policy flip flop (uncertainty)	46.7	43.3	26.7	38.9
Absence of local content of m-applications	0.0	53.3	40.0	31.1
High prices of smart phones	13.3	0.0	60.0	24.4
Low penetration of data service	20.0	36.7	13.3	23.3
Spectrum scarcity and high pricing	26.7	20.0	13.3	20.0
Poor quality of services	0.0	0.0	60.0	20.0
Lower tariff	33.3	0.0	0.0	11.1
High taxes and regulatory charges	20.0	13.3	0.0	6.7
Others	23.3	25.0	8.0	16.8
Total (N)	100(30)	100(30)	100(30)	100(90)

* Percentages do not add to hundred because of multiple responses
Source: Same as Table 7.1

Stakeholders' wish

The stakeholders' wishes asked in order of rank as presented in Table 7.9 were: encouragement of data and value added services (82.2 per cent), rural rollout of the mobile services (77.8 per cent), appropriate spectrum sharing and trading (28.9 per cent) and merger and consolidation rules (17.8 per cent); creation of more jobs or employment opportunities (22.2 per cent); encouragement of local equipment manufacturing (20 per cent) and local and social content mobile application (20 per cent); establishment of telecom financial corporation (13.3 per cent), creation of fibre optic for broadband in rural areas (8.9 per cent), and provision of technology-neutral liberalized spectrum (6.7 per cent). They think that these steps are necessary for the growth of the mobile telecom sector in the country.

These issues differ across type of stakeholders as operators and public interest groups aspired for allowing spectrum sharing and trading and creation of telecom financial corporation. Consultants and public interest groups desired creation of jobs or employment opportunities. Operators also wished for smooth merger and consolidation rules, consultants for encouragement of local equipment manufacturing, and public interest groups for encouragement of social m-application and creating of fiber optic for broadband in rural areas.

Table 7.9: Stakeholders wish for the mobile phone sector (in per cent)

Wish	***Type 1***	***Type 2***	***Type 3***	***Total***
Higher data and value added services rollout	86.7	73.3	86.7	82.2
Higher rural rollout of mobile services	100.0	53.3	80.0	77.8
Allow spectrum sharing and trading	33.3	53.3	0.0	28.9
Creation of more employment opportunities	0.0	26.7	40.0	22.2
Encouragement of local manufacturers	0.0	60.0	0.0	20.0
Encouragement of social m-applications	0.0	0.0	60.0	20.0
Proper merger and consolidation rules	46.7	6.7	0.0	17.8
Creation of telecom financial corporation	20.0	20.0	0.0	13.3
Fibre optics for broadband in all rural areas	0.0	0.0	26.7	8.9
Technology-neutral liberalized spectrum	13.3	6.7	0.0	6.7
Total (N)	100(30)	100(30)	100(30)	100(90)

* Percentage do not add to hundred because of multiple responses
Source: Same as Table 7.1

7.3. CHAPTER SUMMARY

This chapter presents stakeholders' views about mobile telecom regulatory environment and rural consumer perception about impact and difficulties in accessing mobile phone services. The results highlight that most noteworthy achievements in the mobile telecom sector are generating competition, reduction in tariff, successful auction of 3G/BWA, implementation of mobile number portability (MNP) and announcement of National Telecom Policy, 2012. These initiatives have helped in growth of the sector, affordable tariff, improved the quality of services and availability of internet service to consumers.

However, cancellation of 2G licenses and further unsuccessful spectrum auction has deteriorated mobile telecom regulatory environment. The stakeholders viewed that regulations on interconnection, tariff, quality of service are satisfactory due to continuous review of interconnection charges, affordable tariff and regular reporting of quality indicators. On the other hand stakeholders were unsatisfied with regulations on market entry, scarce resources spectrum, anti-competition and universal service obligations due to cancellation of 2G licenses compelled few operators to exit; high spectrum reserve prices and non-transparent process of spectrum allotment made spectrum scarcity, high presence of operators turned intense competitive market and huge unutilized USO fund.

The stakeholders were concerned about high cost of 4G services, intense competition, absence of local content of mobile-application, high prices of smart phone and low penetration of data services. Their wish list includes government should give more attention to rural rollout of the mobile phone services; encouragement of local equipment manufacturing, help in development of mobile application with local and social content, establish telecom financial corporation and provide technology neutral liberalized spectrum; and formulate appropriate merger and consolidation and spectrum sharing and trading policy.

8

Conclusions and Policy Suggestions

Indian economic growth led by service sector has attributed to the expansion of modern services like financial services, communication services (a category that include mobile telephone services) and business services (a category that include information technology services), which emerged due to opening of the economy in the early nineties and technological changes over the years. In particular mobile telecom services have emerged as a growth engine of the economy and transformed India as the fastest growing and the second largest network in the world. This sector contributes to economy, foreign investment and generates employment with a high spill over effect to other sectors.

The mobile phone has long history and has been available commercially after mid-eighties in several countries of the world and launched in 1995 in India. It argued that proactive policies and regulations by the governments of several countries are mainly responsible for the growth of mobile phone. These policies and regulations ensure competitive behaviour in the mobile telecom market and ensure public interests of affordable and wider service coverage. There are several interrelated economic and non-economic characteristics that relate to growth of mobile phone sector, where state intervention is necessary for its smooth functioning. The factors are interconnection, market entry and competition, spectrum tariff, and universal services.

In this context, telecom services were not perceived as one of the key infrastructure during the formative years of India. It was only in early nineties the government recognised its importance and. unveiled the national telecom policy, 1994 and allowed private participation in fixed and mobile phone and foreign investment in the sector. The government further initiated national telecom policy, 1999 that allowed private operators to pay financially viable revenue sharing licence fee from earlier fixed fee, introducing competition by allowing 3rd and 4th mobile operator in a telecom circle, constituting universal obligation fund to facilitate rural and remote area coverage, allowing unified access services licensing that provide both basic and cellular services under the ambit of one license, introducing calling party pays, reducing tariff for national roaming services, hiking foreign direct investment limit, abolishing access deficit charges, reducing interconnect usage charges, introducing country wide mobile number portability, telecom policy 2012 provide roadmap for all India roaming, spectrum sharing and trading, re-framing exercise, merger and acquisition.

In addition, various institutions involved in policy making viz. Department of Telecom (DoT) and regulator viz. Telecom Regulatory Authority of India (TRAI) and dispute settlement body, Telecom Dispute Settlement and Tribunal (TDSAT) facilitated the growth of telecom services in India. Policy makers and their critics often cited the success of mobile telephone services, where government initiated efficient proactive policies.However, the sector has also experienced many ups and downs during its success journey. The performance of sector has slowed in 2010-2013 due to excessive competition in the market, fall of tariff, reduction in foreign investment, and increased debt, which attributed to regulatory and policy uncertainty. Again after the entry of RJio in 2017-18, the price war for mobile phone services among the operators has resulted downturn in the performance of the sector. This has started the wave of consolidation among operators to survive in the market and for some to exit. This situation has benefited the sector in terms of consolidation of hyper competitive market, and availability of data services at low and affordable prices, which has not happened in the past after several efforts made by government. However, this is also an area of great concern for the growth of the sector.

In view of the above discussion, the main objective of book is to understand how the successful journey of mobile phone sector has contributed to economy; impact on people; and role played by government policies and regulations. In spite of the limited previous empirical literature on the topic, and constraints of data in public domain, this book has come out with plausible approaches to analyze the objectives and used comprehensively both primary and secondary information. The highlights, conclusions, and policy implications from the analysis are summarized and discussed in the subsequent section.

8.1. SUMMING-UP

Telecom Policies and Regulatory Institutions

Several policies and regulatory bodies discussed in the chapter two have changed the face of the Indian mobile phone sector. But the success of the sector was also accompanied by poor policy decisions and manip-ulation of rules from time to time. For example licenses provided for wireless services within the local loop (WLL) to fixed service operators by using the CDMA technology that created a potential disadvantage to the GSM cellular operators and public sector operators in 2003; Spectrum licenses allocated on a first-come-first-served basis in 2008, cancelled later by the Supreme Court in 2012; 3G licenses granted to public sector operators (BSNL and MTNL) before the auction by the department of telecom; Fixation of high reserve price in recent auctions (2012 and 2013) to enhance the government exchequer and subsequent mute response, and free services by RJio in 2016 has distorted the market economics. All these reflect some of the poor regulatory decisions. The government has also taken several positive steps as long awaited National telecom policy in 2012 and successful spectrum auctions, merger and acquisition guidelines, sharing and trading guidelines, reduction of spectrum usage charges, reduction in spectrum usage charges, re-farming exercises and announce draft new telecom policy, 2018 for comments are welcoming sign for the industry.

Journey of the Indian Mobile Phone Sector

The Indian mobile phone sector was characterised by slowdown between 2009-10 and 2012-13 in terms of revenue, investment, subscriber additions with saturation in urban market and average revenue per user. It is dominated by private and GSM operators with a highly-competitive market having more than 10 operators. There isstill a huge rural and urban digital divide with tele-density. The concentration index shows the new or small operators in each telecom circle have a small share of subscribers and it is dominated by only three or four operators. The high number of operators in each circle was not only creating spectrum scarcity but also adversely affecting the quality of services. Most of the mobile operators, except Airtel, RJio and Vodafone, could not utilize their available spectrum optimally. The sector has started improvement after 2013 due to several positive policy initiatives such as approved spectrum trading & sharing norms, eased merger & acquisitions guidelines, reduced spectrum usage charges (SUC) from 5 per cent to 3 per cent, approved active infrastructure sharing, spectrum auctions held to enhance operators spectrum portfolio.

In addition, high regulatory charges that include licence fee, spectrum fee, USO charges, frequent penalties on non-compliances of regulations, and high investment for purchasing licenses and its rollout left operators with virtually no capital and rising debt. The consistent non-utilisation of the USO fund also raised questions on continuation of such high levies (5 per cent of revenue) on the operators.

The entry of Reliance Jio (RJio) in September 2016, which offered free voice and data upto March 31, 2017 and crossed the target of 100 million customers. This situation continued even after the free period was over, the tariffs introduced by the RJiowas significantly lower than the prevailing tariffs. The adverse consequence of free and lower prices mobile and internet services of RJioresulted in declining of subscribers and revenue of other operators FY2018. Because these operators are forced to reduce their voice and data tariff charges and are in the process of either merger or spectrum trading & sharing with other operators. The sector isnow heading in consolidation mode with smaller operators are virtually out or merged with big players.

Further, the performance analysis of mobile operator'supto 2017 shows that subscriber and revenue growth of the operators has slowed down, while revenue growth for Reliance and BSNL has turned negative after 2009-10. Current ratio of the operators declined, debt equity ratio increased and earnings per share reduced since 2009-10. This indicates operators had a bad liquidity position or insufficient cash reserves for investment and their recent investment was largely funded by debt. The earnings before interest, depreciation and amortization and return on capital investment of the operators either declined or stagnated over the years.

Partial productivity of the operators in terms of average revenue per asset, average revenue per unit of expenditure and the average revenue per user has also either declined or stagnated between 2009-10 and 2012-13. Airtel and Idea are still performing better than others and have invested more than other operators for expansion of their mobile telephone operations as they adopted outsourcing, infrastructure sharing (Airtel outsource its IT-related services to IBM, and tower and other infrastructural maintenance to Indus) and revenue model (Idea focusing more on high revenue generating circles), while BSNL turned into a loss-making entity due to its high operating cost on its high manpower and asset maintenance and its technological obsolescence.

Data envelopment analysis shows that Airtel was fully efficient in terms of proper investment in assets and management of expenditure, followed by Reliance and Idea, and BSNL was inefficient. Sensitivity analysis reveals that expenditure influenced efficiency of Reliance and Idea, whereas expenditure as well as assets played an important role in the case of Airtel's efficiency and BSNL inefficiency. The analysis shows that other mobile operators in the market can take a lesson from efficient operators like Airtel for increasing their efficiency.

The analysis also shows that entry of RJiois good for the expansion of telecom sector and consumers, who have benefitted in terms of lower charges or free services. As a result, the internet data service has increased substantially during the recent year. Although, such type of strategy may be good for operator and consumers initially for short term but disruptive for longer period.The sign of disruption has already seen as discussed earlier in terms of consolidation wave of mergers and acquisitions of small operators. The scenario is likely to be similar for most of the developed countries four to five large operators' would remain in each telecom circle of India. However, the experts argued that this predatory pricing to have market share and grab customer is always questionable (GhuhaTahakurta, 2017; Bhatia and Rao, 2017).

Contribution to the Economy

Mobile phone sector contributes Indian economy both directly and indirectly. It ranges from the contribution to Gross Domestic Product (GDP) and creation of jobs to public spending, it also enhances the productivity level of other associated sectors, and also creates multiplier effect in job creation. However, the sector is facing some challenges in recent years with declining contribution in government revenue and reduction in job creation due to exit by some operators and consolidation in the market.

The Government has taken numerous measures to lift the sector out of its crisis but its efforts have not been fruitful. For instance, it formulated the Inter-Ministerial Group to suggest solutions. The body made a number of suggestions, such as slashing the spectrum charges and license fees as well as other levies. For decades now, there have been demands for rationalisation of various duties, fees, spectrum charges, and taxes by industry, as well as recommendations for the same by organisations with stakes in the sector. But the license fees and spectrum charges have not been cut. This shows that the government is well-aware of the problems that are ailing the sector but is not serious about acting. The reason behind this may be that the telecom sector is the highest revenue generator for the government. Also, Digital India is entirely based on providing cheap internet services to the electorate.

The granger causality test indicates that GDP per capita is associated bi- directionally with mobile phone revenue and "mobile phone penetration", and uni-directionally with government regulation index, investment and wireless Internet penetration. This indicates that income level of people and mobile phone penetration has a long term causal association with revenue of the sector and *vice versa.* In addition, regression results reveal that the government's policy and regulations, investment and internet penetration also positively associated with revenue and income level of people.

Impact on Mobile Phone Consumers

The consumer survey showed that mobile phones can play an important role in socio-economic empowerment of people belonging to rural or underdeveloped areas. They are benefited by mobile phone use and getting timely information on agriculture, education, health, employment opportunities, able to transfer money and can contact their near and dear ones regularly. However, they still faced many difficulties while using mobile phones such as lack of electricity for charging, lack of knowledge of MVAS, high cost of mobile handsets (smartphone), poor signal, non-functional base stations or mobile towers in the absence of electricity, and fraudulent money deduction practices of the operators. These are some policy concerns for bridging the digital divide or gap between information rich and poor people or areas.

Evaluation of the Current Telecom Policies and Regulations

The findings of the survey of stakeholders reveal they were satisfied with effective regulations for interconnection charges, tariff of voice/data, quality of service, and telecom policy 2012 on account of continuous review of interconnection, tariff and regular monitoring of quality of services by regulators. On the other hand, they were dissatisfied with ineffective regulations for market entry, scarce resources (spectrum), and universal service obligations (USO) on account of non-transparent process of spectrum allotment in 2008 and subsequent cancellation of 2G licenses in 2012, high spectrum reserve prices, higher number of operators in the market and improper utilization of the USO fund.

However, the responses differ across type of stakeholders. Operators were satisfied with effective regulations for entry policy, quality of services, and new telecom policy, 2012 because of recent market consolidation (exit by few operators), but dissatisfied with regulations for access to scarce resources and tariff, on account of spectrum scarcity and low tariff. Public interest groups and consultants were satisfied with effective regulations for tariff on account of affordable services to consumers. Operators and other stakeholders were dissatisfied with ineffective regulations for market entry and competition, USOF policy due to presence of large number of operators in the market, and improper management of the huge USO fund.

They were concerned about high cost of 4G services, intense competition, absence of local content of mobile-applications, high prices of smart phones, and low penetration of data services. Their wish list was that the state should give more emphasis on rural rollout of the mobile phone services; encourage local equipment manufacturing to make handsets, encourage development ofmobile applications with local and social content, establish a telecom financial corporation to help the sector in financing,provide technology-neutral liberalized spectrum, andformulate an appropriate merger and spectrum sharing and trading policy.

Future Growth Drivers

The mobile phone sector is one of important sector, which has huge future growth potential in India. There are several factors, which are considered as future growth drivers for the sector. These are ranging from rising per capita income, rural areas, data and internet services, value added services, mobile commerce, manufacturing services, smart phones, internet of things, and others government efforts such as digital India etc.

8.2. POLICY SUGGESTIONS

In this book, the attempt to examine the impact of mobile phone sector at macro (sectoral), meso (operators) and micro (stakeholders) level by using various data sources is a novel attempt and therefore, the analysis provides some important suggestions, which can contribute in the future policy making.

The government should initiate and prepare a sound policy to set up financial institutions that can help to fund the present Indian mobile phone operators, who do not have enough capital for investment in infrastructure development of 4G and 5G. This is also adversely affecting the quality of services and increasing the call drops cases in recent years.

Mobile phone operators made huge investments that started from buying spectrum (in 2010), when they expected that these services would give them high returns in future. The operators find it very difficult to recover these investments, primarily due to slow rollout of 3G services and expensive smart phones. Instead of high returns they were in debt and scaling down their investments. Further, the spectrum auctions held in 2014, 2015 and 2016 has increased their debt level at INR4.9 trillion in 2018. The debt-to-equity ratio for the industry was largely stable during the non-auction years (2001 to 2010), but it has steadily deteriorated thereafter. The current interest coverage ratio is less than one which means the industry's Earnings before Interest, Taxes, Depreciation and Amortisation (EBITDA) is insufficient to repay debt.

Banks are reluctant to give more loans to mobile telecom operators/investors. This kind of reluctance assumes significance at a time when mobile operators needs additional funds for rolling out of 4G, fibre,Wi-Fi and upcoming 5G networks across the country. The operators require additional funds for not only payment of loan installment but also for the development and operation of the necessary infrastructure. The lack of proper capital investment in infrastructure development resulting in significant number of call drops cases.

The recent government decision to hike the cap of foreign investment from 74 per cent to 100 per cent is a welcome step which has provided some relief to operators who are willing to raise equity and reduce their debt burden. As a result foreign investment flow in recent years was huge. However, more steps need to be taken to improve the financial conditions of the sector *e.g.,* promoting green environment by setting up solar power stations in rural areas with the help of USO fund which will replace the diesel run power backup system. The government should also initiate measures to set up specialised financial institutions that could help to fund the mobile phone operators and other related investors for the development of the telecom sector.

The government should take proactive policy steps in tune with new telecom policy, 1999 to restore the confidence of mobile phone operators.

The journey of the Indian economy since the big-bang reforms of 1991 has been nothing short of a roller-coaster ride, and no other sector encapsulates it better than India's telecom sector. Some of the promised fruits of liberalization-high competition and low product prices- indeed materialized in this sector, leading to a phenomenal rise in tele-density in the country. Yet, some of the darker aspects of the liberalization process-cronyism, resource-grab and corruption-also manifested themselves quite starkly in the sector. In 2012, the Supreme Court struck down the licences of several telecommunication companies citing corruption and arbitrariness in the allocation of spectrum, ruling that the process had enriched telecom firms at the expense of the exchequer. Five years after that verdict, the telecom sector is at the cross-roads once again. Faced with a new rival with deep pockets-RJio-heavily indebted telecom incumbents have rushed to the government for a bailout package, which the government is considering.

The telecom firms are reportedly seeking a bailout deal that would reduce various statutory payments such as the spectrum user charge and the interconnect charge, besides extending the timeframe for making spectrum-related payments to government. Incumbent telecom firms such as Bharti Airtel have often complained that frequent changes in telecom policies have often hurt them while favouring some rivals. For example, the government in 2002-03 allowed companies with fixed telephony licences to offer mobile telephony services, which favouredRCom and Tata Tel. Similarly, when the government changed rules in 2007-08 to allow companies offering mobile services on the CDMA platform to also do so on the dominant GSM platform, the major beneficiaries were again RCom and Tata Tel.

Subsequently, in 2012, the government allowed operators with a broadband wireless license to offer voice services, which benefitted Reliance Industries Ltd. Governments and regulators on their part have often cited changes in technology and consumers' interests while changing rules and regulations. This is not the first time telecom firms have lobbied for a bailout package, though. The first such package was in 1999. Eighteen years later, the sector is in crisis once again. To understand how this has happened, it is helpful to rewind to the mid-1990s when the first country-wide telecom spectrum auctions took place. The auctions were poorly designed, and complaints regarding lack of transparency in the auction process and frequent change of rules were common.

The net result of those auctions was slow roll-out of services because of the financial stress borne by auction-winners, slow clearances for frequency allocations, and the lack ofsuitable framework for managing the interconnect arrangements. Eventually, the problems snowballed and the telecom sector successfully lobbied to obtain a bailout in 1999. The then-NDA government waived existing obligations of telecom firms in lieu of a revenue-sharing agreement; the license fees fixed earlier were waived. However, this move was criticized among others by the Comptroller and Auditor General (CAG) at that time, as providing undue favour to telecom firms. But the rapid expansion of the telecom sector after the 1999 bailout package quelled criticism about the move, and the move was hailed retrospectively.

After the 1999 bailout, the government conducted one more auction in 2001, which was designed better than the previous one. But faced with shortage of spectrum, the government began to allot additional spectrum on a first-come-first-served basis and abandoned the auction route. This allegedly led to certain malpractices, with operators trying to inflate their subscriber numbers. According to an explosive 2010 CAG report, this policy led to losses worth INR 1.76 trillion. The abuse of the first-come-first-served policy led the government to revert to the auction route. A subsequent court verdict cancelling licences granted under the earlier policy in 2008 only put the final nail on the coffin of the first-come-first-served policy.

Partly because of the government's urge to maximize revenues in order to be perceived as honest administrators of public resources, and partly owing to the aggressive bidding by telecom firms to access a scarce resource, telecom firms are today among the most indebted firms in the Indian economy. The exaggerated claims of the CAG did not help matters as it helped raise public expectations from the spectrum auctions. The CAG's maximum estimate of loss-INR 1.76 trillion-was based on revenues generated by 3G auctions, which seem to have been inflated by aggressive bidding.

The moral hazard created by the 1999 bailout might have played a part in the aggressive bidding by telecom firms since they might have anticipated a bailout in the event of financial distress. While there are some striking parallels between the latest crisis and the one in the 1990s, the one big difference is the entry of RJio. RJio's launch has been disruptive for the sector and its expansion plans may put further pressure on incumbents. Yet, it is the burden of repaying high spectrum costs which lies at the root of the crisis as it did in the 1990s. Heightened competitive pressures have only aggravated the crisis. The outstanding debt of mobile operators was around INR 4.9 trillion, besides another INR 3 trillion owed to the government as deferred payment obligations for spectrum.

There kind of mistrust between the mobile phone operators and authorities is not a good sign for the future development of the sector. Both are constrained to spend a lot of their time, money and energy on litigation/dispute settlements related to regulatory compliances, which have a negative bearing on the planning and development of this sector. The government (DoT) has imposed penalties for violating the regulatory framework related to roll-out obligations, subscriber verification, roaming pact, additional taxes etc. The operators challenged various penalties (INR 200 billion) imposed by the government in various courts of law. Hence, the government needs to bring about necessary amendments in its regulatory framework to be in tune with 1999, and settle all the cases and reduce the debt burden with mutual understanding to restore the confidence among the operators.The government has recently formed a committee to recommend their suggestions on the bailout issue such as reduction of regulatory charges such as license fees, spectrum usage charges etc. But the government has not accepted most of these recommendations yet.

The government should make a proper policy to manage huge unutilised Universal Service Obligation Fund(USOF) for the development of mobile phone services in rural and remote areas.

Expansion of mobile phone services to remote and rural area in the country involves huge capital investments by the service providers. Also, low returns on these investments (low potential revenues, low commercial activity, etc.) make expansion in these areas less profitable for the operators and act as a bottleneck for their investments. Thus, there is a need for change in the market mechanism in order to enable operators to bridge the rural-urban divide. This led to the introduction of USOF in April, 2002 which is calculated as a percentage of the revenue collected by operators under various licenses, aimed at providing connectivity to untapped villages in India.

The government intends to use USOF for various initiatives such as providing network infrastructure and connectivity to remote parts of the country. Multiple schemes like BharatNet initiative which is part of "Digital India" campaign would eventually help in carrying out full-fledged roll out of telecom services in rural areas and connecting the unconnected. GSMA, in their "mobile economy report" highlighted that USO levy of 5 per cent in India as against the 2 per cent in Colombia and Pakistan and 1 per cent levy in Brazil, financially over-burdens for operators in India. Also, as per DoT's annual report, the USOF accumulated has not been completely utilised. Approximately 58 per cent of the total collection remains unutilised. The report also suggests that the Indian government may explore adoption of a more participative approach, with the operators consulted when defining targets and levies. Further, TRAI also recommends that the government may consider reducing USOF from 5 per cent to 3 per cent of annual revenue for all licenses, so that effectively license fee is reduced to 6 per cent.

Hence, the low utilisation rate of USO fund is a major concern. It should be properly managed to provide incentives for pilot projects, use of renewable energy sources, and infrastructure development for broadband in rural and remote areas. It can also be used to encourage mobile application with local & social content and in providing affordable smart phone devices by subsidizing them in rural and remote area. The government has recently started using this underutilize USO fund for connecting villages through broadband fiber optics, whose progress is rather slow.

The government should encourage public sector mobile phone operators to rationalise their cost by proper planning, evaluation and increasing productivity of its manpower. They can also rent out or share unused passive and active infrastructure or assets to other mobile operators and utilise it for other revenue generating activities, and adopt practices of benchmark private operators like Airtel.

The government still continues to subsidise loss-making public sector mobile phone operators (MTNL and BSNL), who failed to face up to the tough competition from private players. The example of Air India should be sufficient to warn the government against pouring money into loss-making public sector enterprises when efficient private sector competition ensures that the PSUs are not likely to earn profits if proper measures are not taken. The Public sector operators lack flexibility and despite having inevitably inflated salary bills, do not match private sector operators in terms of profitability, efficiency and modernisation.

There is a need to explore and utilise individual strengths of these organisations (PSUs) for their mutual benefits. Efforts should be made by all the PSUs to reduce their dependence on government support and become competitive by shedding obsolete technological and non-profitable product lines, reduce huge manpower expenditure and move on to more remunerative activities and services. BSNL needs to properly utilise its huge assets (tower, land and other infrastructure) by sharing them like private operators Airtel; rationalise its manpower by evaluating the need of both skilled and unskilled workforce, so extra manpower can be reduced by offering voluntary retirement schemes and increase productivity. There is also a need to look for newer markets and alliances. Government support should be restricted only to initiatives which address and meet the social obligations of the government and in areas where the market is not fully developed.

Instead of an intense competitive environment, the present Indian mobile phone sector needs policies and regulatory environment that provide a proper contestable market (easy entry and exit) to increase its efficiency. There is an urgent need for a proper exit policy, which prevents non-performing or small operators from leaving the market. As the sunk cost (cost of infrastructure development and spectrum cost) in the sector is very high, there is need to device a proper policy for sharing and trading of spectrum and other infrastructure, so the new players who are finding it difficult to compete in the market and facing continuous losses can surrender their spectrum and get their money back from the government. Proper policies for merger and acquisition, exit, sharing and trading can help in development of contestable market.

The industry has reached a point where most of the operators are running losses and reeling under debt, and the consolidation wave of mergers and exits is on. The intensity of competition in the sector has reduced due to merger and exit of a few small players. The industry is looking at structural changes with the numbers of players reducing to four (three large private sector players and one government sector player) in the short to medium term from 8-10 players per circle till now.

As new entrant RJio continues to remain disruptive, competitive intensity will not subdue in the short to medium term even if the number of players has reduced. The market is already consolidated in terms of spectrum holdings and the exit of smaller players will redefine it further. The competition will be per circle, and players will concentrate on top revenue generating circles to protect the customer base. The exit of smaller operators is good for industry structure in the long-term but painful for the stakeholders including lenders. But cartelization amongst the operators is a genuine fear in time to come. It is for the competition commission of India to ensure that it does not happen.

The Governments recent (May, 2018) steps to ease spectrum holding caps and extended the payment period for spectrum dues to 16 years from 12 years at present (including the initial two-year moratorium) is a welcome sign for the debt ridden operators. The restructuring of the deferred payment liability, the cash flow for the telecom service providers will increase in the immediate time frame providing them some relief. The spectrum holding cap limit increased to 35 per cent from 25 per cent earlier. Current government rules bar any merged entity from holding more than 25 per cent of the spectrum allocated in a service area or circle, and over 50 per cent in a particular band. Revising the limit for the spectrum cap holding will facilitate consolidation of telecom licenses and may encourage the participation in future auctions.

There must be a balance between spectrum resource allocation and government revenue generation policy in auctions for the development of the sector.

The government should target a long term plan to maximise the overall revenue for the exchequer. Due to high reserve prices, spectrum auctioned recently remained unsold, which resulted in loss of revenue and upfront spectrum charges and fees. The prices of spectrum should be reasonable, affordable and determined through a transparent e-auction. The total cost of spectrum for the operator must be viewed as a combination of the upfront spectrum price and the recurring spectrum charges, and not as a means to enhance the government exchequer only. High spectrum prices will result in an immediate increase in tariff, thereby impacting affordability. The government and regulator should consider future investment cost, sunk cost, optimum utilisation of infrastructure created, engineering feasibility and quality of services and further humanization of spectrum. Otherwise this will have huge financial implications for the telecom operators for expansion of 4G and upcoming 5G services in the country.

The allocation of additional spectrum to operators is critical to address the service quality for both voice and wireless internet services. In this direction the government needs to carry out regular audits of spectrum available with the defence services, railways and other security organisations. The un-utilised spectrum should be vacated and used for telecom services. The sharing and trading of spectrum available with telecom operators will help in ensuring efficient utilisation and encourage healthy competition. The government approval of spectrum cap recently has also helped in consolidation and ensuring the efficient use of spectrum in future.

The government must encourage mobile application developers for creating applications having local and social content, and ensure availability of cheap or subsidised smart phones for the faster rollout of 4G or data services and 5G services in near future.

The rollout of 4G data services is yet to reach out across the country at affordable prices and now 5G is on the way to start. This is affecting the value added services and other applications, which required higher bandwidth. The high cost of smart phones is one of the main reasons for poor rollout of data services. There is an urgent need to encourage local manufacturing of cost effective smart phones for expanding penetration of data services. Further, availability of low cost handsets is necessary as Indian mobile telecom operators can establish necessary infrastructure in partnership with foreign major telecom manufacturing companies to provide smart mobile handsets at low cost. The government should keep taxes low on handsets as it will reduce gray market activity and enhance the affordability of the mobile handsets for the masses.

Apart from policy to bridge the rural-urban digital divide across space and socio-economic groups', the government should take appropriate steps to stop the private operators from cheating rural consumers, who deduct money by fraudulent means and providing poor quality services like infrequent signal and call drops.

Therural tele-density was 57.4 per cent by March, 2018, which means around 43 per cent of rural market is yet to be covered by the mobile phone services. It is argued that private operators were less interested in serving rural areas because of less profit. But over the years, due to saturation of urban market, they are also penetrating in rural areas. The government like most of the countries in the world, has made rural rollout mandatory and also put in place the Universal Service Obligation Fund(USOF) to encourage telecom services in rural and remote areas. But the results are still not satisfactory and close to 55,669 villages in the country are still devoid of telecom services.

Government of India (GoI) has launched ambitious scheme of the 'Digital India' initiative focussed on rural telecomby implementing 'BharatNet' which involves roll out of 'National Optical Fibre Network (NOFN). Under 'BharatNet', government has deployment target of high-speed optical fiber cables to connect 258 thousand Gram Panchayat across the country and every Indian will have a smartphone by 2019. This has increased the use of smartphone and fiberized in more than 100,000 gram panchayats. However, the pace of bridging the rural-urban gap is still very slow.

The low return and paying capacity of people in the rural area discourages the private operators from investing and expanding. Therefore, private operators should be encouraged by providing them subsidy and infrastructural help to expand in rural and remote areas. In addition, government should also formulate some schemes for the poor and other excluded groups to connect them with the information age. Provision of more funding in the tune of 'BharatNet'and support to encourage rollout of broadband in rural and remote areas will be crucial and more focus on the national optical fibre network will be needed to connect villages. The government should simplify the policy for right of way to facilitate rollout of fixed infrastructure and installation of towers in rural areas across the circles.

The government could also embark on a mission to increase awareness of the technology's benefits among rural India, with the help of telecom operators, mobile application content for students in universities, colleges and schools, and content on governance for local administration and other welfare schemes. Mobile applications are useful in providing information on health (m-health), education (m- education), banking (m-banking), and government welfare schemes (m-governance). It is important that the target audience be trained and adept at using mobile applications for successful adoption. Imparting mobile-awareness would help users in understanding and appreciating the value of mobile phone technology and ultimately help in the development of the region. The regulator also needs to devote attention in terms of awareness regarding non-functional towers in the absence of electricity, and fraudulent deduction money by operators.

There is an urgent need to ensure proper co-ordination between multiple policy and regulatory institutions, which create confusion and delay in implementing the policies and regulations.

There are multiple regulatory institutions functioning in the telecom sector without any autonomy. TRAI recommends and DoT facilitates coordination amongst various institutions such as the Telecom Commission, Wireless Planning and Coordination and EGoM for functioning of such policies. But most of the TRAI officials are on deputation or retired from DoT or other related organizations, due to shortage of skilled manpower (Malik, 2010), which raised many questions on its autonomy and transparency of its policy recommendations. There is a need to revisit the TRAI Act, 1997 and revise its provisions to address the emerging issues. There is also need to review the executive functions of DoT for greater autonomy and fuller authority.

There has been an increase in converged regulators with responsibility over broadcasting, telecommunications and information technology, which is prevalent in most countries including Finland, Italy and the UK, Australia, Hong Kong, China, Malawi, Malaysia, South Africa and Tanzania. This is because such structures are considered to be better equipped to address convergent environments where different services are offered over the same platform. Such a move facilitates the regulatory hurdle in next generation networks in India.

The "regulatory cost" that includes service taxes, licence fees, universal service obligation and spectrum usage charge are nearly 30 per cent of the gross revenue of operator. Apart from these regulatory costs, operators are also heavily penalised for non-regulatory compliances.

There is need to rationalise high regulatory charges after proper consultations. Therevision of these charges is required to reduce the costs of mobile network deployment, including but not limited to the rollout of fibre (fast tracking rights of way at nominal rates), tower installation, costs of deploying sites, and affordable power for sites etc. There is a need to revisit the higher spectrum usage charge (recover only administrative cost of managing spectrum), significantly cut the USO levy and other input taxes/fees. Spectrum should be allocated and released under reasonable terms and conditions.

The future growth drivers of mobile phone services lies in broadband or data services, rural market, mobile applications, Internet of Things (IoT), and 5G services. There is need to Right of Way and Fiberisation for further expansion of broadband and 5G services particularly in rural areas. The new telecom policy, 2018 should focus on provision of telecom infrastructure development and better regulatory environment to implement these growth derivers.

Benefits of consolidation, restoration of pricing power, and increased data usage are expected to result in steady improvement in future. The growth in data consumption is likely to remain high in future, given the sharp decline in prices and a favourable ecosystem. Broadband subscriber growth mainly stems from growing adoption of data in the wake of digitalisation. The faster data penetration and consumption could support revenue over the medium term if the ecosystem remains favourable. Consolidation has led to sufficient spectrum availability and top mobile operators have strengthened their business model *via* acquisition of spectrum at attractive prices. The much awaited telecom consolidation is in the final lap, but the tangible benefits are some time away to be reaped.

At one end of the spectrum, IoT driven point solutions will be adopted to solve a specific business issues, and at the other end of the spectrum, IoT driven enterprise solutions would help organizations redefine their business models and provide innovative services for their customers.

The Government, through the new telecom policy, seeks to spur the socioeconomic development up to the bottom of the pyramid by ensuring voice, video and data connectivity for all. It seeks to provide reliable and secured connectivity with assured quality of service, facilitate development of infrastructure and services for new technologies including 5G and IoT, encourage innovation and manufacturing, and develop a large pool of digitally skilled man-power, by restructuring regulatory and licensing frameworks impacting the telecom sector.

This growth of data communication services will help in enhancing the economic conditions in rural and remote areas, and spurring new businesses by enabling access of markets to a large number of small and medium enterprises (SMEs). Above all, growth of digital communication networks is boosting competitiveness, enabling innovation, and improving productivity. Enhanced investments in telecom network infrastructure, which allow fast, reliable, and affordable internet connectivity, are leading to socio-economic growth and job creation in India.

The speedy rollout of telecom infrastructure is vital for meeting the increasing demand of data, improving competitiveness, productivity, innovation, implementation of 5G services and enabling the Fourth Industrial Revolution in the country. The rollout of fibre networks is critical for backhauling the large amount of data, improving reliability, and reducing latency. For speedy rollout of infrastructure, it is necessary that Right of Way permissions, to be granted by the respective local authorities, are granted expeditiously at reasonable charges and in non-discriminatory manner to the service providers. Accordingly, there is need for coordinated efforts among the Central, State, and Local authorities so that a common online portal for granting all kind of Right of Way permissions in time bound manner is put in place swiftly. It will improve ease of doing business in the sector and in attracting required amount of investments.

The rollout of 5G networks will connect wearable computers, a vast array of sensors, and other devices, leading to better health, economic gains, and other advantages. 5G networks not only addresses Internet of Things (IoT) deployment on a massive scale, but also of applications previously not possible that depend on ultra-reliable and low latency communications.

Annexure 1

GRANGER CAUSALITY TEST

The Granger causality method is a statistical hypothesis test based on time series study that can be used to understand the correlation between the dependent variable(s) and the independent variable (s). This causality test captures the effect of long term changes in one factor on the changes in other factors and *vice versa*. It examines the long run relationship between variables – as x and y variables – x said to be 'Granger-cause' y if and only if the forecast of y is improved by using the past value of x together with the past values of y, then by not doing so. To make time series stationary, unit root test is applied, which required lag and differentiation to achieve stationary. Before applying Granger causality test, pre examination of the data has been done in order to avoid the problem of non-stationary- one whose statistical properties such as mean, variance, autocorrelation are not constant over time, which can lead to spurious results. The Augmented Dickey Fuller test for stationary found that all the variables were non-stationary at initial level and turned into stationary after first differentiation. Granger causality model test rejects the hypothesis at 5 per cent standard of probability, *i.e.,* P value of below 0.05.

HERFINDAHL-HIRSCHMAN INDEX (HHII)

The Herfindahl Hirschman Index (HHI) is used to measure the level of competition within a market or industry, as well as provide an indication of how the distribution of market share occurs across the firms. This is an important indicator to understand the level of competition in the market and help in formulating a strategic plan for the firms to establish its products or services. The formula for calculating HHI is as follows:

$$HHI = S_1^2 + S_2^2 + S_3^2 + S_4^2 \ldots + S_n^2$$

Where S indicate the share of each firm upto n number of firms in a market

It ranges from close to zero to 10,000. If there is only one firm in the market (monopoly), which has 100 per cent share and HHI of the firm will be 10,000. If there are a great number of market participants with each company having a market share of close to 0 per cent then its HHI will be close to zero. These values define the market concentration (Scott Sehlhorst, 2009) as follows

- When the HHI value is less than 1000, the market is highly competitive.
- When the HHI value is between 1000 and 1800, the market is said to be concentrated.
- When the HHI value is above 1800, the market is said to be highly concentrated or duopoly monopolized.

Feature of Mobile Phone Services

Table 1: Mobile phone subscribers by operators (in Millions)

Service Provider	*2000*	*2005*	*2010*	*2011*	*2012*	*2013*	*2014*	*2015*	*2016*	*2017*	*2018*
Bharti	0.4	11.0	127.6	162.2	181.3	188.2	205.4	226.0	251.2	273.6	304.2
Vodafone	0.5	7.8	100.9	134.6	150.5	152.4	166.6	183.8	198.0	209.1	222.7
RJio	-	-	-	-	-	-	-	-	-	108.7	186.6
Idea/Spice	0.3	6.5	63.8	89.5	112.7	121.6	135.8	157.8	175.1	195.4	211.2
Reliance.com	0.1	10.5	102.4	135.7	153.1	123.0	110.9	109.5	102.4	83.5	0.2
Aircel/Dishnet	0.0	1.8	36.9	54.8	62.6	60.1	70.2	81.4	87.1	90.9	74.2
BSNL	0.0	9.9	69.5	91.8	98.5	101.2	94.7	77.2	86.4	101.0	111.7
Tata	0.0	1.1	65.9	89.1	81.8	66.4	63.0	66.3	60.1	49.0	31.2
Telenor	0.0	0.0	0.0	0.0	0.0	0.0	35.6	45.6	52.5	50.5	38.0
MTNL	0.0	1.1	5.1	5.5	5.8	5.0	3.4	3.5	3.6	3.6	3.6
Loop	0.0	0.0	2.8	3.1	3.3	3.0	2.9	0.0	0.0	-	-
Quadrant	0.0	0.1	0.3	1.5	1.3	1.4	2.2	2.7	3.2	0.0	0.0
Sistema	0.0	0.0	3.8	10.1	15.8	11.9	9.0	8.9	7.7	4.9	0.0
Unitech	0.0	0.0	4.3	22.8	42.4	31.7	0.0	0.0	0.0	-	-
S Tel	0.0	0.0	1.0	2.8	3.4	0.0	0.0	0.0	0.0	-	-
Videocon	0.0	0.0	0.0	7.1	6.0	2.0	5.0	7.1	6.6	-	-
Etisalat	0.0	0.0	0.0	1.0	0.8	0.0	0.0	0.0	0.0	-	-
Shyam	0.0	0.0	0.0	0.0	0.0	0.0	0.0	0.0	0.0	-	-
BPL	0.3	2.6	0.0	0.0	0.0	0.0	0.0	0.0	0.0	-	-
Escotel	0.1	0.0	0.0	0.0	0.0	0.0	0.0	0.0	0.0	-	-
Hexacomm	0.0	0.0	0.0	0.0	0.0	0.0	0.0	0.0	0.0	-	-
Total	1.7	52.2	584.3	811.6	919.2	867.8	904.5	969.9	1034	1170	1183

Source: TRAI

Table 2: Mobile subscribers (in millions) and Tele-density, 2018

State	***Subscribers (in million)***			***Tele-density***		
	Total	***Rural***	***Urban***	***Rural***	***Urban***	***Total***
AP	84.3	38.1	46.2	59.1	184.1	94.1
Assam	22.6	14.3	8.3	51.6	152.6	68.3
Bihar	84.3	49.3	35.0	40.7	180.1	60.0
Delhi	55.6	2.8	52.8	-	-	247.8
Gujarat	70.6	27.1	43.5	72.5	157.9	108.8
Haryana	25.5	11.2	14.3	63.1	136.6	90.3
HP	10.6	7.5	3.1	117.6	362.0	146.9
JK	13.1	6.4	6.7	70.5	188.4	103.8
Karnataka	67.2	22.6	44.6	58.9	178.5	106.1
Kerala	41.0	18.5	22.5	68.7	246.5	113.6
MP	73.1	33.3	39.8	43.4	134.9	68.8
Maharashtra (incl. Mumbai)	131.7	45.2	86.5	71.3	141.1	105.6
North East	12.8	6.6	6.2	62.3	171.2	90.1
Orissa	34.0	20.5	13.6	58.0	174.2	79.0
Punjab	38.1	13.9	24.2	79.7	171.4	120.8
Rajasthan	65.8	32.9	32.9	58.2	181.4	88.1
Tamil Nadu (incl. Chennai)	87.0	25.7	61.3	93.2	138.8	121.2
UP (East and West)	163.1	81.1	82.0	44.9	150.9	69.4
WB(incl. Kolkata)	87.1	42.2	44.9	61.6	161.7	90.5
All India	1167.4	499.0	668.4	56.3	163.4	90.1

Source: TRAI

Table 3: Mobile phone operators circles wise presence

Sl. No.	***Service provider***	***Area of operation***
1	Bharti Airtel	All India
7	IDEA Cellular Ltd	All India
5	Vodafone	All India
14	Reliance JioInfocom Ltd	All India
2	Aircel Group	All India
3	Reliance Communications	All India (except Assam & NE)
4	Reliance Telecom	Kolkata, MP, WB, HP, Bihar, OR, Assam & NE
6	Tata Teleservices	All India except Assam, NE & J&K
9	BSNL	All India (except Delhi & Mumbai)
10	MTNL	Delhi & Mumbai
13	Telenor Communications (India) Pvt. Ltd.	MH, Guj., AP, UP(W), UP(E), Bihar

Source: TRAI, 2018 *Upto December, 2017

Table 4: Number of internet subscriber and internet density per 100 population

Sl. No.	*Circle*	*Internet subscribers (in million)*			*Internet density per 100 population*		
		Rural	***Urban***	***Total***	***Rural***	***Urban***	***Total***
1	Andhra Pradesh	9.1	15.7	24.9	14.3	63.7	28.1
2	Assam	3.2	3.5	6.8	11.8	67.7	20.8
3	Bihar	8.9	10.8	19.6	7.5	56.6	14.3
4	Delhi	–	–	20.6	–	–	96.5
5	Gujarat	6.1	15.0	21.1	16.4	56.4	33.2
6	Haryana	3.0	4.6	7.6	16.9	46.1	27.5
7	HP	1.8	1.3	3.0	28.1	153.5	42.8
8	JK	1.8	1.8	3.6	20.5	51.6	29.1
9	Karnataka	5.5	17.1	22.6	14.5	70.4	36.3
10	Kerala	5.6	9.0	14.6	20.8	99.6	40.8
11	Kolkata	6.2	14.2	20.4	8.3	49.8	19.7
12	Madhya Pradesh	9.8	19.7	29.5	16.0	59.3	36.9
13	Maharashtra	0.3	15.4	15.7			
14	Mumbai	2.0	2.1	4.1	18.8	59.7	29.1
15	NE	3.4	4.9	8.3	9.6	65.5	19.5
16	Orissa	4.7	8.8	13.5	27.2	64.5	43.5
17	Punjab	7.0	10.3	17.3	12.7	58.1	23.6
18	Rajasthan	6.9	21.2	28.0	24.0	49.7	39.4
19	TN	11.2	11.3	22.5	10.0	40.7	17.0
20	U.P.(E)	6.5	10.0	16.5			
21	U.P.(W)	0.6	8.7	9.3	12.1	53.1	23.9
22	WB	7.6	5.8	13.4			
	All India	111.9	230.7	342.7	12.8	58.3	27.0

Source: TRAI, 2017

Table 5: Spectrumal location (in MHz) by circle to operators (GSM) in 900 and 1800 bands

Operator	*Bharti Airtel*	*Voda-fone*	*Idea*	*Reli-ance*	*Tata*	*BSNL*	*Aircel/ Dishnet*	*MTNL*	*Uni-tech*	*Vide-ocon*	*Loop*
A. P.	10.0	6.2	12.4	4.4	4.4	10.0	4.4		4.4		
Assam	6.2	4.4	4.4	6.2		10.0	6.2				
Bihar	9.2	4.4	4.4	8.0	4.4	10.0	4.4		4.4	4	
Delhi	10.0	10.0	8.0	4.4			4.4	12.4			
Gujarat	6.2	7.8	6.2	4.4	4.4	7.4	4.4		2.0	4	
Haryana	6.2	6.2	10.6	4.4	4.4	10.0	4.4			4	
H. P.	6.2	4.4	4.4	6.2	4.4	10.0	4.4				
J&K	6.2	4.4	4.4	4.4		8.0	4.4				
Karnatka	10.0	8.0	10.6	4.4	4.4	10.0	4.4				
Kerala	6.2	6.2	8.0	4.4	4.4	10.0	4.4				
Kolkata	8.0	9.8	4.4	6.2	4.4	10.0	4.4				
M.P.	8.0	4.4	8.0	6.2	4.4	10.0	4.4			4	
Maharashtra	8.2	6.2	14.2	4.4	4.4	10.0	4.4		4.4		
Mumbai	9.2	10.2	4.4	4.4	4.4		4.4	12.4			10
North East	6.2		4.4	6.2		10.0	4.4				
Orissa	8.0	4.4	4.4	6.2	4.4	10.0	4.4				
Punjab	7.8	6.2	7.8	4.4	4.4	6.2	4.4				
Rajasthan	8.2	6.2	6.2	4.4	4.4	8.0	4.4				
TamilNadu	9.2	8.0	4.4	4.4	4.4	10.0	9.8				
U.P. (E)	6.2	6.2	8.0	4.4	4.4	10.0	4.4		4.4	4	
U.P.(W)	7.2	8.2	6.2	4.4	4.4	10.0	4.4		4.4	4	West
Bengal	6.2	6.2	4.4	6.2	4.4	8.0	4.4				

Source: TRAI, 2013

Table 6: Spectrum efficiency (GSM in 900 and 1800 bands) by circles, (per MHz Subscriber in 000'), 2013

Operator	*Bharti Airtel*	*Voda-fone*	*Idea*	*Reli-ance*	*Tata*	*BSNL*	*Aircel/ Dishnet*	*MTNL*	*Uni-tech*	*Vide-ocon*	*Loop*
A.P.	18252	946	903	848	1089	9290	400		978		
Assam	640	530	90	476		1144	797				
Bihar	2106	1538	1373	826	541	5691	1059		989	5	
Delhi	9293	8534	612	981			669	202			
Gujarat	1147	2059	1373	1152	471	565	42		2474	138	
Haryana	376	747	2364	382	408	3090	8			184	
H.P.	319	113	107	215	21	1576	162				
J&K	384	142	51	142		136	186				
Karnataka	16230	855	3904	972	1191	6951	383				
Kerala	565	1000	990	254	346	7436	24				
Kolkata	461	427	312	456	492	2271	426				
M.P.	1265	979	1945	1530	715	5031	22			171	
Maharashtra	1231	2169	1154	1257	787	6724	270		1269		
Mumbai	416	5344	707	626	474		352	186			3008
North East	440		67	138		1609	528				
Orissa	866	693	249	571	408	4443	666				
Punjab	900	717	742	589	336	708	213				
Rajasthan	1797	1445	830	1029	329	724	674				
Tamil Nadu	1466	1528	525	1015	1109	9482	3421				
U.P. (E)	2458	2399	926	1298	757	10015	454		1715	4	
U.P. (W)	920	1157	1741	997	612	4769	127		1126	1	
West Bengal	1496	1871	605	949	398	442	684				
Average	2865	1676	980	759	582	4105	526	194	1425	84	3008

Source: TRAI, 2013

Table 7: Net profit margin (%)

	2007	*2008*	*2009*	*2010*	*2011*	*2012*	*2013*	*2014*	*2015*	*2016*
Idea	11.5	15.5	10.2	8.9	5.5	3.0	3.7	6.5	9.0	7.3
Reliance	18.6	17.5	30.5	3.5	–6.2	1.4	5.5	6.5	–1.4	–16.3
Airtel	22.5	24.0	22.6	26.5	20.3	13.8	11.2	13.2	23.8	12.5
Tata	11.3	8.9	13.3	14.5	4.5	4.2	10.8	12.4	15.6	2.4
BSNL	20.8	11.6	4.1	–6.3	–21.3	–31.0	–28.7	–24.8	–	–

Table 8: Return on capital employed (%)

	2007	*2008*	*2009*	*2010*	*2011*	*2012*	*2013*	*2014*	*2015*	*2016*
Idea	15.0	16.9	11.2	10.7	7.5	10.0	8.3	9.7	13.9	9.4
Reliance	11.0	9.7	4.8	2.0	0.0	2.0	4.1	1.7	0.1	0.7
Airtel	29.1	28.0	28.4	23.9	16.7	13.1	12.1	13.2	17.3	11.3
Tata	10.3	6.5	6.2	3.0	4.6	5.7	7.5	8.9	11.0	6.8
BSNL	8.4	3.3	0.6	–2.1	–7.8	–10.7	–12.4	–10.0	–	

Annexure 2

UNIT ROOT TEST RESULTS

The Augmented Dickey Fuller test for stationary for all the five variables have been found to be non-stationary at level and became stationary after taking the first difference of their log values as presented below:

(A) Results at Level

(i) Result of unit root test for revenue (levels)

Null Hypothesis: LREV has a unit root

Lag Length: 0

Augmented Dickey –Fuller Test Statistics: –2.446

Test critical value 1% level: –3.675

Test critical value 5% level: –2.969

Test critical value 10% level: –2.617

T-statistics probability: 0.1293

(ii) Result of unit root test for GNP per capita (levels)

Null Hypothesis: LGNPPC has a unit root

Lag Length: 0

Augmented Dickey –Fuller Test Statistics: –1.602

Test critical value 1% level: –3.675

Test critical value 5% level: –2.969

Test critical value 10% level: –2.617

T-statistics probability: 0.4827

(iii) Result of unit root test for FDI (levels)

Null Hypothesis: LFDI has a unit root

Lag Length: 0

Augmented Dickey –Fuller Test Statistics:-1.079

Test critical value 1% level: –3.675

Test critical value 5% level: –2.969

Test critical value 10% level: –2.617

T-statistics probability: 0.7235

(iv) Result of unit root test for mobile phone subscribers (levels)

Null Hypothesis: LSUB has a unit root

Lag Length: 0

Augmented Dickey –Fuller Test Statistics: –1.074

Test critical value 1% level: –3.682

Test critical value 5% level: –2.972

Test critical value 10% level: –2.618

T-statistics probability: 0.725

(v) Result of unit root test for government effectiveness index (levels)

Null Hypothesis: LGOV has a unit root

Lag Length: 0

Augmented Dickey –Fuller Test Statistics: –1.738

Test critical value 1% level: –3.675

Test critical value 5% level: –2.969

Test critical value 10% level: –2.617

T-statistics probability: 0.4119

(vi)Result of unit root test for internet subscribers (levels)

Null Hypothesis: LINT has a unit root

Lag Length: 0

Augmented Dickey –Fuller Test Statistics: 0.857

Test critical value 1% level: –3.675

Test critical value 5% level: –2.969

Test critical value 10% level: –2.617

T-statistics probability: 0.9925

(B) Results After First Difference

(i) Result of unit root test for revenue (differences)

Null Hypothesis: LREV has a unit root

Lag Length: 0

Augmented Dickey –Fuller Test Statistics: –7.097

Test critical value 1% level: –3.682

Test critical value 5% level: –2.972

Test critical value 10% level: –2.618

T-statistics probability: 0.0000

(ii) Result of unit root test for GNP per capita (differences)

Null Hypothesis: LGNPPC has a unit root

Lag Length: 0

Augmented Dickey –Fuller Test Statistics: –6.644

Test critical value 1% level: –3.682

Test critical value 5% level: –2.972

Test critical value 10% level: –2.618

T-statistics probability: 0.0000

(iii) Result of unit root test for FDI (differences)

Null Hypothesis: LFDI has a unit root

Lag Length: 0

Augmented Dickey –Fuller Test Statistics: –1.079

Test critical value 1% level: –3.675

Test critical value 5% level: –2.969

Test critical value 10% level: –2.617

T-statistics probability: 0.7235

(iv) Result of unit root test for mobile phone subscribers (differences)

Null Hypothesis: LSUB has a unit root

Lag Length: 0

Augmented Dickey –Fuller Test Statistics: –5.702

Test critical value 1% level: –3.675

Test critical value 5% level: –2.969

Test critical value 10% level: –2.617

T-statistics probability: 0.0000

(v) Result of unit root test for government effectiveness index (differences)

Null Hypothesis: LGOV has a unit root

Lag Length: 0

Augmented Dickey –Fuller Test Statistics: –3.012

Test critical value 1% level: –3.682

Test critical value 5% level: –2.972

Test critical value 10% level: –2.618

T-statistics probability: 0.0038

(vi) Result of unit root test for internet subscribers (differences)

Null Hypothesis: LINT has a unit root

Lag Length: 0

Augmented Dickey –Fuller Test Statistics: –4.129

Test critical value 1% level: –3.682

Test critical value 5% level: –2.972

Test critical value 10% level: –2.618

T-statistics probability: 0.0009

Annexure 3

RATIO ANALYSIS

Ratio analysis is an approach to understand the strength and weakness of a firm, company or mobile phone operator. It also tells about successful and unsuccessful firms in the market. It is a very powerful analytical tool useful for measuring performance of an operator and set goals for improvement. The financial ratios of an operator can be compared with the industry standard ratios. This comparison provides an overview of the firms over a period of time, its condition and stability in the market. These trends and patterns provide clues on trend and future problems to the firms. Ratios also facilitate firms in taking proper decisions regarding various important business strategies including investment.

Ratio analysis includes five main indicators in the study, which are (i) Current Ratios, (ii) Debt Equity Ratio, (iii) Earning per Share, (iv) Earning before Interest Depreciation and Amortization and (v) Returns on Capital Employed (RoCE). The detail definitions of these ratios are given in this chapter, where these ratios have been analysed.

PARTIAL FACTOR PRODUCTIVITY

Productivity is the measure of how specified resources are managed to accomplish timely objectives as stated in terms of quantity and quality. It is useful as a relative measure of actual output of production compared to the actual input of resources, measured across time or against common entities. The ratio of output to a single input factor is called partial factor productivity. It shows how much output has increased in relation to inputs over a time period by holding the quantity of that particular input constant. The ratio reflects an increase in productivity, when output increases for a level of input, or as the amount of input decreases for a constant level of output.

Partial factor productivity analysis includes four indictors in the study, which are (i) Revenue per unit of Asset, (ii) Revenue per unit of Expenditure, (iii) Average Revenue per user and (iv) Net Profit per User.

These are self-explanatory terms as Revenue per unit of Asset is an indicator of how much revenue a firm can generate per unit of asset and it's a way to determine the efficiency by which a company converts investment into assets and assets into revenue. Revenue per unit of Expenditure indicate that how much revenue a firm can generate on per unit of expenditure and it's a way to determine the efficiency by which a firm converts expenditure into revenue. Subscribers' data has been used as a proxy of employees to understand the productivity patterns because employee detail is not available or provided by the operators. Average revenue per users indicates that how much revenue is generated from a single subscriber, and Average net profit per user reflects the average net profit generated by a subscriber.

DATA ENVELOPMENT ANALYSIS

Data Envelopment Analysis (DEA) has emerged as one of the important tool for evaluating the performance of manufacturing and services units or firms. It is used extensively to measure the efficiency level of a unit or firm by using linear programming technique. It allows multiple inputs and outputs at the same time and measure efficiency score of the firms in terms of a proportional change in inputs or outputs.

The efficiency score is defined as ratio of weighted sum of outputs to the weighted sum of inputs used in the DEA analysis. Assuming that there are n firms, each with *m* inputs and *s* outputs, the relative efficiency score of a firm is represented by the following formula:

$$\max h_0(u,v) = \sum_r u_r \, y_{r0} \Big/ \sum_i v_i \, y_{i0}$$

$$\text{Subject to } \frac{\sum_r u_r y_{rj}}{\sum_i u_i y_{ij}} \leq 1, \text{for } j = 0,1 \ldots \ldots \ldots, n$$

$$0 < \in \leq u_r; r = 1,2 \ldots, s; 0 < \in \leq v_i, i = 1,2 \ldots \ldots, m$$

Where ho is the efficiency ratio of the first firm or mobile operator in this study.$v_i$and $u_r$are virtual multipliers (weights) for i^{th} input and r^{th} output respectively; m is the number of inputs, s is the number of outputs and n is the number of firms . $x_{io}$is the value of the ith input for first firm.$y_{r0}$is the value of the output r for first firm.

Overall Efficiency from Charnes A., W. W. Cooper, and E. Rhodes (CCR) model can be decomposed into Technical Efficiency and Scale Efficiency in the Data Envelopment Analysis. Scale Efficiency can be measured for a firm by using CCR model as follow: SE = OE / TE, If the ratio is equal to 1 then a firm is scale efficient, otherwise if the ratio is less than 1 then a firm is scale inefficient.

Description of objectives, Analysis tools, Variables and data sources of performance of mobile phone operators study

Objective/Analysis tools	*Variables*	*Sources*
Financial Ratios Current Ratio Debt Equity Ratio EBITDA Return to Capital Employed	Current Asset, Liabilities Debt, Equity, Turn over, Net Profit, Earnings per Share	TRAI, Operator's Annual Reports & website:moneycontrol.com
Partial Factor Productivity Revenue per Asset Revenue per Expenditure Average Revenue per User Average Return per user	Revenue, Debt, Total Expenditure, Net Profit, Subscribers,	-do-
Efficiency Analysis Data Envelopment Analysis Sensitivity Analysis	Revenue, Total Asset; Total Expenditure	-do-

INDIAN TOP MOBILE OPERATORS

Bharti Airtel Ltd

Telecom giant Bharti Airtel is the flagship company of Bharti Enterprises. The Bharti Group has a diverse business portfolio and has created global brands in the telecom sector. Airtel comes from Bharti Airtel Limited, India's largest integrated and the first private telecom services provider with a footprint in all the 23 telecom circles. Bharti Airtel since its inception has been at the forefront of technology and has steered the course of the telecom sector in the country with its world class products and services.

Reliance Communications Ltd.

Reliance Communications is the flagship company of the Anil Dhirubhai Ambani Group (ADAG) of companies. It is India's leading integrated telecommunication company. Their business encompasses a complete range of telecom services covering mobile and fixed line telephony. It includes broadband, national and international long distance services and data services along with an exhaustive range of value-added services and applications.

Bharat Sanchar Nigam Ltd.

Bharat Sanchar Nigam Ltd. formed in October, 2000, is World's 7th largest Telecom Company providing comprehensive range of telecom services in India. BSNL is the only service provider, making focused efforts and planned initiatives to bridge the Rural-Urban Digital Divide ICT sector. In fact there is no telecom operator in the country to beat its reach with its wide network giving services in every nook and corner of country and operates across India except Delhi and Mumbai.

Idea Cellular Ltd

IDEA Cellular is India's leading GSM mobile services operator. It has licenses to operate in 11 circles. A brand known for many firsts, Idea was the first to launch GPRS and EDGE in the country. IDEA Cellular is part of the Aditya Birla Group, India's first truly multinational corporation. IDEA has seen phenomenal growth since its inception, the company's footprint idea is to first achieve critical mass, then drill deep instead of spreading thin, however, does not increasing geographic footprint only, it also drills deep and successfully attempts to provide excellent network coverage in all its circles of operations.

Reliance Jio

Reliance JioInfocomm Limited (RJio) is an Indian mobile operator. Owned by Reliance Industries and headquartered, it operates a national LTE network with coverage across all 22 telecom circles. RJio does not offer 2G or 3G service, and instead utilizes voice over LTE to provide voice service on its network. The company commercially launched its services on 5th September, 2016, and within three months times it crossed 100 million subscribers. Today, it is third largest mobile subscribers in India, and highest wireless broadband or data subscribers in India.

Annexure 4

OPERATORS PERFORMANCE

Table 1: Share of subscribers (%)

	2007	*2008*	*2009*	*2010*	*2011*	*2012*	*2013*	*2014*	*2015*	*2016*
Airtel	22.5	23.7	24.0	21.8	20.0	19.7	21.7	22.7	24.1	24.3
Idea	10.1	10.8	12.1	10.9	11.0	12.3	14.0	15.0	17.0	16.9
BSNL	18.8	15.6	13.3	11.9	11.3	10.7	11.7	10.5	8.2	8.4
Reliance	17.0	17.5	18.5	17.5	16.7	16.7	14.2	12.3	10.0	9.9
Vodafone*	16.0	16.9	17.6	17.3	16.6	16.4	17.6	18.4	19.2	19.2
Others	15.6	15.4	14.5	20.6	24.4	24.3	20.9	21.1	21.6	21.3
All	100.0	100.0	100.0	100.0	100.0	100.0	100.0	100.0	100.0	100.0

Source: Telecom Regulatory Authority of India, operators' annual reports and moneycontrol.com, 2018

Table 2: Share of revenue (%)

	2007	*2008*	*2009*	*2010*	*2011*	*2012*	*2013*	*2014*	*2015*	*2016*
Airtel	17.6	20.9	24.5	28.1	28.5	27.9	28.6	28.7	29.3	30.2
Idea	4.2	5.2	6.7	10.2	12.0	13.4	14.2	15.6	17.3	18.4
BSNL	37.7	29.5	23.5	18.7	13.9	11.7	10.9	10.6	8.6	8.8
Reliance	13.7	14.8	14.6	10.1	9.7	8.1	7.0	6.8	5.6	5.1
Vodafone*				17.8	19.4	20.5	21.0	21.4	21.8	21.7
Others	26.8	29.6	30.7	15.0	16.5	18.4	18.2	17.0	17.4	15.8
All	165	261	392	100.0	100.0	100.0	100.0	100.0	100.0	100.0

Note: Vodafone data for 2007-09 not available
Source: Telecom Regulatory Authority of India, operators' annual reports and moneycontrol.com, 2017

Table 3: Current ratio

	2007	*2008*	*2009*	*2010*	*2011*	*2012*	*2013*	*2014*	*2015*	*2016*
Airtel	0.50	0.60	0.70	0.70	0.70	1.00	0.70	0.90	0.70	0.70
Idea	0.90	0.40	1.00	1.00	0.50	0.30	0.50	0.40	0.40	0.30
Reliance	1.80	1.00	1.50	1.40	1.00	0.90	0.90	0.70	1.50	0.80
BSNL	2.50	2.50	2.30	1.10	0.90	1.00	0.90	1.10	0.80	1.10

Source: Telecom Regulatory Authority of India, operators' annual reports and moneycontrol.com, 2017

Table 4: Debt-equity ratio

	2007	*2008*	*2009*	*2010*	*2011*	*2012*	*2013*	*2014*	*2015*	*2016*
Airtel	0.47	0.33	0.28	0.14	0.27	0.29	0.24	0.13	0.26	0.50
Idea	1.95	1.84	0.67	0.57	0.86	0.79	0.78	1.14	0.74	1.56
Reliance	0.71	0.82	0.60	0.48	0.65	0.62	0.91	0.96	0.76	0.87
BSNL	0.16	0.14	0.13	0.11	0.13	0.13	0.13	0.13	0.20	0.20

Source: Telecom Regulatory Authority of India, operators' annual reports and moneycontrol.com, 2017

Table 5: EBITDA margin (%)

	2007	*2008*	*2009*	*2010*	*2011*	*2012*	*2013*	*2014*	*2015*	*2016*
Airtel	40.7	41.4	38.7	39.1	35.3	33.0	29.7	32.7	35.0	37.0
Idea	37.0	37.1	31.6	27.4	23.6	25.2	26.5	27.8	30.9	33.0
Reliance	43.2	41.7	34.7	16.2	12.9	28.3	24.2	16.3	15.3	21.1
BSNL	20.5	11.7	3.6	–6.9	–22.2	–31.6	–29.3	–24.8	–30.9	–12.7

Source: Telecom Regulatory Authority of India, operators' annual reports and moneycontrol.com, 2017

Table 6: Return to capital employed(%)

	2007	*2008*	*2009*	*2010*	*2011*	*2012*	*2013*	*2014*	*2015*	*2016*
Airtel	29.10	28.00	28.40	23.90	16.70	13.10	12.10	13.20	17.30	11.30
Idea	15.00	16.90	11.20	10.70	7.50	10.00	9.60	9.70	13.90	9.40
Reliance	11.00	9.70	4.80	2.00	1.00	3.30	4.60	1.70	0.10	0.70
BSNL	8.40	3.30	0.60	–2.10	–7.80	–10.70	–12.40	–10.10	–15.90	–7.40

Table 7: Revenue per Rs. of investment (in Rs.)

	2007	*2008*	*2009*	*2010*	*2011*	*2012*	*2013*	*2014*	*2015*	*2016*
Airtel	1.07	0.97	0.97	0.85	0.68	0.66	0.70	0.67	0.62	0.48
Idea	0.68	0.69	0.54	0.68	0.67	0.84	0.87	0.79	0.83	0.58
Reliance	0.37	0.34	0.23	0.21	0.18	0.18	0.18	0.20	0.22	0.17
BSNL	0.66	0.66	0.60	0.40	0.39	0.40	0.28	0.31	0.39	0.47

Source: Telecom Regulatory Authority of India, operators' annual reports and moneycontrol.com, 2017

Table 8: Revenue per Rs of Expenditure (in Rs.)

	2007	*2008*	*2009*	*2010*	*2011*	*2012*	*2013*	*2014*	*2015*	*2016*
Airtel	1.70	1.70	1.60	1.70	1.60	1.50	1.50	1.50	1.70	1.60
Idea	1.60	1.60	1.50	1.40	1.30	1.30	1.30	1.40	1.50	1.50
Reliance	1.80	1.80	1.00	1.40	1.20	1.50	1.40	1.30	1.50	1.30
BSNL	1.30	1.10	1.00	0.90	0.80	0.80	0.80	0.80	0.80	0.90

Source: Telecom Regulatory Authority of India, operators' annual reports and moneycontrol.com, 2017

Table 9: Revenue per subscribers (2012 constant prices, in Rs.)

	2007	*2008*	*2009*	*2010*	*2011*	*2012*	*2013*	*2014*	*2015*	*2016*
Airtel	845	670	552	372	232	190	147	128	122	131
Idea	485	406	373	261	174	146	112	105	102	115
Reliance	840	544	407	210	106	66	55	56	56	55
BSNL	1134	873	687	449	255	146	104	102	106	111

Source: Telecom Regulatory Authority of India, operators' annual reports and moneycontrol.com, 2017

Table 10: Earnings per share (in Rs.)

	2009	*2010*	*2011*	*2012*	*2013*	*2014*	*2015*	*2016*
Airtel	40.8	24.8	20.3	15.1	13.4	16.5	33.0	18.9
Idea	3.2	3.2	2.6	1.7	2.5	5.1	7.8	7.3
Reliance	23.3	2.3	–3.7	0.8	3.0	3.6	–0.6	–6.5
BSNL	1.2	–3.7	–12.8	–17.7	–15.7	–14.0	–16.4	–7.8

Source: Telecom Regulatory Authority of India, operators' annual reports and moneycontrol.com, 2017

Table 11: Profit (in Rs.) per subscriber (2012 constant prices)

	2007	**2008**	**2009**	**2010**	**2011**	**2012**	**2013**	**2014**	**2015**	**2016**
Airtel	191	161	125	98	47	26	21	24	39	21
Idea	55	61	36	22	9	4	5	9	12	11
Reliance	156	92	102	6	–6	1	4	5	–1	–11
BSNL	135	210	61	9	–22	–58	–75	–65	–62	–83

Source: Telecom Regulatory Authority of India, operators' annual reports and moneycontrol.com, 2017

Annexure 5

QUESTIONNAIRE (STAKEHOLDERS) ON TELECOM REGULATORY ENVIRONMENTAL IN INDIA

Dear Participants

Thank you very much for your consent to participate in this study. The seven dimensions used in this study are broadly based on the reference paper of the fourth protocol of the general agreement on trade in services and assessed on a five-point scale. The broad definition of seven dimensions is following:

(1) Market entry and competition

- Transparency of licensing- applicants should know the terms, conditions, criteria and length of time needed to reach a decision on their application, licence conditions and exclusivity issues.
- Anti-competitive cross subsidization.
- Using information obtained from competitors with anti-competitive results.
- Not making technical information about essential facilities and commercially relevant information available to competitors on a timely basis.
- Excessive prices.
- Price discrimination and predatory low pricing.
- Refusal to deal with operators and other parties.
- Vertical restraints.
- Technical disruption of interconnection.

- Sharing of towers and facilities by parent company and subsidiaries in different segments of the market.

(2) Access to scarce resources

- Timely, transparent, non-discriminatory allocation to spectrum
- Numbering and rights of way: frequency allocation, telephone number allocation, tower location rights.

(3) Interconnection

- Interconnection with a major operator should be ensured at any technically feasible point in the network.
- Quality of interconnection comparable to similar services offered by own network.
- Reasonable rates for interconnection.
- Unbundling of interconnection and Interconnection offered without delay.
- Sharing of incoming and outgoing and IDD revenue.
- Payment for cost of interconnection links and switch interface.
- Payment for cost of technical disruption of interconnection.

(4) Tariff regulation

- Regulation of tariffs charged from consumers.

(5) Universal service obligation (USO)

- Administration of the universal service program/fund in a transparent, non-discriminatory and competitively neutral manner and is not more burdensome than necessary for the kind of universal service defined by the policymakers.

(6) Quality of service (QoS)

- The actual performance of a service with respect to what is promised, depending upon the network traffic control mechanisms.

- Specific criteria may be call quality, connection speeds or throughput (for broadband).

I. Identification		
Q1	Name	
Q2	Designation	
Q3	Organization/Company	

Please fill 1 in the suitable box that best represents the quality of the recent regulatory environment for each dimension that best suits your perspective. The lower number represents Highly Ineffective and the higher number represents Highly Effective. If you feel you do not have sufficient information about a particular question, you may choose to leave it blank.

II. Telecom regulatory assessment

Sl.No.	Dimension	Quality of telecom regulatory environment				
		Highly effective				Highly ineffective
		1	2	3	4	5
Q1	Market Entry and Competition	1	2	3	4	5
Q2	Access to Scarce Resource	1	2	3	4	5
Q3	Interconnection	1	2	3	4	5
Q4	Tariff Regulation	1	2	3	4	5
Q5	Universal Service Obligation (USO)	1	2	3	4	5
Q6	Quality of Service (QoS)	1	2	3	4	5
Q7	New Telecom Policy (NTP12)	1	2	3	4	5

III. Major challenges/concern (order of importance)

1
2
3
4
5

IV. Regulatory wish list (order of importance)

1
2
3
4
5

Annexure 6

CONSUMER SURVEY QUESTIONNAIRE

Identification Number________________

Section 1: Demographic Information

1.1. Name of the Respondent ____________________

1.2. Gender
[Male-1; Female-2]

1.3. Caste
[ST-1; SC-2, OBC-3; Others-4]

1.4. Religion
[Hindu-1; Muslim-2, Others-3]

1.5. Main Occupation

Section 2: Mobile Ownership and Access

2.1. Do you own a mobile phone
[Yes-1; No-2]

2.2. If yes, who purchased
[Self-1; Parents-2; Brother/Sister-3; Spouse-4; Son/Doughter-5; Relative-6; provided by employer or landlord-7; other (specify)]

2.3. Reasons for Mobile Ownership

____

2.4. If no, how do you access to mobile phone? [Family members-2; Relative/Friends-2; Co-workers-3; Neighbours-4; Not Acess-5; other (specify)] ☐

2.5. How many mobile connections does your family have? ☐

2.6. Frequency of outgoing call

2.6.1. Daily ☐ 2.6.2. Weekly ☐ 2.6.3. Monthly ☐

2.7. Frequency of Incoming call

2.7.1. Daily ☐ 2.7.2. Weekly ☐ 2.7.3. Monthly ☐

2.8. If yes, three main purpose of calls [Three in order of importance] ☐ ☐ ☐

Interact with spouse-1; Relative and friends-2; parents-3; Agriculture related- 4; Employment or Work related-5; Migration or family member away-6; Business or Trading-7; Health Information-8; Education Information-9; Credit or other financial information-10; Entertainment-11; Emergency-12; Others Information (Specify)

2.9. Do you also use the following facility [Yes-1; No-2]

2.9.1. SMS ☐ 2.9.2. Internet ☐ 2.9.3. Music ☐

2.9.4. Others (Specify) ______________________

2.10. Total Monthly Expenditure on Mobiles ________________

Section 3: Use & Impact of Mobile Phone on End-Users

3.1. Use of mobile and impact (agriculture crops and vegetables) and other allied activities

Cycle	*Activities#*	*Information Source**	*Benefits [Impact]***
i) Crop planning & other inputs			
ii) Planting & Growing			
iii) Harvesting, packing and storing			
iv) Pre-trading			
v) During-trading			
vi) Post-trading			
3.1.1. Animal Husbandry			
3.1.2. Dairy			

 # Activities

1. ***Crop planning & other inputs*:** Buying Seed or crop variety (option new crops or new variety, like higher value crops or better seed varieties)-1; Fertiliser Availalbilty-2; Weather Information-3; Others (specify)
2. ***Planting & Growing:*** Best time to plant-1; Cultivation and plantation best techincs-2; Pest Control-3; Crop Insurance-4; Electricity Timing for Irrigation-5; Others (specify)
3. ***Harvesting, packing and storing*:** Best harvest time-1; Packing or storing-2; Government subsidy or scheme for storage etc-3; Protection of produce-4; others (specify)

4. ***Pre Trading*:** Check/confirm prices of various products from different Market and comparative find best prices-1, Market demand-2; Plan and Co-ordinate with traders or middlemen-3; trying to find improved trade-4; more geographical areas coverage-5; others (specify)
5. **During Trading:** Find Best prices -1; Transport-2; Storage-3; Negotiations of prices-2; Finalisation of price or deal-3; others (specify)
6. **Post Trading:** Trade of agreed terms-1; Customer satisfaction-2; others (specify)

Information Sources

Other progressive farmers-1; input dealer-2; trader-3; middlemen-4; co-operative society-5; Extension workers-6; farmer call centre-7; others (specify)

Benefit or Outcome

1. ***Benefits during Agriculture practice*:** Reduce traction cost-1; More productivity-2; Time Saving-3; Improved Farming Practices-4; Reduce wastage/spoilage of crop infection-5, timely decision making on crop pattern and other inputs-6; more credit available-7; others (specify)
2. ***Benefits during trading of produce:*** Reduce wastage/spoilage of stock-1; Time to provide services-2 ; Reduce cost of procure/ providing services-3; More return on products-4;More Access to existing suppliers/Mandi/Customers-5;Finding new suppliers/customers-6; Access to source of credit-7, others (specify)]

3.2 Use of mobile for non-agricultural purposes

	Purposes	*Activities*	*Information Sources*	*Benefits*
(i)	Social Networking	______	______	______
(ii)	Employment or	______	______	______
	Work Related	______	______	______
(iii)	Migration or other	______	______	______

family member away ______________________

(iv) Business or ______________________

other trading ______________________

(v) Health Information ______________________

(vi) Educational Information

(vii) Credit/Financial ______________________

information ______________________

(viii) Entertainment ______________________

(ix) Emergency ______________________

(x) Others (specify) ______________________

3.3. Innovative practices

3.3.1. Use of Missed Call (Flash)

3.3.2. Use of SMS

3.3.3. Use of Internet

____

____

____

3.3.4. Other innovative practices (describe) (like use of one mobile sim by several people; For Informal Money transfer or Courier)

____

____

____

3.4. Other Barriers

3.4.1. What are the three major barriers in accessing mobile phone?

[Cost of handset-1; Cost of call-2; Difficulty in using mobile phone-3; Difficulty in charging-4; Not enough knowledge about value of mobile-5; others (specify) _______________]

3.4.2 What are the negative impacts of mobile phone (Describe?)

____

____

____

Annexure 7

ABOUT THE STUDY AREAS

Bihar's economy is dominated by the rural sector, which is characterised by high poverty (37 per cent) and low per capita state gross income (Rs. 69,870). Around 70 per cent of the population in the state lives in the rural areas. The state has 38 districts, which consist of sub-divisions, *tehsil*s and blocks. Agriculture has been the mainstay of the people's livelihood in the state. The contribution of agriculture to the economy has, however, been declining over the years and remains only one-fifth of the total contribution at present. The structure of the economy has also undergone a change over time with a shift from agriculture to the service sector. The latter made a contribution of 59 per cent to the state economy.

The telecommunication infrastructure in Bihar has also been playing a major role in the growth of the service sector in the state. The number of mobile phone subscribers has reached to 84.3 million and internet users to 12 million in January, 2018. However, the tele-density in Bihar (61 per cent) is still far behind than all India average (93 per cent) with huge rural and urban gap. The tele-density in rural Bihar is lowest in India around 42 per cent. Therefore to understand the socio-economic impact on consumer, a survey among 394 mobile phone consumers was carried out across seven districts and twelve villages in the rural areas of the state.

Annexure 8

SAMPLING METHODOLOGY OF PRIMARY SURVEY

The sample of the study has been taken from a census survey conducted by the Rodger *et al.*(2013) in Bihar. In the study, they selected a sample of 12 villages from six districts (2 villages from each district) namely Gaya, Nalanda, Rohtas, Gopalganj, Madhubani and Purnea, which represent the geographical clusters of the state. A total, 5934 households were covered under the census survey including a questions that whether household having access to mobile phone or not (Table 1).

Table 1: Total number of households in different villages.

Districts	*Village*	*Number of Households*
Gaya	Alalpur–Bishnupur	185
	Salempur–Rupaspur	436
Gopalganj	PaharpurDayal	84
	Dewanparsa	289
Madhubani	Mahisan	1490
	Khangaon	731
Nalanda	Chandkura	446
	Mohiuddinpur	111
Purnea	Belabadan	1296
	Jitwarpur	356
Rohtas	Samhutibuzurg	280
	Amarhi	230
All	Total	5934

From the census survey, 10 per cent sample from those who had access to mobile phone from the large villages and 20 per cent from smaller villages with at least minimum, 10 sample from each village was selected for the study. The selection of the sample households was done using systematic circular random sampling with replacement method[1] and an interview was conducted with household members, who use mobile phone. The final survey was conducted with 394 mobile phone users as given in Table 2.

Table 2: Distribution of total number of households covered under the census and the number of households covered under the sample survey.

	Village	*Number of Households*	*Mobile phone HHs*	*Sample Size*
Gaya	Alalpur–Bishnupur	185	55	11
	Salempur–Rupaspur	436	140	28
Gopalganj	PaharpurDaya	84	75	15
	Dewanparsa	289	150	30
Madhubani	Mahisan	1490	560	56
	Khangaon	731	450	45
Nalanda	Chandkura	446	125	25
	Mohiuddinpur	111	50	10
Purnea	Jitwarpur	1296	1040	104
	Belabadan	356	160	32
Rohtas	Samhutibuzurg	280	100	20
	Amarhi	230	90	18
	Total	5934	2995	394

Note: In the mobile phone study, only member (of sample households) having access to a mobile phone were interviewed.

[1] Sample to select every ith item on the list by using random numbers to pick up the unit with which to start, for instance if 10 per cent sample is desired, the first item would be selected randomly from the first 10 and thereafter every 10 nth item would automatically be included in the sample. If the selected sample is not available, it can be replaced by the just next item like 10 can be replaced by 11^{nth} and so on.

Bibliography

Abraham, R. (2006). Mobile phones and economic development: Evidence from the fishing industry in India. *Information Technologies and International Development,* 4(1): 5–17.

Achar, A. (1999). Untangling a telecom revolution. *Telecommunication,* 33(10): 181–183.

Acharya, S. (2006). *Essays on Macro Economic Policy and Growth in India,* New Delhi: Oxford University Press.

Ahn, H. and Myeong, H.L. (1999). An econometric analysis of the demand for access to mobile telephone networks. *Information Economics and Policy,* 11(3): 297–305.

Amulaya, D. and Anand, D. (2012). Privatization of telecom: Public sector on the wane. *SCMS Journal of Indian Management, 9*(1): 23–35.

Arrow, K.J. (1962). The economic implications of learning by doing. *Rev. Econ. Stud.,* 29(3): 155–73.

Arthreya, M.B. (1996). India's Telecommunication Policy, A Paradigm Shift. *Telecommunications Policy,* 20(1): 11–22.

Aschauer, David A. (1989). Is Public Expenditure Productive? *Journal of Monetary Economics,* 23(2): 177–200.

Bagchi, P. (2000). Telecommunications Reform and the State in India: The Contradiction of Private Control and Government Competition, Center for the Advanced Study of India (Occasional Paper No., 13), USA: University of Pennsylvania.

Baijal, P. (2004). Telecommunications: Regulatory Wild West? *Economic and Political Weekly,* 39(8): 771–77.

Bart, V. and Barasia,S. (2010). *How Global Telcos Can Profit from India's Wireless Experience, Bain and Company Asia-Pacific Telecommunications, Media & Technology practice, New Delhi.* accessed on 18 April, 2013 from www.bain.com.

Baumaol, W.J. (1967). Macroeconomics of Unbalanced Growth: The Anatomy of Urban Crisis. *American Economic Review,* 57(3): 415–426.

Bedi, A.S. (1999). The Role of Information and Communication Technologies in Economic Development – A Partial Survey, ZEF (Discussion Papers on Development Policy, No. 7), Germany: Center for Development Research. Bonn.

Berg, S. (2009). Characterizing the Efficiency and Effectiveness of Regulatory Institutions, University of Florida: Public Utility Research Center (Working Paper No 1).

Bernardo, B., Megginson W., D'Souza, J. and Fantini, M. (2002). Sources of performance Improvement in privatized firms: A Clinical Study of the Global Telecommunication Industry. *Telecommunication Policy,* 26: 243–268.

Besen, S.M. (1999). Innovation, Competition and the Theory of Network Externalities, the World Economy in the 21st Century, Paper presented at the Yale University Department of Economics Reunion, The World Economy in the 21st Century.

Bhagwati, J. (1984). Splintering and Disembodiment of Services and Developing Nations. *The World Economy,* 7(2): 133–144.

Bhatia, J. and Palepu Rao A. (2017). Reliance Jio, Predatory Pricing or Predatory Behaviour? *Economic & Political Weekly,* 51(41): 33–39.

Braandt, L. and Rawski, T. (2008). *China's Great Economic Transformation*, New York: Cambridge University Press.

Braff, A., Passmore, W.J. and Simpson, M. (2003). Going the Distance with Telecom Customers. *The McKinney Quarterly,* (4): 83.

Brock, G.W. (1996). Interconnection Policy and Technological Progress. *Federal Communications Law Journal,* 58(3): 445–451.

Brookings (2015). Spectrum policy in India, Centre for Technology Innovations at Brookings accessed on 10 Feb, 2016, from https://www.brookings.edu/wp-content/uploads/2016/06/Spectrum-Policy-in-India8515.pdf

Buigues, P.A. and Rey, P. (2004). *The Economics of Anti-Trust and Regulation in Telecommunications*, UK and USA: Edward Elgar Publishing.

Canning and Bannathan (2002). The Social Rate of Infrastructure Investment, World Bank Policy Research (Working Paper Series Number 2390), Washington, DC: World Bank, accessed on 12 June, 2013 from http://papers.ssrn.com/sol3/

Canning, D., Fay, M. and Perotti, R. (1994). Infrastructure and Growth in Baldassari M., Paganaetto, M. and Phelps, E.S. (*eds.*). International Differences in Growth Rates: Market Globalization and Economic Areas, New York: St. Martin Press, pp. 277–304.

Capello, R. and Nijkamp, P. (1996). Telecommunications, Technologies and Regional Development: Theoretical Considerations and Empirical Evidences. *The Annals of Regional Science,* 30(1): 7–30.

Capgemini (2008). Lessons from the Indian Mobile Market: How Operators Can Sustain Margins. *Low ARPU Market, Telecom & Media & Entertainment*, accessed on 12 March, 2013 from www.capgemini.com/tme

CARE Research (2013). Indian Telecom Wireless Industry – Story of policy surprises and subdued growth continue. Industry Update – Telecom Wireless, accessed on 15 March, 2014 from www.capgemini.com/tme

CARE (2013). The Indian Telecom Tower Industry, Care Research. Accessed on 24 May, 2015, from http://www.careratings.com/upload/Research/Industry Research/Telecom%20Tower.pdf

Carter, M. and Wright, J. (1999). Interconnection in Network Industries. *Review of Industrial Organization,* 14(1): 1–25.

Cave Martin, E (2006). *Handbook of Telecommunication, Vol. I, Structure, Regulation and Competition*, UK: Elsevier.

Charnes, A., Cooper, W.W. and Rhodes, E. (1978). Measuring the efficiency of decision making units. *European Journal of Operations Research,* 2(4): 429–444.

Chenery, H.B. (1960). Pattern of Industrial Growth. *American Economic Review,* 57(3): 415–426.

Chenery, H.B. and Syrquin, M. (1975). *Pattern of Development*: 1950-1970, London: Oxford University Press.

Chowdary, T.H. (2000). Telecoms to the Villages. *Economic and Political Weekly,* 35(24): 1995–1997.

Chowdary, T.H. (2001). Opening basic telephone service to competition. *Economic and Political Weekly,* 36(02): 94–95.

Chowdary, T.H. (2003). Telecom: Migration to Unified Multiple-Service Licences. *Economic and Political Weekly,* 38(38): 1231–1294.

Chowdary, T.H. (2004). Telecom reforms: A decade on. *Economic and Political Weekly,* 39(21): 2085–2087.

Chun-Hsiung Liao and Shaw-Er Wang (2003). Comparing the Operational Performance of Taiwan Private Mobile Telecommunications Operations, Proceeding of the first workshop on knowledge economy and electronic commerce. Accessed on 6 January, 2014 from http://moe.ecrc.nsysu.edu.tw/English/workshopE/2003/31.pdf

Claire, M. (1998). Stages of Universal Service Policy. *Telecommunication Policy,* 22(9): 775–780.

Clark C. (1940). *The Conditions of Economic Progress*, London: McMillan and Co. Ltd.

CramptonP. (2006). Spectrum Auctions, *In*: Cave, M.,Majumdar, S. and Vogelsang, I. (*eds.*). *Handbook of Telecommunication, Vol. I, Structure, Regulation and Competition*, Elsevier, Oxford UK, pp. 606–637.

Cronin, F.J., Colleran, E.K., Gold, M.A.P., Herbert, L. and Lewitzky, S. (1993). Factor Prices, Factor Substitution and the Relative Demand for Telecommunications across US Industries. *Information Economics and Policy,* 5(1): 73–85.

Cronin, F.J., Colleran, E.K., Gold, M.A.P., Herbert, L. and Lewitzky, S. (1993). Telecommunications and Growth. *Telecommunications Policy,* 27(9): 677–96.

Cronin, F.J., Colleran, E.K., Gold, M.A.P., Herbert, L. and Lewitzky, S. (1991). Telecommunications infrastructure and economic growth: An analysis of causality. *Telecommunications Policy,* 15(6): 529–34.

Daniel, F.S. (2002). Transaction Innovation and the Role of the Firm. *In*: Baye M.R. (*ed.*), *The Economics of the Internet and E-commerce, Advances in Applied Microeconomics: Volume 11*, Bingley, West Yorkshire, England: Emerald Group Publishing Limited, pp. 159–189.

Daniel, Š. (2009). The waves of the technological innovations of the modern age and the present crisis. *Studia Politica Slovaca,* 1:32–47

Dasgupta, S.and Singh, A. (2005). Will services be the new engine of Indian economic growth. *Development and Change,* 36(6): 1035–1057.

Datta, A. and Agarwal, S. (2004). Telecommunication and economic growth: A panel data approach. *Applied Economics,* 36(15): 1649–1654.

Desai, A.V. (2006). *India's Telecommunications Industry: History, Analysis, Diagnosis,* India: Sage Publications.

Dilorenzo, T.J. (1996). The myth of natural monopoly. *Review of Austrian Economics,* 9(2): 43–58.

Domar, E.D. (1946). Capital expansion rate of growth and employment. *Econometrica,* 9(14): 137–147.

Dossani, R. (2002). *Telecommunications Reform in India, Westport, Connecticut* (USA): Quorum Books.

DoT (2010). Performance Audit Report on the by the Department of Telecommunications Ministry of Communications and Information Technology Issue of Licences and Allocation of 2G Spectrum, Comptroller and Auditor General of India accessed on 10th, March, 2013 from http://cag.gov.in/html/reports/civil/2010-11_19PA/Telecommunication%20Report.pdf

Dudley, L.(1997). Communications and Economic Growth. *European Economic Review,* 41(9): 595–619.

Duncombe, R. and Boating, R. (2009). Mobile phones and financial services in developing countries: A Review of Concepts, Methods(s): Evidence and Future

Research Directions (Working Paper No 37), Manchester (UK): Institute for Development Policy and Management, accessed on 5 January, 2014 from http:/ /www.sed.manchester.ac.uk/idpm/research/publications/wp/di/di_wp37.htm

Eichengreen, B. and Gupta, P. (2010). The Service Sector as India's Road to Economic Growth (ICRIER Working Paper Series Number 249), New Delhi (India): Indian Council for Research on International Economic Relations, accessed on 1 March, 2014 from http://www.icrier.org/pdf/Working%20Paper%20249.pdf

Eichengreen, B. and Gupta, P. (2013). The two waves of services sector growth. *Oxford Economic Papers*, 65(1): 124–146

Falch, M. (2005). Cost and Demand Characteristics of Telecom Networks in Telecom Reform: Principles, Policies and Regulatory Practices (Ed.), Denmark: Schultz Docu Center, accessed on November, 10, 2013 from http://www.lirne.net/ resources/books/books.htm.

FICCI (2013). Telecom Sector in India,FICCI, DoT and A.T. Kearney Study. Accessed on 28th January, 2014 from http://www.ficci.com/sector.asp?secid=39

Fink, M. and Rathindran, R. (2002). An Assessment of Telecommunications Reform in Developing Countries (Policy Research Working Paper No. 2909), Washington D.C. USA: World Bank, accessed on 3 March, 2014 from http://elibrary. worldbank.org/doi/book/10.1596/1813-9450-2909.

Fisher, A.G.B (1935). *The Clash of Progress and Security*, London, UK: Macmillan and Co. Ltd.

Freeman, C. (2007). A Schumpeterian Renaissance, *In:* Hanusch H. and Pyka A. (*eds.*), *Elgar Companion to Neo-Schumpeterian Economics*, Northampton, UK: Edward Elgar Publishing, pp. 130–141.

Freeman, C. (1994). The Economics of Technical Change. *Cambridge Journal of Economics,* 18(5): 463–514.

Ghani Ejaz (2011). The Service Revolution, Paper presented at ILO Conference, Geneva, 2011 accessed on 5 March, 2014 from http://www.ilo.org/wcmsp5/groups/ public/documents/presentation/wcms_175061.pdf

Ghose, A.K. (2013). India's Services -led Growth and its discontents? Paper presented in 'Labour and Employment Conference held in Mumbai: IGIDR.

Ghose, A.K. (2014). India's services-led growth (Working Paper No 01), Institute for Human Development, New Delhi, accessed on 8 January, 2013 from http:// www.ihdindia.org/Working%20Ppaers/2014/Ajit%20K.%20Ghosh.pdf

Giokas, D.I. and Pentzaropoulos, G.C. (2000). Evaluating productive efficiency in telecommunications: Evidence from Greece. *Telecommunications Policy,* 24(8):781–794.

Goswami, D. and Malik, P. (2007). Telecom growth in poor regulatory environments: A comparative analysis of Indonesia and India, Paper Presented at Paris: International Association for Media and Communication Research (IAMCR) conference.

Griliches, Z. (1992). Output Measurement in the Service Sector, Chicago (USA): The University of Chicago Press.

Gruber, H. and Frank, V. (2001). The Evolution of Markets under Entry and Standards Regulation— The Case of Global Mobile Telecommunications (Centre for Economic Policy Research Working Paper No DP2440), London, UK: 77 Bastwick Street.

Gual, J. and Francesc, T. (2006). Telecommunications policies: Measurement and Determinants (Working paper No 630), Barcelona (Spain): IESE Business School-University of Navarra.

Guha, T.P.and Roy, G. (2012). TRAI Recommendation, the Next Round of Telecom Tussles. *Economic and Political Weekly,* 47(22): 51–58.

Guha, T.P. and Kaushal, A. (2010). Underbelly of the Great Indian Telecom Revolution. *Economic & Political Weekly,* 45(49): 49–53.

Guha, T.P. (2017). A call for review, Supreme Court's Decision on Reliance Jio. *Economic & Political Weekly,* 51(24): 32–43.

Sai H.C.T. *et al.* (2006). The comparative productivity efficiency for global telecoms. *International Journal of Production Economics,* 103(2): 509–526.

Hardy, A. (1980). The role of the telephone in economic development. *Telecommunications Policy,* 4(4): 278–286.

Harrod, R.F. (1939). An essay in dynamic theory. *Economic Journal,* 49(193): 14–33.

Headrick, D. (1988). The tentacles of progress: Technology transfer in the age of imperialism, New York: Oxford University Press, pp. 1880–1940.

Hill, T.P. (1977). On Goods and Services. *Review of Income and Wealth,* 32(2): 3–10.

Hu Jin-Li and Chu Wei-Kai (2008). Efficiency and productivity of major Asia-pacific telecom firms. *Chang Gung Journal of Humanities and Social Sciences,* 1(2): 223–245.

ICRA (2017). Telecom Industry: Consolidation may lead to scale and synergy benefits, but pricing pressure unlikely to ease, accessed on 5 June, 2013 from https://www.icra.in/

Ingle, B.D. (2012). Growth of Telecom Industry in India. *Global Economic Research Journal,* 1(2): 85–105.

Islam, S. (2011). Evaluation of an M-Service for Farmers in a Developing Region—A Case Study from Rural Bangladesh. *Media Asia,* 38(1): 41–51.

ITU (2014). *'ICT statistics - ITU'* accessed, from www.itu.int/en/ITU-D/Statistics/Pages/stat/default.aspx?utm

Jain R. (2002). WLL, Government Corporatisation and SWANS: A review of Institutional Development, *The Infrastructure Report,* IIM Ahmadabad and IIT Kanpur: 3i Network, pp. 54–59.

Jeffery, R. and Assa, D. (2013). *Cell phone Nation: How Mobile Phones Have Revolutionized Business, Politics and Ordinary Life in India*, USA: Harvard University Press.

Jensen, R. (2007). The digital provide: Information (Technology), market performance, and welfare in the South Indian fisheries sector. *Quarterly Journal of Economics,* 122(1): 879–924.

Jha, V. (2012).*India Emerging: The Reality Checks*, New Delhi: Academic Foundation.

Joshi, S. (2004). Tertiary Sector Driven Growth in India: Impact on Employment and Poverty. *Economic and Political Weekly,* 39(37): 879–924.

Kaldor, N. (1966). Causes of slow rate of growth in the United Kingdom, Cambridge: Cambridge University Press.

Kaldor, N. (1967). *Strategic Factors in Economic Development*, New York (USA): Cornell University Press.

Kathuria, R. (2000). Telecom policy reforms in India. *Global Business Review,* 1(2): 301–26.

Kathuria, R., Uppal, M. and Mamta (2009). An econometric analysis of the impact of mobile, Moving the debate forward: India the Impact of Mobile Phones, (The Policy Paper Series, Vodafone Group Number 9).

Kessides, I.N. (2004). *Reforming Infrastructure: Privatization, Regulation and Competition*, Washington, DC: World Bank and Oxford University Press.

Kongsamut, P., Rebalo, S. and Xie, D. (2001). Beyond Balance Growth. *Review of Economic Studies*, 68(4): 869–882.

Kotwal, A., Ramaswami, B. and Wadhwa, W. (2010). Economic liberalization and indian economic growth: What's the evidence? (BREAD Research Working Paper Series, Working Paper Number 294), USA: Duke University.

Kuznets, S. (1971). Economic Growth of Nations: Total Output and Production Structure, Cambridge, Massachusetts (USA): Harvard University Press.

Laffont, J.J. and Tirole, J. (2000). *Competition in Telecommunication*, Cambridge: MIT Press.

Lam, P.L. and Lam, T. (2005). Total factor productivity measures for Hong Kong telephone. *Telecommunications Policy,* 29(1): 53–68.

Lee, S., Levendis, J. and Gutierrez, L. (2009). Telecommunications and economic growth: An empirical analysis of sub- Saharan Africa (Working Paper No. 64), *Facultad de Economia:* Universidad del Rosario.

Lee, Y.Y., Park, Y.T. and Oh, H.S. (2000). The impact of competition on the efficiency of public enterprise: The case of Korean Telecom. *Asia Pacific Journal of Management,* 17(3): 423–442.

Leff, N.H. (1984). Externalities, Information Costs and Social Benefit-Cost Analysis for Economic Development: An Example from Telecommunications. *Economic Development and Cultural Change,* 32(1): 255–275.

Levy, B. and Spiller, P.T. (1994). The Institutional Foundations of Regulatory Commitment: A Comparative Analysis of Telecommunications Regulation. *Journal of Law, Economics and Organization*, 10(2): 201–246.

Lewis, W.A. (1954). Economic Development and Unlimited Supplies of Labour.*Manchester School of Economic and Social Science,* 22(2): 139–191.

Liao Chun-Hsiung *et al*. (2007). Comparing Operational Efficiency among Mobile Operators in Brazil, Russia, India and China,accessed on 18 June, 2013 from http://www.cprsouth.org/wp-content/uploads/drupal/

Lichtenberg, F. (1995). Output Contributions of Computer Equipment and Personnel: A Firm-Level Analysis. *Economics of Innovations and New Technology,* 3(3): 201–218.

Lucas, R.E. Jr. (1988). On the Mechanics of Economic Development. *Journal of Monetary Economics,* 22(1): 3–42.

Malik, P. (2006). Indian Telecommunications in Competition and Regulation, (Working Paper), New Delhi: NCAER, accessed on 10 June, 2013 from repository.mdp.ac.id/ebook

Malik, P. (2008). *Telecom Regulatory Environment in India: Results and Analysis of the TRE Survey* accessed on 12th March, 2013 from http://lirneasia.net/projects/2008-2010/indicators-continued/telecom-regulatory-environment

Malik, P. (2009). *Telecom Regulatory and Policy Environment in India: Results and Analysis of the 2008 TRE Survey*, accessed on 10 August, 2013 from http://lirneasia.net/projects/2009-2011/indicators-continued/telecom-regulatory-environment

Malik, P. (2010). *Telecom Regulatory and Policy Environment in India: Results and Analysis of the 2008 TRE Survey*, accessed on 20 May, 2016, from http://papers.ssrn.com/sol3/papers.cfm?abstract_id=1555459,

Mani,S. (2012). A Compendium on the Indian Telecommunications Industry. *Economic and Political Weekly,* 47(10): 16–19.

Maximo, T., Shyamal, C. and Arjun, S.B. (2002). Telecommunications Infrastructure and Economic Growth: A Cross-Country Analysis in Torero M. and Braun J.V. (*eds.*). *Information and Communication Technology for Development and Poverty Reduction,* Baltimore: Johns Hopkins University Press, pp. 21–63.

Meera, S.N., Jhamtani, A. and D.U.M. Rao (2006). Information and Communication Technology in Agricultural Development: A Comparative Analysis of Three Projects from India (Network Paper No. 135), London: Overseas Development Institute.

Mehta B.S. (2012). Employment in the Information and Communication Sector. *The Indian Journal of Labour Economics*, 55(4): 389–406.

Mehta, B.S. (2013). Capabilities, Costs, Networks and Innovations: Impact of Mobile Phones in Rural India Capturing the Gains (Working Paper No., 29), UK: The University of Manchester.

Melody, W.H. (2001). *Telecom Reform, Principal, Policies and Regulatory Practices*, Den Private Ingeniørfond, Technical University of Denmark, Lyngby, *pp.* 77–89.

Ministry of Finance, Government of India (2011-12). *Economic Survey* accessed on 18th, January, 2014 from http://indiabudget.nic.in/survey.asp

Ministry of Finance, Government of India (2012-13). *Economic Survey* accessed on 11th, January, 2014 from http://indiabudget.nic.in/survey.asp

Mittal, S., Momaya, K. and Sushil (2009). Technological competitiveness of telecommunication industry in India: Glimpse of reality, opportunities and challenges, Proceedings of the Global Conference, Mumbai (India): National Institute of Industrial Engineering.

Mittal, S., Sanjay, G. and Tripathi, G. (2010). Socio-economic Impact of Mobile Phones on Indian Agriculture (Working Paper No. 246), New Delhi: Indian Council for Research on International Economic Relations.

Mody, B. (1995). State Consolidation through Liberalization of Telecom. *Journal of Communication,* 45(4): 107–24.

Mowery, D.C. and Rosenberg, N. (1989). *Technology and the Pursuit of Economic Growth*, Cambridge (UK): Cambridge University Press.

Mukherji, R. (2004). Managing Competition: Politics and the Building of Independent Regulatory Institutions. *India Review*, 3(4): 278–305.

Mukherji, R.(2009). Interest, Wireless Technology and Institutional Change: From Government Monopoly to Regulated Competition in Indian Telecommunications, The Association for Asian Studies. *The Journal of Asian Studies,* 68(2): 491–517.

Nadiri, M.I. and Nandi, B. (2003). Telecommunications Infrastructure and Economic Development in Madden G. (*ed.*), *Telecommunications Network: The International Handbook of Telecommunications Economics*, Northampton, UK: Edward Elgar Publishing, pp. 293–314.

Nayyar, G. (2012). *The Service Sector in India's Development*, New Delhi: Cambridge University Press.

NCAER and TRAI (2012). *Telecom Sector in India: A Decadal Profile*, accessed on 10 September, 2013 from at www.trai.gov.in.

NERA (1998). *Governance and Regulatory Regimes for Private Sector Infrastructure Development.* A report of Asian Development Bank, accessed on 5 July, 2013 from http://www.nera.com/67_4682.htm

Noam E.M. (2006). Interconnection Practices in Cave, M., Majumdar, S. and Vogelsang I. (*eds.*). *Handbook of Telecommunication, Vol I, Structure, Regulation and Competition*, Elsevier, Oxford UK, pp. 606–637.

Noll, R. (2000). *Telecommunications Reform in Developing Countries* (SIEPR Policy Paper), Stanford (USA).

Nørgaard, O. and Møller, L. (2002). Beyond Commitment: Telecom Development in Hungary in the 1990s, paper presented on ECPR Joint Sessions, Turin, March 22-27. from www.demstar.dk

Norton, S. (1992). Transaction Costs, Telecommunications and the Microeconomics of Macroeconomic Growth. *Economic Development and Cultural Change*, 41(1): 175–96.

Nuechterlein, J.E. and Weiser, P.J. (2005). *Digital Crossroads American Telecommunications Policy in the Internet Age*, Cambridge (USA): Massachusetts Institute of Technology Press.

Panagariya, A. (2002). India's Economic Reforms: What has been accomplished? What Remains to be done? *Economic Research Department Policy Brief Series*, Number 2, Asian Development Bank.

Pentzaropoulos, G.C. and Giokas, D.I. (2002). Comparing the Operational Efficiency of the Main European Telecommunications Organizations: A Quantitative Analysis. *Telecommunications Policy,* 26(11): 595–606.

PWC (2011). Indian Mobile Services Sector-Struggling to Maintain Sustainable Growth, PWC, accessed on 5 June, 2013 from https://www.pwc.in/

PwC (2012). Fostering Economic Growth through Next Generation Reforms in Enterprise Services and Data Sector, PwC and FICCI, 2012, accessed on 8th June, 2013 from www.ccaoi.in/.../FICCI-PwC%20Report-Inputs%20for%20NTP %202011

Qiang, C.Z.W. (2009). *Telecommunications and Economic Growth*, Mimeo: World Bank.

Ramachandran, T.V. (2005). *The Indian Cellular Industry – Current Status & Opportunities Ahead.* TIDC, Bangalore, accessed on 18 June, 2013 from www.slideserve.com/.../the-indian-cellular-industry

Rodrik, D. and Subramaniam, A. (2005). From Hindu Growth to Productivity Surge: The Mystery of the Indian Growth Transition, IMF Staff papers, 52(2): 193–228.

Rogders, G. *et al.* (2011). Inclusive Development in Rural Bihar, Report Published by Institute for Human Development, New Delhi.

Rohlfs, J. (1974). A Theory of Interdependent Demand for a Communications Service. *The Bell Journal of Economics and Management Science,* 5(1): 16–37.

Röller, L.H. and Waverman, L.(2001). Telecommunications Infrastructure and Economic Development: A Simultaneous Approach. *The American Economic Review,* 91(4): 909–23.

Röller, L.H. and Waverman, L. (1996). *The Impact of Telecommunications Infrastructure on Economic Development, The Implications of Knowledge-based growth for Micro-Economic Policies*, Canada: University of Calgary Press Calgary.

Romer, P. (1986). Increasing Returns and Long-Run Growth. *Journal of Political Economy,* 95(5): 1002–1037.

Romer, P. (1990). Endogenous Technological Change. *Journal of Political Economy,* 98(5): 71–101.

Rowthorn, R.E. and Wells, J.R. (1987). *De-Industrialization and Foreign Trade*, Cambridge: Cambridge University Press.

Rushdi, A.A. (2000). Total Factor Productivity Measures for Telstra, *Telecommunications Policy,* 24(2): 143–154.

Samarajiva, R. (2009). How the developing world may participate in the global Internet Economy: Innovation driven by competition, *In*: OECD (2010), *ICTs for Development: Improving Policy Coherence*, The Development Dimension, OECD Publishing, pp. 75–117.

Samarajiva, R. and Dokeniya, A. (2005). Regulation and Investment: Sri Lanka Case Study, *In*: Mahan A.K. and Melody W.H. (*eds.*), *Stimulating investment in network development: Roles for regulators*, Monte Video: World Dialog on Regulation, pp. 141–76.

Samarajiva, R., Galpaya, H., Goswami, D. and Ratnadiwakara, D. (2007). Telecom Regulatory Environment (TRE) Assessment: Methodology and Implementation Results from Five Emerging Economies, paper presented at the USA: 35th Telecommunications Policy Research Conference.

Sanchez-Robles, B. (1998). Infrastructure Investment and Growth: Some Empirical Evidence. *Contemporary Economic Policy,* 16(1): 98–108.

Sappington, D.E.M. (2006). Interconnection Practices in Cave, M., Majumdar, S. and Vogelsang, I. (*eds.*). *Handbook of Telecommunication, Vol. I, Structure, Regulation and Competition,* Elsevier, Oxford UK, pp. 227–287.

Sappington, D. (2002). Price Regulation in Cave, M., Majumdar S.K. and Vogelsang, I. (*eds.*). *Handbook of Telecommunications Economics*, Amsterdam: Elsevier, pp. 225–293

Sarkar, S. and Balwant, S.M. (2010). Labour Market Patterns and Trends in India's ICT Sector in Posthuma A. and Nathan D. (*eds.*). *Labour in Global Production Network*, New Delhi: Oxford University Press, pp. 321–47.

Saxena, V. *et al*. (2009). Evaluating the Performance of Mobile Telecom Operators in India. *International Journal of Engineering and Technology,* 10(2): 40–45.

Sehlhorst, S. (2009). *Measuring Market Concentration (Competition)*, report accessed on 11 January, 2012 from http://tynerblain.com/blog/2009/04/13/measure-market-concentration/

Seth A., Momaya K.and Gupta H.M. (2008). Managing the Customer Perceived Service Quality for Cellular Mobile Telephony: An Empirical Investigation. *Vikalpa-The Journal for Decision Makers,* 33(1): 19–34.

Shanthi, N.M. (2005). *Indian Telecom: Growth and Transition,* Business Today, accessed on 18 June, 2013 from shodhganga.inflibnet.ac.in:8080/jspui/bitstream/.../10_chapter%202.pdfý

Sharma, E. (2011). Comparison of BSNL with other telecom industries. *Asia Pacific Journal of Research in Business Management*, 2(1): 11–25

Sharma, S., Kirankumar, M. and Manohar, K. (2010). Assessing the Performance of Telecommunication Industry in India: A Data Envelopment Analysis. *Journal of International Business and Economy,* 11(2): 29–47.

Singh, H.V., Anita, S. and Rajat K. (1999). *Telecom Policy Reform India*, 2009, accessed on 5 June, 2012 from http://siteresources.worldbank.org/INTRANETTRADE/Resources/Singh.pdf

Smith, A. (1776).*The Wealth of Nations*: *Volume I*, London (UK): Methuen and Company Ltd.

Sood, A.D. (2006). *The Mobile Development Report,*Research Report, Bangalore: Nokia Centre for Knowledge Societies (CKS), accessed on 5 March, 2012 from cks.in/wp-content/

Souter, D., Christopher, G., Jain, R., Mascarenhas, O. and McKemey, K.(2005). *The Economic Impact of Telecommunications on Rural Livelihoods and Poverty Reduction: A Study of Rural Communities in India (Gujarat), Mozambique and Tanzania*, accessed on 5th May, 2012 from www.telafrica.org/R8347/files/pdfs/FinalReport.pdf

Spulberg, D.F. (2006). Competition Policy in Telecommunication in Cave, M.,Majumdar, S. and Vogelsang, I. (*eds.*). *Handbook of Telecommunication, Vol. I, Structure, Regulation and Competition,* Elsevier, Oxford UK, pp. 478–506.

Sridhar, K.S. and Sridhar, V. (2007). Telecommunications Infrastructure and Economic Growth: Evidence from Developing Countries. *Applied Econometrics and International Development,* 7(2): 37–56.

Sridhar, V. (2004). Network Externalities in Telecom. *Economic and Political Weekly*, 39(32): 3586.
Stern, J. and Holder, S. (1999). Regulatory Governance: Criteria for assessing the performance of regulatory systems: An application to infrastructure industries in the developing countries of Asia. *Utilities Policy*, 8(1): 33–50.
Stern, J. and Cubbin, J. (2005). Regulatory Effectiveness: The Impact of Regulation and Regulatory Governance Arrangements on Electricity Industry Outcomes, (World Bank Policy Research Working Paper 3536).
Strother, N. (2004). *Boom Times for India's Wireless Market Wireless*, 425: 827–7150, Report No. IN0401742WH, In-Stat/MDR 2004, accessed on 4th May, 2012 from www.itu.int/ITU-D/ict/newslog/
Subramanian, R. (2008). The Continuing of India's Telecom Policy. *Communications of the IIMA*, 8(3): 33-48.
The Economist (2009). Mobile Marvels: A Special Report on Telecoms in Emerging Markets, accessed on 5th September, 2013 from www.economist.com/node/
Thomas, J. (2011). The sun is setting on the telecom sector in India. *The Management Accountant*, 5(1): 201–203.
Todaro, M.P. and Smith, S.C. (2009). *Economic Development*: Tenth Edition, Boston (USA): Addison-Wesely.
TRAI (2012). Telecom Sector in India: A Decadal Profile, report prepared by Telecom Regulatory Authority of India and National Council of Applied Economic Research, accessed on 5 January, 2013 from www.trai.gov.in
TRAI (2015). *Performance Indicator Report*, Telecom Regulatory Authority of India, accessed on 10 March, 2016 from www.trai.gov.in
TRAI (2016). *Performance Indicator Report*, Telecom Regulatory Authority of India, accessed on 8 January, 2017 from www.trai.gov.in
TRAI (2012). *Consultation paper on draft guidelines for unified licensing regime*, accessed on March 15, 2013 from http://www.trai.gov.in/WriteReadData/ConsultationPaper/Document
TRAI (2012). *Recommendations on Auction of Spectrum,* accessed on 10 March, 2013 from http://www.trai.gov.in/WriteReadData/Recommendation/Documents
Upadhyay, R. (2008). Uniform Licence Fee in Telecom: Way Forward. *Economic & Political Weekly,* 44(55):71–74.
Uppal, M., Nair, S.K.N. and Rao, C.S. (2006). India Telecom's Reform: A Chronological Account (IIPA working paper series), accessed on January, 2014 from www.iipa.org.in
Ure, J. (2010). *Telecommunication Development in Asia*, Hong Kong: Hong Kong University Press.
Uri, N.D. (2001). Measuring the impact of price caps on productive efficiency in telecommunications in the United States. *The Engineering Economist*, 49(2): 81–115.
Venkatesh,S.(2008).Analysis of gaps in telecommunication services – a study with respect to service gaps in fixed-line segment. *Innovative Marketing*, 4(1): 64–76.
Vittal, N.(1997). Government initiatives, regulation and financing of the telecommunications sector. *Vikalpa,* 20(3): 3–9.
Waverman, L., Meschi, M. and Fuss, M. (2005). The Impact of Telecoms on Economic Growth in Developing Countries, (Working paper The Vodafone Policy Paper Series- 3), pp. 10–24.
World Bank (2011). *Global Wireless Matrix,* Bank of America Merrill Lynch, accessed on 12, March, 2013 from www.gsmamobilewirelessperformance.com

Subject Index